BOUND AND GAGGED

A Secret History of Obscenity in Britain

Alan Travis

BOUND AND GAGGED

A Secret History of Obscenity in Britain

P

PROFILE BOOKS

LONDON

First published in Great Britain in 2000 by
Profile Books Ltd
58A Hatton Garden
London EC1N 8LX
www.profilebooks.co.uk

This edition published in 2001

10 9 8 7 6 5 4 3 2 1

Typeset in Bembo by MacGuru
info@macguru.org.uk

Printed and bound in Great Britain by
Bookmarque Ltd, Croydon, Surrey

ISBN 1 86197 286 5

Contents

Acknowledgements

With thanks to: Andrew Franklin and Profile Books; Owen Bowcott; Lorna Donlan; Carolyn Holder; Jackie Rafferty; Beth McHattie; Harvey Starte for giving it a legal once-over; Professor Tim Newburn; Geoffrey Robertson; Jo Lorenz; Philippa Drew; Anne Crawford, Nick Forbes and the staffs of the Public Record Office, the British Library, Chelsea Art College and the London Library; Emma West, archivist at Birmingham City Archives, and not least my colleagues at the *Guardian*.

List of illustrations

1

Before the damning began

The arrival of the Internet on a promise to illuminate our personal and our working lives has already sparked a furious debate over how this new mass medium should be regulated. It is not an academic question. People have already lost their jobs and some sent to prison for using the Net for criminal, or even just 'inappropriate', purposes. When the Internet was still a specialised secret shared only by the universities and research communities, its pioneering developers were able to operate in an anarchic atmosphere of unfettered free speech. But by the late 1990s the desire of affluent young men to view the more explicit pornography available on American or European websites than could be found in a high street newsagent helped to accelerate its early growth. Those generations have now been joined by a mass public audience who enjoy the boundless universe of the Net but already show signs of anxiety about what they or their children may come across while they are cruising the search engines of cyberspace.

As the Net has become more popular so the state has started to ensure that the rule of law is applied as much on the Net as it is in the rest of society. 'What is illegal offline remains illegal online' is the clarion call of the Home Office under Jack Straw. In Britain it must be doubted whether that will ever prove totally successful. Already the authorities concede that attempts to censor the content of individual websites will not succeed as they will be 'mirrored' by others as soon as they are closed down. But in one small corner of the forest an entirely new system of self-regulation is being developed complete with a network of rating systems, filters and blocking tools. It is being put together under the banner of giving people more choice and more power about how they and their families use the Internet.

Once it was the bookseller, the newsagent, the film company, the television scheduler or the video store manager who were legally responsible for deciding what could or could not be seen, heard or read by the general public, including by children. Now the advent of the Internet leaves it, at least in theory, to individual adults to decide what comes into their home and who should have access to it. On the Internet a much more sophisticated system of classification is promised than has ever been seen in television or the film industries. It raises the prospect that parents will be able to choose exactly what kind of material their children can and cannot have access to. Parents not only can block illegal sites involving for example explicit hard-core sex or neo-Nazi propaganda but also have the opportunity to grade the material their children see on screen by degree of sex and violence. Some programmes operate by blocking any site that falls foul of a list of key words, to which you can add your own. Others stop access to sites on a blacklist or allow access only to specified sites.

Pornography is only the beginning. Children can be banned from sites that promote heroin or cocaine abuse or even stopped from visiting those that advertise alcohol or tobacco. It is a system of regulation that goes far beyond the 18-rated film or the 9 o'clock watershed on television. Every page that a child visits on the Net can now in theory be classified; if it is regarded as undesirable it is possible to ensure that access is denied. An indelible diary of each session on the Internet ensures that a child's use can also be monitored and checked. All the parent has to do is to check the 'history' section to reveal a list of the sites that have been visited.

The British Internet industry is already heavily involved in operating this system of self-regulation. It started by blocking access mainly to child pornography sites but more recently has turned its attention to those which incite racial hatred by carrying criminally racist material. There will always be those computer 'techies' who have the skills to ensure that they can access whatever they want on the Net. But for the vast majority of Internet users in Britain who log on through British Telecom (BT), AOL, CompuServe, Freeserve, Demon or any of the other big Internet service providers, self-regulation already means that they are denied access to such illegal content. This is because the government-backed and industry-funded Internet Watch Foundation advises them to remove sites that contain potentially illegal material. It is advice that the Internet service providers consistently comply with, as they have no desire to find themselves being prosecuted at the Old Bailey on obscenity or race hate public order charges. This system of self-regulation is similar to that which the film industry in Britain has long subscribed to. The underlying politics imply that the creation of a family-friendly Internet should be left up to the individual parent or teacher. But that material which may be offensive to some, but is not illegal under British law, should also be available to any adult who is in full possession of their civil liberties. Some Internet service providers already restrict access to such sites by operating a built-in family filter for its subscribers. You the individual are no longer given the choice of what material, short of that which is illegal, you should receive if you want to use their services.

The more draconian alternative, which has already become law in Australia and is the subject of repeated attempts in the United States, is to make the big Internet companies criminally liable for the content of the millions of sites that their subscribers can access through their servers. It is a new form of censorship that would make Mrs Mary Whitehouse's attempt to shut up Alf Garnett as part of her 1960s campaign to clean up television look like a quick flick around the house with the duster. So far Tony Blair and his Labour government have shown all the signs of refusing to follow the Australians and Americans down that particular path.

But for this industry self-regulation to work, even through the good offices of the Orwellian-sounding Internet Watch Foundation, without sacrificing the hard-won civil liberties of fully grown adults on the altar of 'protecting the little ones', then the law itself must be credible and in fully working order. One purpose of this book is to demonstrate that the case for the reform of Britain's obscenity laws is once again long overdue. The central argument is that it is time, not to abandon the attempt at regulation, but to base the law on the test of proving significant and substantial harm. The 150-year-old test based on the 'tendency to deprave and corrupt' is now mostly useless and unenforceable as are vague community standards of 'obscenity' or 'indecency', the definition of which change depending on who is charged with the task of enforcing them.

This is a difficult debate for it tries to balance our classic notions of freedom of speech or expression with the need to protect the health or morals of the public from either real or imagined diseases. The classic definition of freedom of speech remains that coined by John Milton in 1643 in protest at the reimposition of the licensing of printing. It is contained in his manifesto, *Areopagitica*, a copy of which is still presented to every new incoming president of the Liberal Democrats. Milton in his speech to Parliament demanding the liberty of unlicensed printing asked Members of Parliament (MPs) and peers to consider:

> What nation is it whereof ye are: a nation not slow and dull, but of a quick, ingenious and piercing spirit. It must not be shackled or restricted. Give me the liberty to know, to utter, and to argue freely according to conscience, above all liberties.[1]

The bedrock of Britain's obscenity laws remains a monument to

Victorian respectability and prudery, the 1857 Obscene Publications Act. It was passed as a result of the crusading zeal of the
early Methodist anti-vice societies. They were trying to curb the
growth of the flourishing Victorian underworld trade in
pornography to be found at the heart of the imperial capital –
or at least based around Holywell Street in the Aldwych area of
London. Despite the best efforts of the Society for the Suppression of Vice, including by its founder member John Bowdler,
which mounted forty prosecutions under the common law in
five years, this trade continued to expand as the Victorian
reading public began to take on a mass character for the first
time. The critic, the Reverend Sydney Smith, suggested that a
more appropriate title for this social morality lobby might be 'a
society for suppressing the vices of persons whose incomes do
not exceed £500 p.a.'. In a criticism that all modern regulators
should bear in mind, the Revd Smith noted that all such bodies,
however good their intentions, soon degenerated into a recep-
tacle for every species of tittle-tattle, impertinence and malice.
'Men whose trade is ratcatching love to catch rats ... and the
suppressor is gratified by his vice,' he observed.

The 1857 bill was the work of the then Lord Chief Justice,
Lord Campbell. He had been presiding over a particularly lurid,
and unsuccessful, pornography trial at the same time as a bill to
control the sale of poisons was going through Parliament. Lord
Campbell was convinced that the failure of the pornography
trial demonstrated the need to restrict 'the sale of a poison more
deadly than prussic acid, strychnine or arsenic', as he described
the Holywell Street trade. Lord Campbell's bill introduced a
new aspect into the law of obscenity. His target was not the publisher but the books themselves, which were to be liable to
summary destruction by the magistrates. Campbell's bill met
fierce resistance in Parliament. It passed only after he gave the
explicit, but long forgotten, assurance that it would apply
'exclusively to works written for the single purpose of corrupting the morals of youth and of a nature calculated to shock
the common feelings of decency in any well regulated mind'.

Literary works, even if they were of a polluting character, would be damned only by the force of public opinion not by the law, Lord Campbell assured his critics.

The Lord Chief Justice must have thought that he had made his intentions clear. The idea was to seize and burn the porn, leave the publishers alone and strictly avoid action against works which could be described as being of literary or artistic merit. It was a qualification that appears to have been quickly forgotten and the 1857 Obscene Publications Act was to provide the legal framework for the banning in Britain of some of the greatest literary works of the twentieth century. The police and the courts were to pay little attention to Campbell's qualification in the decades that were to follow, even if several historians have sought to exonerate the former Lord Chief Justice of the blame.

Instead responsibility is laid at the door of another Lord Chief Justice, Lord Cockburn, whose interpretation of the Campbell Act was to remain the law of the land for more than a century. Its effects are still being felt today. The Cockburn definition of obscenity was to give the Victorians a weapon powerful enough to ban any work to which they took offence, and dictated the proper judicial tone for four generations of judges not only in Britain but also in the United States and throughout the English-speaking empire.

Lord Chief Justice Cockburn made his ruling on obscenity in 1868. The case involved a pamphlet published by the Protestant Electoral Union, a militant anti-Catholic society, and entitled *The Confessional Unmasked Showing the Depravity of the Romish Priesthood, the Iniquity of the Confessional, and the Questions Put to Females in Confession*. The Wolverhampton magistrates had ordered that 250 copies seized under the Campbell Act should be burned despite the protests of their owner that he was concerned only to expose the Church of Rome and not to harm anybody's morals. Lord Cockburn upheld the decision of the Wolverhampton magistrates and in the process laid down his now famous definition. The Lord Chief Justice ruled:

> The test of obscenity is whether the tendency of the
> matter charged as obscenity is to deprave and corrupt
> those whose minds are open to such immoral influences
> and into whose hands a publication of this sort may fall.[2]

He completely ignored Campbell's explicit warnings about the 'single purpose' of the works to be banned and any judgment about their effect on a 'well regulated mind'. Indeed Cockburn made clear his sympathy with the anti-Catholic motive of the tract but said it did nothing to excuse its obscenity. The many critics of Cockburn's 'deprave and corrupt' definition have since claimed that had it ever been applied consistently by the courts in Britain, it would have reduced the published ranks of English literature to the level of the nursery. Instead they argue that the 'deprave and corrupt' test has been used in such an arbitrary way that it has proved a major source of injustice and caused untold damage to science and literature. Lord Cockburn confirmed his own intentions when a decade later he upheld the conviction of Charles Bradlaugh and Annie Besant in 1877 for republishing a pioneering pamphlet on birth control, *The Fruits of Philosophy: An Essay on the Population Question*. The two defendants were sentenced to six months' imprisonment for a work that did little more than outline primitive forms of contraception. That sentence was quashed only on a technicality on appeal. One significant point about the Bradlaugh and Besant case was that it involved a jury. It was a troublesome jury at that, for they returned a verdict of some sophistication. They said that while they believed that the book in question was calculated to deprave public morals, they exonerated the defendants from any corrupt motives in publishing it. It was a distinction that this Lord Chief Justice had no wish to draw and he simply ruled that the jury had returned a guilty verdict and sentenced these pioneering radical social reformers to six months each. He had established that in obscenity cases alone, the question of motive was irrelevant to the issue of guilt.

The first prosecution of a publisher of a work of serious

THE SOIL.

(LA TERRE.)

A REALISTIC NOVEL.

BY

ÉMILE ZOLA.

WITH A FRONTISPIECE DESIGNED BY H. GRAY.

LONDON:
VIZETELLY & CO., 42 CATHERINE STREET, STRAND.
1888.

The Soil (La Terre) by Emile Zola. The title page of the 1888 Vizetelly edition which was condemned at the Old Bailey.

literature using the Cockburn test followed soon after. It involved an Old Bailey prosecution of a publisher, Henry Vizetelly, who in 1889 had been responsible for the first British translation of Emile Zola's novel, *La Terre*, and Gustave Flaubert's *Madame Bovary*. The prosecution of *La Terre* was initiated by the National Vigilance Association only three weeks after Zola had been decorated with the French Legion of Honour for his services to literature and freedom. Vizetelly was fined and he withdrew the books from circulation, a ban that was applauded by *The Times*. The next year Vizetelly repeated the offence but this time was forced to serve three months in prison. An old man of

70, he died a ruined man while inside prison. Two years later that leading organ of British public opinion was forced to join in literary London's acclamation of Zola. Similarly the reviewers who saw the first London production of Ibsen's *Ghosts* greeted it as 'garbage' and 'offal', and 'foul' and 'filthy'. Six years later it was being performed in front of Queen Victoria herself. In the same year Thomas Hardy's *Tess of the D'Urbevilles* was denounced as immoral and *Jude the Obscure* was the subject of an even more virulent attack. The newspapers condemned it as indecent. The Bishop of Wakefield threw it in the fire. W.H. Smith withdrew it from circulation. It broke Hardy. He turned from writing novels to drama and poetry.

It was not just literature that fell foul of the Campbell Act. The prosecution of *Sexual Inversion*, the first volume of Dr Havelock Ellis's *Study in the Psychology of Sex*, which dealt dispassionately with the subject of homosexuality, was also a victim. Its prosecution illustrated another major weakness in the Campbell Act. Only three years before, in 1895, the trial of Oscar Wilde had left the British public with the clear impression that homosexuality was so evil that it was probably the real cause of earthquakes.

Havelock Ellis had arranged an elaborate defence and assembled a team of medical experts to prove the book's scientific merits. Horace Avory, the George Carman of his day, had been briefed. All was ready. But it was not Havelock Ellis's name that appeared on the indictment but that of his bookseller, Thomas Bedborough. At the last moment the bookseller pleaded guilty and Havelock Ellis was left powerless to defend his work. Sir Charles Hall, the magistrate involved, told the bookseller that at first he might have been gulled into the belief that somebody might say it was a scientific work: 'But it is impossible for anybody with a head on his shoulders to open the book without seeing that it is a pretence and a sham, and that it is merely entered into for the purpose of selling this obscene publication,' said Sir Charles.[3] So without a hearing, Havelock Ellis was condemned in the public mind as a 'purveyor of literary garbage'. It is a theme that was to recur throughout the unhappy history of literary censorship in Britain over at least the next sixty years.

This book sets out to show that these judgments suppressing some of the greatest books of the nineteenth and twentieth centuries were not just isolated cases brought on in a fit of Victorian puritanical pique. Instead I have attempted to trace a secret history of obscenity and censorship through the twentieth century that demonstrates that the track record of even enlightened British governments in this area has not been good.

The account draws heavily on many Whitehall papers – from the restricted and confidential files of the Home Office, the Director of Public Prosecutions, the Metropolitan Police and others – that have only recently been made public. Some Home Office files were released four years earlier than the 30-year rule permits specifically for the purposes of this book, for which I am grateful. It is a story in which some of the English literary masterpieces of the twentieth century were banned and burned as no more than cheap pornography, often in the name of offending 'not the least of the little ones' and sometimes on the basis of the most cursory of examinations. In a few instances they are simply stories of good old-fashioned British bungling.

The starting point is an account of the moral crusades of Stanley Baldwin's Conservative government and the history and origins of the British bans on James Joyce's *Ulysses* and Radclyffe Hall's celebrated lesbian novel, *The Well of Loneliness*. It looks at the pulp fiction purge of the 1950s that even extended to banning cheeky seaside postcards and the background to Roy Jenkins's 1959 landmark obscenity legislation. It explains for the first time the inside story of how the Crown lost the trial of *Lady Chatterley's Lover*.

The book also seeks to demolish one of the main myths of the 'permissive sixties'. It reveals that Roy Jenkins's Home Office defended 'hippie' publications, such as *Oz* and *IT*, not out of sympathy for their amoral anarchism but because they were trying to come to terms with a police force that was becoming involved in a web of corruption. It also discloses the behind-the-scenes deal that went on in the corridors of power over the death of theatre censorship in Britain.

The final chapters look at the more recent history of the obscenity laws and examine the chaotic way they have developed to deal with every new technological advance, be it the cinema, home video, satellite television and finally the challenge of the Internet. Nearly every episode underscores the vague and conflicting nature of the law in this area.

The 1959 Obscene Publications Act, with its defence of being justified as being for the public good if it is in the interests of science, literature, art or learning, has ensured the liberty of literature in Britain. There is now hardly a taboo that has not been explored in print. Child abuse, necrophilia and the more bizarre sexual fetishes are now discussed in detail in novels and books produced by mainstream publishing houses. One illustration of this is the changing role of the Director of Public Prosecutions (DPP). In many parts of this book the DPP appears as the villain of the piece. The current DPP, David Calvert-Smith, had on the shelves of his office near London's Old Bailey a copy of the first British edition of the Marquis de Sade's *Juliette* and a copy of an American novel, Bret Easton Ellis's *Less Than Zero*. It is a measure of the changing standards of our times that before he took up his present job, Mr Calvert-Smith had a crucial role in ensuring their publication in Britain.

At the same time some ancient Victorian statutes are still in use in this area. Indeed the law is scattered among so many statutes that overlap with each other that many commentators have described it as a complicated mess. For example, while books published in Britain come under the 1959 and 1964 Obscene Publications Acts' 'public good' defence, no such protection is given to books that are imported into Britain. These are covered by section 42 of the 1876 Customs Consolidation Act. It is still in force today. Under this Customs law, there is no need to prove a tendency to deprave or corrupt. Instead all a Customs officer has to do is prove that the book or item crossed the much lower threshold of being 'indecent or obscene'. It is

said that like the elephant, Customs officers know what is indecent when they see it. This 'indecent or obscene' formula is used
to establish what can be sent by post or put on public display.
There are also common law offences of conspiracy to corrupt
public morals and conspiracy to outrage public decency, not to
mention the more modern offences of downloading computer
pornography or making indecent photographs of children.
Alongside these laws sit other statutes to curb video nasties and
horror comics.

The three separate police units dealing with this issue in
London, Birmingham and Manchester apply the law as it exists
in wholly different ways. Material that a police officer working
for the Scotland Yard Vice and Clubs Unit regards as innocuous
may be seized if found in Manchester. This whole area of law is
in such chaos and in such desperate need of overhaul and sim-
plification that nothing less than a new comprehensive approach
is required if it is not to be swept aside in the face of the global
development of the Internet. Scotland Yard already regards the
'deprave and corrupt' test as a dead letter, with its officers unable
to persuade juries to convict even in the most extreme cases of
filmed bestiality. Senior officers bemoan the fact that the public
think they are trying to ban the kind of soft porn that appears in
top-shelf magazines whenever the subject is mentioned rather
than the abuse of children and the kind of extreme sexual violence they come across in the material they seize.

In 1969 an Arts Council working party, whose members included John Mortimer and the publisher, John Calder, proposed
that the law in this area should be completely repealed for an
experiment for an initial five years until 'we had all grown up'.
The Arts Council report was compiled while under the influence of the 1960s Danish experiment in the liberalisation of the
porn laws, which it was claimed had been accompanied by a fall
and not a rise in sex crimes in Copenhagen. Times and attitudes
have changed sharply since then. Indeed the kind of explicit
pornography that was being published in Denmark then is now
available in mainstream newspapers and magazines in Britain.

Even so a libertarian position which allows the sale of hard-core pornography on the same shelf as the sweets in the local newsagent is no longer regarded as acceptable.

So if not the current law, what then? Well for me, the answer is to be found in the pages of a dusty Home Office report on obscenity and film censorship which was convened by the previous Labour government under the chairmanship of the distinguished Cambridge philosopher, Professor Bernard Williams. Although it was condemned then as a 'pornographer's charter' because it developed the concept of the licensed sex shops and the R-18 film category, other recommendations of the Williams committee have stood the test of time. It suggested that the current obscenity laws be scrapped and replaced with a single, comprehensive statute based on a test of significant and substantial harm rather than the current useless concepts of depravity, obscenity or indecency.

Williams also suggested that only one small class of material should be banned outright. This involved any photographs or films that involved the sexual exploitation of a child under the age of 16 in their production or those that included scenes in which actual physical harm was inflicted on the participants. The kind of material to be covered by the ban was not that depicting consensual sex but films and videos that involved paedophilia, torture and coercion. The ban was to be aimed at material produced for pornographic purposes. News and documentary material was to be exempt. The Williams committee suggested that there should be no bans or restriction on the publication of the printed word. However, it did recommend that there should be restrictions on the access or display of other specified kinds of material so that the 'reasonable person' was protected from being caused offence and to prevent it being made available to young people.

The Williams committee suggested that it was unacceptable to allow the unrestricted availability of offensive material that portrayed violence, cruelty or horror, or sexual, faecal or urinary functions or genital organs. Their solution to the widespread feeling that many people want to be able to go through their daily lives without having such images being thrust in their face was to restrict their sale to licensed sex shops or by mail order. Children under 18 were banned from entering the sex shops, which were supposed to display prominent warnings in their windows. In the event the sex shops died under the combined weight of local public morality campaigners and a feminist backlash and the soft-core porn mag a few shelves away from the sweets became a staple of the corner newsagent.

This kind of regime has a far better chance of success in regulating the Internet. It ensures that children, and for that matter adults, do not come across the kind of material they regard as offensive while allowing all but a small category of illegal material to be accessed by all adults who want it. This I believe could form the basis for a liberal approach to regulating the Internet. But it means that British law needs to be reformed if it is to work. Already the law surrounding video releases is governed by the 'significant harm' rather than the 'deprave and corrupt' test, with the result that the sexual violence of *Straw Dogs* remains banned while the *Texas Chainsaw Massacre* is allowed into the home.

The question is no longer whether or not it is possible to police the Internet. Most developed countries are already busy devising ways of limiting what can and cannot be seen in cyberspace. Half a dozen countries have already insisted that the Internet service providers, such as AOL and CompuServe, which operate within their boundaries use filtering technologies. It means that the pre-censorship of online communications is already a reality for some Internet users. Online content providers, or indeed anyone with their own website, will soon be required to start rating their content according to sophisticated classification systems or face the penalty of being denied a public audience.

The development of such rating and filtering technology has firmly put on the agenda the question of what should be banned or restricted on the Net. An intense debate is already raging over whether to ban sexually violent pornography, or racist and hate speech sites, through to those that promote illegal drugs or terrorist techniques. Increasingly police forces and security services in Britain, North America and Europe are working out ways of snooping on the Net, so that they can monitor online communications, often in the name of combating organised crime.

In the United States a constitutional battle struck down the first attempt to pass a Communications Decency Act. But in 1998 President Clinton signed into law the Child Online Protection Act, which makes it illegal to distribute material on the web which is harmful to minors. In a move designed to curb the use of cyberspace for child abusers, it also regulates the circumstances in which children under 13 can be asked for personal information.

In Britain, as in North America, the rush to limit access to parts of the Net has centred on child pornography and the self-evident risks to children involved in the rapid growth of a new market for the paedophiliac exploitation of sexual and violent images. The Gary Glitter case demonstrated how the growth of the Internet has already led to changes in the law and demonstrated that the very act of possession of pornographic material is now illegal in Britain – because the law says that downloading such images amounts to manufacture.

The dangers to the children involved in the production of such material are self-evident and rightly produce public revulsion. The material itself should be used as evidence of abuse and often assault of those children involved in its production. But public debate often concentrates on the most hideous dangers facing those children who surf the Net – the possibilities of being lured into a face-to-face meeting by a predatory paedophile and physically abused or abducted – and yet they are the least likely to occur. Children are far more likely to face the problem of being confronted accidentally with inappropriate material. For example a child looking for Spice Girls websites might well need to be protected from the hundreds of naked

images on sites that some search engines might throw up. So
there is already a strong demand for voluntary filtering systems,
such as Cyber Patrol and Net Nanny, so that parents can feel
assured that they can leave their children to surf the Net safely.

Every school, college and library in Britain will be online by
2002. The Department for Education and Employment (DfEE)
has already advised teachers and librarians that they should be
aware that the right to freedom of speech and freedom of choice
must be balanced by the rights of younger children.[4] The official guidance, *Superhighway Safety*, refuses to be alarmist. It
clearly says that the educational benefits of using the web far
outweigh the minimal possible dangers. It advises that parents
should make sure that computers are used in shared parts of the
house, to talk to their children about what they encounter on
the Net and to answer questions truthfully.

The official advice also suggests using an Internet service
that filters material or buying control or filtering software for
the computer activity of children. For example it suggests that
'walled gardens' might be a good idea to be used both in school
and at home. These are collections of websites that have been selected, vetted and approved for access by children who can only
access these particular sites. It also recommends the use of filters,
such as Cyber Patrol and Net Nanny, which allow access to all
but the blocked sites. The DfEE even points out the limitations
of such filters, saying that there are issues of censorship about
who selects the sites and noting that many perfectly safe sites can
fall outside these 'walled gardens'.

All well and good, but these self-same filtering systems are
not just used in schools to protect children from inappropriate
material. The most popular Cyber Patrol forms the basis of the
screening system used by the big Internet service providers, such
as AOL and CompuServe, for their millions of subscribers and
are also used by companies to filter the websites accessible to
their staff during working hours. Some have already lost their
jobs for using their work computers for inappropriate purposes.
In practice a whole new classification system for access to the

web for most of the adult population as well as for children is being put into place without any real public or political debate about how it works or who is and is not excluded by it.

Already there are examples emerging of the kind of rough justice which discredited the Obscene Publication Acts. Internet freedom campaigners claim that already perfectly legal forums have been closed by Internet service providers, including a news site about Basque separatism, a Northern Ireland discussion group and a site criticising Britain's judicial system. Others worry that the very kinds of filtering and rating systems developed to deal with child pornography are now being used by the Chinese to try to prevent millions of 'Net worms' (as Internet addicts are called) accessing sites with information not released through official channels.

The current political mood in Tony Blair's Britain carries with it a social authoritarian undercurrent that makes the prospect of reform of the law in Britain less rather than more likely. Officially the obscenity laws are regarded as 'a flexible tool that have stood the test of time'. A recent fundamental review of the law on sex offences was carried out with any consideration of obscene law reform expressly excluded. But as the Williams committee's report shows, this remains a piece of unfinished business from the previous Labour government. The Williams committee was set up in 1977 by James Callaghan's government. It had the misfortune not to finish its work until Mrs Thatcher had taken over 10 Downing Street and found itself born an orphan child. Tony Blair and Jack Straw would do well to reconsider its principles as the basis for a new comprehensive obscenity law that would prove practical in the age of the global frontier.

The case of *Ulysses*

The tone of the Empire comes from you the authors of our land. If the tone is pure, the blood will go on pulsating through the whole world.

William Joynson-Hicks, Home Secretary, to the Authors' Club,
11 December 1928.[1]

Police notwithstanding, I should like to put everything into my novel.

James Joyce.[2]

The British Foreign Office had made up its mind about one of the greatest writers of the twentieth century long before English Customs officers started burning copies of the first two editions of *Ulysses* when they were published in 1922. Unpublished Foreign Office papers show that during an obscure diplomatic incident in Joyce's life in the summer of 1918, the British authorities developed such an enmity towards him that they even considered revoking his British passport – an act that would have confined him to Dublin.[3]

In that final summer of the First World War, Joyce was touring French-speaking Switzerland with an English theatrical company performing Oscar Wilde's *Importance of Being Earnest*. His apparently innocent request to the British Legation in

THE CASE OF ULYSSES

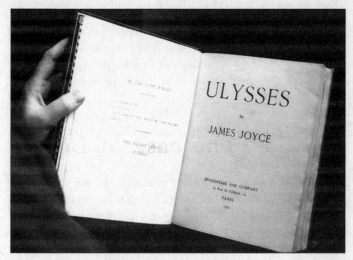

Ulysses, *James Joyce, Shakespeare and Co. Paris. Inside title page of the 1922 first edition, 500 copies of which were seized by the British customs at Folkestone.*

Berne asking if they could help stage a performance ended in an exchange of telegrams with London. As Sir Horace Rumbold at the British Legation in Berne put it in his official communication to the Foreign Office during the subsequent inquiry: 'Mr Joyce informed me that he had been insulted by a member of the Consulate-General at Zurich on whom he had called for payment of some money which was owing to him.' Sir Horace had asked the consul-general for an explanation of the incident and was told:

> Mr Joyce and his company are the most undesirable people and their performances are very mediocre and are neither socially nor professionally in the interests of British propaganda.[4]

Worse was to follow:

> Mr Joyce is an Irishman of military age [he was 36 at the

time] and returned to the Consulate-General a circular which had been sent him on the subject of military service with the remark that it had been evidently sent to him by mistake. In view of this I told Mr Joyce that I could give no assistance in his theatrical undertaking.

The Foreign Office in London applauded Sir Horace Rumbold's judgment: 'We most certainly agree with the action taken,' noted one senior official, who went on to discuss the idea of revoking Joyce's passport. The suggestion had come from a Mr Beak, who noted that Joyce was engaged in 'the wrong kind of cultural propaganda' and speculated that he did not suppose that the Irishman was so mischievous that they need consider cancelling his passport. The files show it was an idea that was seriously considered:

> Mr Joyce is a novelist of some note – his novel *Portrait of the Artist as a Young Man* was received favourably here some few months ago. His later work is bad and what he is doing in Switzerland is not very much to our artistic credit, but these are hardly reasons for revoking his passport.[5]

Joyce's version of the incident is rather different. He had got along badly with Henry Carr, a young member of staff at the British consulate, who had played the role of Algernon Moncrieff in the English Players' production of the Wilde play. Joyce went to the Zurich consulate to collect some money that Carr owed him for tickets that the Englishman had sold. Carr had in turn demanded more money after Joyce had paid him less than what he considered to be the going rate for playing the role of Algernon. He called Joyce a 'cad and a swindler' and threatened to throw him down the stairs. As to the question of military service, Joyce told the consulate that he had promised the Austrians in Trieste to remain neutral in the war.

It is no wonder then that when the Whitehall files were opened recently they revealed an unremitting hostility towards

Joyce. The Home Office papers on *Ulysses* were to have remained secret until 2037 under the hundred-year rule but were opened by ministerial discretion.[6] They show that the British law officer responsible for banning one of the greatest literary works of the twentieth century made his decision after reading only 42 of its 732 pages. Sir Archibald Bodkin, the Director of Public Prosecutions, who was responsible for driving James Joyce's Irish masterpiece underground in Britain for more than a decade, then went on to compound this gross error. He threatened to prosecute the legendary Cambridge literary critic, F. R. Leavis, who was regarded by officialdom as 'a dangerous crank or worse'. Bodkin was even prepared to intimidate the Vice-Chancellor of Cambridge University, who, it was said, needed 'to be brought to his senses' to take action against Leavis.

The ban on the British publication of *Ulysses* lasted from 1922 to 1936 and the Post Office ensured that it was enforced throughout the British Empire. The British Home Office was first alerted to the nature of *Ulysses* by the reviews that had sporadically appeared after instalments of the book had been published in an American magazine, the *Little Review*. At the instigation of the New York Society for the Prevention of Vice, three US judges had found extracts published in the *Little Review* to be obscene in February 1921, although two of the judges were reported to have found them incomprehensible.

But the Home Office files show that it was not news of this trial but a notice by a critic, Shane Leslie, in Britain's *Quarterly Review*, which determined the initial official reaction in London to *Ulysses*. Leslie said that he had found the book 'unreadable, unquotable, and unreviewable' but, in the words of the senior civil servant who wrote the Home Office secret report:

> [Leslie] has promptly proceeded to read it, review it and
> to quote from it. The price is, to the multitude,
> prohibitive. In the circumstances no general harm is
> likely to be caused by its contents. But if it is ever found
> open in the post it should be detained.

Copies of the second edition of *Ulysses* were on sale in Paris at 136 francs (about £2), but the reviews had provoked such a demand that imported copies were fetching £40 a time in London. Shane Leslie's review described the book as a massive volume, whose resemblance in size and colour to the London Telephone Book made it a danger to the unsuspecting, written by a well-known Dublin author and published in Paris at an excessive price.

> It is not the kind of book to be met with on Messrs W. H. Smith's ubiquitous bookstalls. It is doubtful that the British Museum possesses a copy as the book could not be printed in England and no copy could fall by law to the National Collection.

Shane Leslie did, however, recognise its literary significance by describing it as 'an attempted Clerkenwell explosion [a reference to a famous Irish Fenian bombing of a London jail] in the well-guarded, well-built, classical prison of English Literature. The bomb has exploded ... All that is unmentionable, according to civilised standards, has been brought to the light of day without any veil of decency.' Its only redeeming feature, he noted, was Joyce's 'cumbersomeness of style', which he concluded was 'its most effective screen against prying eyes'.[7]

British Customs records show that the first copy of *Ulysses* seized in England was confiscated at Croydon Airport, London, on 12 December 1922. The first edition of *Ulysses* had been published in Paris on 22 February 1922 with a print run of 1,000 copies. Five hundred of these copies were to be seized and destroyed by the United States Postal Services. Customs and Excise pressed the Home Office for an early decision on whether it should be banned as being indecent or returned to its owner. 'The importer describes it as a noteworthy work of art by an author of considerable repute which is being seriously discussed in the highest literary circles,' said the Customs report. Five days later Sidney W. Harris, a senior Home Office official, decided to dispatch the book to the DPP, Sir Archibald Bodkin, with a note saying: 'There is no doubt as to the obscenity of the passage referred to on pages 704 and 705.'

The offending texts include a passage in which Molly Bloom is talking about having her breasts sucked. She goes on to compare the beauty of her breasts to a man

> with his two bags full and his other thing hanging down
> out of him or sticking up at you like a hatrack no
> wonder they hide it with a cabbageleaf the woman is
> beauty of course that's admitted ....[8]

Mr Harris was also no doubt greatly shocked by the passage on page 705 in which she lets 'Master Poldy' drink her breast milk, saying:

> I had to get him to suck them they were so hard he said
> it was sweeter and thicker than cows then he wanted to
> milk me into the tea well hes beyond everything ....[9]

But the final passage on page 705 probably contains the crucial lines that sealed the fate of *Ulysses* for the next 30 years.

> O Lord I must stretch myself I wished he was here or
> somebody to let myself go with and come again like that
> I feel all fire inside me or if I could dream it when he
> made me spend the 2nd time tickling me behind with
> his finger I was coming for about 5 minutes with my legs
> round him I had to hug him after O Lord I wanted to
> shout out all sorts of things fuck or shit or anything at all
> only not to look ugly or those lines from the strain who
> knows the way hed take it you want to feel your way
> with a man theyre not all like him thank God.[10]

The sound of Molly Bloom's orgasmic cries had penetrated to the highest reaches of Whitehall. A week later Bodkin delivered his learned and considered opinion:

As might be supposed I have not had the time, nor may I add the inclination to read through this book. I have however read pages 690 to 732. I am entirely unable to appreciate how those pages are relevant to the rest of the book or indeed what the book itself is about. I can discover no story. There is no introduction which gives a key to its purpose and the pages above mentioned, written as they are as if composed by a more or less illiterate vulgar woman, form an entirely detached part of this production. In my opinion, there is more, and a great deal more than mere vulgarity or coarseness, there is a great deal of unmitigated filth and obscenity.

The book appears to have been printed as a limited edition in Paris, where I notice the author, perhaps prudently, resides. Its price no doubt ensures a limited distribution. It is not only deplorable but at the same time astonishing that publications such as the *Quarterly Review*, the *Observer* and the *Nation*, should have devoted any space to a critique upon *Ulysses* ... I do not suppose that many people could read this book cover to cover; if they did they would come across, so far as I can tell from glancing at the earlier pages, various indecencies and suggestiveness. It is in the pages mentioned above that the glaring obscenity and filth appears. In my opinion the book is obscene and indecent, and on that ground the Customs authorities would be justified in refusing to part with it.

It is conceivable that there will be criticism of this attitude towards this publication of a well-known writer; the answer will be that it is filthy and filthy books are not allowed to be imported into this country. Let those who desire to possess or champion a book of this description do so.

So on New Year's Day 1923 Sidney Harris, armed with Bodkin's legal opinion, sat down at his desk at the Home Office and drafted his memorandum for the Home Secretary:

I have discussed this with the DPP and agree entirely with his opinion. The passages, which he has marked, are foul in their obscenity and cannot be justified by any literary motive. It seems to me that the *Quarterly Review* and other papers which have published notices of the book have done a disservice both to English literature and to public decency. But for these notices few people would have heard of the book which is being talked about and being obtained no doubt by private purchase in Paris. Fortunately the book is too expensive to command a wide circle of readers. The fear is that other writers with a love of notoriety will attempt to write in the same vein. I think we may safely advise the Customs that the book is obscene and should be forfeited.

The question arises whether we ought not to make discreet enquiry among the booksellers in London as to whether the book is being obtained; but on the whole I think it is best to take no further action at present. A prosecution might only give the book further publicity. The Customs should also be asked to seize any further copies that may be forfeited and the Post Office and the police informed.

Mr Harris also advised that intercept warrants should be signed by the Home Secretary to allow postal parcels to be searched for copies of the book. A confidential note was sent from the Home Secretary to the Customs and the Post Office telling them to forfeit any further copies that came their way.

Archibald Bodkin's admission that he had declared *Ulysses* obscene after reading only 42 of its 732 pages can only be regarded as breathtaking. That he was able to ban this literary masterpiece without any reference to a court, let alone a jury, must still be regarded as shocking. The 1876 Customs legislation used against *Ulysses* is still in force today and gives Customs officers the power to seize 'indecent or obscene prints, paintings, books, cards, etc'. The person bringing the book into Britain is given one month to challenge the decision, not initially in the courts, but before a Customs commissioner either in person or in writing. Only then can the aggrieved person go before a court. Few were even aware that this power of protest existed at the time of the ban on *Ulysses*, let alone had the inclination to challenge a decision to seize an individual copy.

The effect of the ban was initially fairly complete. In January 1923, 500 further copies of the second edition bearing the imprint of the Egoist Press were printed in Paris to replace those seized by the US postal service. A copy was sent by post to the founder of the Egoist Press, Harriet Shaw Weaver, in London but the remaining 499 were shipped to England in April. At Folkestone, in accordance with Bodkin's advice, Customs officers seized the consignment and destroyed the books by burning them in 'the King's Chimney'. A Home Office circular was sent to all chief constables to establish how effective the ban had been. In only one instance 'was a trace of *Ulysses* found': it was reported that a single copy had been sold in Manchester.

But a year later Shakespeare and Co. published an unlimited edition which was sold by Paris booksellers at 60 francs or just under £1. Joyce's reputation ensured that academic and literary interest remained strong in *Ulysses* and individual copies were no doubt circulating in London. However, it was never that easy to get your hands on a copy. As late as 1932 George Orwell talks of 'the friend who was going to lend me *Ulysses* has at last got his copy back, and I shall go up to town one day to collect it'.

Two years later he tells another friend 'I managed to get my copy of *Ulysses* through safely this time.'[11]

So when in the summer of 1926 a request from a Cambridge bookseller asking if Dr F.R. Leavis of Emmanuel College, Cambridge, could have permission to import a copy of *Ulysses* arrived at the Home Office, it caused consternation. Leavis, in an account he gave in a letter to the *Times Literary Supplement* (*TLS*) in May 1963, said the idea arose after he was talking to his bookseller about the censorship exercised by the US Customs.

'Well, *we* can't talk: there are books you can't get me,' Leavis told him, adding:

> The upshot was that, at his suggestion I dictated a letter
> to the Home Office requesting permission to import a
> copy of *Ulysses*, by James Joyce, for use by me at
> Cambridge in a course of lectures on English prose. I was
> down on the lecture-list for such a course.'[12]

When the letter in the name of Charles Porter of Galloway & Porter arrived at the Home Office on 17 July 1926 after being forwarded by the Cambridge Chief Constable, Rob J. Pearson, it was greeted with horror. As well as asking for permission to import Leavis's copy, Porter's letter also asked the Home Office if they would consider

> a further copy being placed in a suitable library
> connected with the University, and for use of students
> attending this course only, or … to permit us to supply
> any student a copy for study.

Mr H. Houston of the Home Office noted in the official file:

> Now that this work is to be the subject of a course of
> lectures for the English Tripos at Cambridge there is sure
> to be a large demand for it and the application of these
> university booksellers for a removal of the ban is as
> natural as a Savoy Opera. From my knowledge of the
> book I am inclined to doubt its suitability for the
> education of the boy and girl undergraduates who may
> attend lectures and I am inclined to say that so far from
> removing the ban we should take steps to prevent the
> lectures taking place. The introduction of obscene
> literature into Oxford and Cambridge is a matter that for
> some time past has been handled – and admirably
> handled – by the Director and if we might trespass on his

time in this case I have no doubt but that this somewhat alarming proposal would be suitably and speedily dealt with. Send to Director of Public Prosecutions.

Sidney Harris, the more senior civil servant who had dealt with the original ban, had no doubt:

> This is an amazing proposition. A lecturer at Cambridge who proposes to make this book a textbook for a mixed class of undergraduates must be a dangerous crank. Permission must of course be refused but I agree that it would very useful to have the advice of the DPP.

So Sir Archibald Bodkin was once again recruited to lay down the law. But first he wrote confidentially to the Chief Constable of Cambridge asking him to make a few discreet inquiries about Leavis. He wanted to know if the literary critic intended to deliver his lecture on Joyce to a mixed university class – 'I presume of males and females' – and whether they would be recommended to read the book, and wanted to be sure that the whole thing was not a student prank. 'You have already been informed from the Home Office that *Ulysses* is an obscene work by one James Joyce,' Bodkin told Chief Constable Pearson.

> It has been suggested that it is possible that Galloway and Porter may be the victims of a hoax and that no such lectures are intended – at any rate on the subject of this book.
>
> I shall be obliged if you would cause inquiry to be made and to inform me as to who and what Dr F.R. Leavis of Emmanuel College is; what his position is in the College; whether there is any corroboration to be found either in the 'current lecture list for the English Tripos' or otherwise for the statement quoted by Galloway and Porter … If you can procure a copy of the lecture list, or any other public announcement of such

lectures, and forward it to me, I shall be much obliged.

You will, I am sure, appreciate that the inquiries as to Dr Leavis must be made discreetly. At the same time I am desirous of receiving any information at the earliest moment, for having discussed this matter with the Home Office, it is quite clear that the ban on this disgusting book will certainly not be removed; that no facilities whatsoever will be given for lecturing upon its subject; and that if it be discovered that any other booksellers in Cambridge or elsewhere have in some way procured copies and sell them, I shall have to consider very carefully the advisability of instituting proceedings.

I am further desirous of taking some steps with the University Authorities to prevent such lectures from being delivered, whether to a mixed University Class, or otherwise. It is necessary, of course, however, to be quite sure of the facts before taking further action in the matter.

Within a week the Chief Constable was ready to report. He had done his work thoroughly. Leavis was a member of Emmanuel College, Cambridge, where he had rooms at the K2 hostel. He also lived at 6 Chesterton Hall Crescent. Although Leavis had a doctorate he was not actually a university lecturer by rank but gave lectures arranged by the English faculty and took pupils privately. The *Cambridge University Reporter* confirmed that he was to give a course of lectures on Modern Problems in Criticism during the 1926 Michaelmas Term and again the following term. Students were to be charged 15 shillings (75 pence).

The Chief Constable had also established that women were to be among the students, most probably first- and second-year undergraduates from the women-only Newnham and Girton colleges. There was no question of it being a hoax. Pearson told Bodkin:

I feel quite sure than any communication from you to

the University vice-chancellor will receive immediate
attention. I also feel sure, from enquiries made, that no
copies of this disgusting book can be obtained from any
of the book-sellers in Cambridge, they all having been
previously warned with respect to the sale of this book.

The next day the Director of Public Prosecutions wrote to Professor Albert Seward, the vice-chancellor of Cambridge University, a benign and distinguished botanist:

I trust I am not unduly troubling you but I do not know
to whom else to write upon a delicate and important
matter which has been reported to me by the Secretary
of State, Home Office [Sir William Joynson-Hicks].
There is a notorious book called *Ulysses* by one James
Joyce, which for some reasons, the chief of which is
probably owing to its disgusting character, was published
in Paris in 1922. Attention was drawn to it as an indecent
publication and, not by HM Customs, but by myself
acting under directions of the Home Secretary, every
effort has been made to secure and destroy any copies
found coming into or circulating within this country.

Bodkin, having established that he was acting in the name of the
Home Secretary in insisting that Professor Seward join his
Joyce-hunt, then rehearsed the reasons behind the bookseller's
request to the Home Office. He made much of the outrageous
idea that the lectures should take place in mixed company:

It was hardly credited that this book should be proposed
as the subject of lectures in any circumstances but above
all that it should be the subject of discussion and be
available for the use of a mixed body of students.

Bodkin obviously decided that when it came to university vice-
chancellors, intellectual argument was not what was needed:

I do not pretend to be a critic of what is, as I suppose,
literature, but the book Ulysses which contains 732 pages
is an extraordinary production of which, to use a
colloquialism, I am unable to make head or tail, but there
are many passages in it which are indecent and entirely
unsuitable to bring to the specific attention of any
person of either sex.

The book concludes with reminiscences, as I suppose
they may be called, of an Irish chamber-maid, in various
parts of which grossness and indecency appear. I should
be quite prepared, if you desire it, to lend you a copy of
Ulysses for the purpose of satisfying yourself that my
observations upon it are justified, as also is the
prohibition, which attaches to it. I am confident that no
English publisher would take the risk of publishing such
a book.

After questioning whether the vice-chancellor himself actually
had the authority to stop Dr Leavis's lectures, Bodkin made clear
there would be no surrender in the matter:

It is unnecessary to add that the ban or prohibition upon
this book will not only not be relaxed but additional
vigilance will be impressed upon the Chief Constable to
prevent it becoming available in any manner in
Cambridge, and should I find that any book-seller or any
other person publishes or circulates *Ulysses* I shall, as
Director of Public Prosecutions, have very seriously to
consider whether prompt criminal proceedings shall not
be instituted.

Despite the stilted and pompous legal language used by Bodkin,
he presumably believed that even an academic botanist would
make 'head or tail' of such a clear threat to deal with Leavis and
any accomplice.

Professor Seward took it calmly. He asked Leavis to see him

and wrote back to the DPP saying that the interview would take place in the next day or two and no, there was no need for Bodkin to put himself to the trouble of sending him a copy of Joyce's book. Leavis says that when he saw the vice-chancellor, Professor Seward simply handed him Bodkin's letter.

Leavis told Seward that he had never entertained the 'absurd idea' that he was going to prescribe *Ulysses* for study for the English Tripos. But he did say that he could not see why anyone who wanted to read the book should not be free to do so or at least to try to. He claimed it was a book that everyone who was interested in contemporary literature was already expected to be able to discuss intelligently and, anyway, it was already in wide circulation among Cambridge students.

'I happen to know that there are copies circulating at both Girton and Newnham,' said Leavis, adding that he wanted to eliminate the 'glamour of the clandestine attending the cult', as he reported in his letter to the *Times Literary Supplement* four decades later.[13]

> [Leavis] went on: 'I could easily have got a copy by letting myself be put in touch with one of the disreputable agents every bookseller knows of.' 'I am glad you didn't do that,' the vice-chancellor replied. 'Letters get intercepted.' And he touched with an admonitory finger one of the pigeonholes of the desk at which he was sitting. He didn't seem at all disturbed, and I think he replied to the Public Prosecutor in terms of my explanation.[14]

The vice-chancellor responded to the DPP's bullying by concentrating on Leavis's denial that he had never actually contemplated making *Ulysses* a prescribed text for those students attending his lectures.

> I have today seen Dr Leavis. He tells me that the has not recommended students to buy the book and he adds he

would never think of doing so. He has referred to the book in his lectures and he asked the Cambridge booksellers, Galloway & Porter, if they could obtain permission to import a copy for illustrations and comment in his lectures.

Dr Leavis also says that critiques of the book have been published in the *Nation* and *Athenaeum* and other literary periodicals. The book has also been quoted with approval in the Supplement to the *Times*, he thinks possibly on March 5 of this year.

Bodkin was less than happy with this response:

From your letter it appears to be clear that some efforts were made by Dr Leavis to persuade Messrs Galloway & Porter to import a copy of *Ulysses*, and I do not think it can be doubted that that copy was intended to be available for a mixed University Class attending Dr Leavis's lectures … I can only remark that it is astonishing that the book could have in any manner been introduced into University lectures.

I am aware that criticisms upon this book have appeared but I have considerable doubt whether the reviewers of it had ever waded through its 732 pages; if they did, and their critiques represented their real views, they must have peculiar ideas as to what constitutes literature.

This is not the first occasion on which I have known a book containing disgusting passages being favourably reviewed by the 'literary critics'. What I am concerned in is to prevent any knowledge of this book, *Ulysses*, spreading among University [students] of either sex.

In what is now a classic statement, Bodkin added:

Knowledge of it may awake curiosity, and curiosity may

lead to possibly successful efforts to obtain it. If I learn that any copy has come into the hands of any University student I shall take every step which the law permits to deal with the matter, and I cannot avoid remarking that if I have to take any such steps inevitably the source from which knowledge of the book arose will be known, and the publicity will hardly tend to increase the reputation of the University, or the subject matter of its lectures.

I trust that you will think right to bring every influence to bear upon Dr Leavis to impose upon this book as complete a ban as the authorities impose upon booksellers and others who might be likely to deal with it.

If that sharp jab did not prove effective, Bodkin also took the precaution of writing to the Chief Constable again:

I think it advisable you should inform Messrs Galloway & Porter that the book is entirely prohibited and that should any person be found dealing in it or supplying it in any manner, I shall, on being informed, take every step which the law permits to deal with such a transaction.

Bodkin added that he knew it would be 'exceedingly difficult' but if the Chief Constable could find a way of monitoring Leavis's lectures and see if he referred to *Ulysses* he would be glad to know 'as I should then probably consider it right to address a communication to Dr Leavis personally.'

Bodkin reported back to the Home Office on all he had done to the evident satisfaction of all: 'Mr Leavis must be a crank – or worse,' wrote Ernley Blackwell, the assistant secretary (legal).

If the last 40 pages of this book can be called literature there is a whole lot of it running to waste every day in the airing courts at Broadmoor [the asylum for the criminally insane].

The VC's letter is evasive. Can he have read the book?
He said he would not trouble the Director to send him a
copy. It is to be hoped that the Director's last letter will
have the desired effect. If not a prosecution of any
bookseller found dealing with the publication ... would
bring the vice-chancellor and Mr Leavis to their senses.

His Home Office colleague, Sidney Harris, was impressed by
Bodkin's panache: 'This is a model of the way to address vice-
chancellors,' he noted.

Despite the bluster and pompous threats from Bodkin, Professor Seward appears to have ridden out the storm. Leavis in
his 1963 account says that he heard nothing of any further official action and he used, and went on using, a passage from
Joyce in his lecture course. Presumably in those days Cambridge police officers were too conspicuous to attend university English lectures without being spotted or perhaps even
then they had better things to do with their time. Yet Leavis
was convinced that the episode was held against him throughout his academic career and contributed to his reputation for
'persecution mania':

To say that harm undoubtedly resulted for me isn't
primarily to indict anyone, though naturally I could
make – and substantiate – some severe judgments. The
moral I have in mind regards the potency of convention,
and the way in which it has changed. It was very natural
at the time of [D.H.] Lawrence's death, and later, for
ordinary conventional academics to say, with an
untroubled conscience, when asked how Leavis had
earned so marked a disfavour: 'We don't like the books
he lends undergraduates.' After the notorious scandal to
have gone on to D.H. Lawrence and T.F. Powys[15] was, in
those days, asking for it.[16]

Leavis noted that in those days the Cambridge University

library had the power to refuse to allow undergraduates to
borrow the works of both authors. With hindsight Leavis was
particularly bitter that those who claimed he suffered from persecution mania were quite likely to be heard during the *Lady
Chatterley* trial (which took place a short while before his *TLS*
letter) testifying in court that it would be a good thing and
would tend to strengthen respect for marriage if Lawrence's
book was to be sold cheaply in every Woolworth's in Britain.

Leavis was not the only individual to be harassed by the authorities over Joyce, but these confidential Home Office and
DPP papers show just how much energy and time was exhausted by very senior Whitehall civil servants and law officers
in trying to suppress the news about Molly Bloom's orgasms.
One by-product of the Leavis affair was that in July 1926 Stanley
Baldwin's Home Secretary, Sir William Joynson-Hicks, imposed
a warrant which gave the Post Office the power to open all suspicious parcels going to students.

An equally harsh approach to the next 'request' for official
permission to import a copy of *Ulysses* was made in September
1926. This time it did not come from the privileged quads of
Cambridge colleges but from Stepney in the East End of
London. The Town Clerk's letter says that Joseph M. Lask of
Stepney, a miller, had asked the municipal library for a copy of
the book. The Stepney Libraries committee was meeting to
consider the request and wanted some Home Office guidance.
The Home Secretary's note that was sent to Stepney made the
deluded claim that all copies imported into Britain had been
seized.[17] At the same time, Sir William ordered that Joseph Lask's
post be watched to see if he tried to import a copy from France.
The following month another request from Stepney – this time
for an anonymous reader – produced a more sinister response, a
visit from the police. Inspector C. Chapman of New Scotland
Yard Criminal Investigation Department (CID) rang the Town
Clerk, V.B. Bateson, and arranged an appointment to see him.
Bateson at first did not want to see him, saying that he had
already got a letter from the Home Office about *Ulysses*. But the

inspector insisted and when he met him, asked for the name of the person who had applied for the book.

> Mr Bateson said: 'I expected that was what you wanted to see me for. I am very sorry, but I have been forbidden to give the name of the applicant to the Police. I would gladly do so, but I have an Oxford University man to deal with and he is a red hot Socialist. I told him you were coming to see me and would probably want the name of the person who applied for the book and he told me he had read the book and would not consent to the Police having the name of the person who applied for it.

'Mr Bateson did not tell me who the University man was, but probably he is the Librarian,' says the police report. The file does not record what further action was taken.

These repeated attempts to enforce the ban were to last for years. In April 1930, Arthur Mee, the editor of the *Children's Newspaper*, wrote to Scotland Yard saying that he had noticed that Davis and Orioli, booksellers of Museum Street, London, were advertising a mint-condition 1922 first edition of *Ulysses* at a price of 12 guineas (£12.60) and saying that it was one of only 150 copies in existence. A different CID inspector was sent round to the shop near the British Museum. The owner, Joseph Davis, claimed that the book had been bought in a parcel of books from a private library. He knew that it was banned. He explained that the catalogue had been made up by an assistant and *Ulysses* had been accidentally included in it. The book was sold to a personal friend. He would not have offered it publicly for sale.

Similarly, no action was taken in the case involving a former Lord Chancellor, who most definitely did not come from Stepney. Alfred Noyes, who held the distinction of being a best-selling poet and who then lived at Hanover Terrace in Regent's Park, London, telephoned Scotland Yard in December 1930.

According to the police constable, H. Grub, who took the message, Noyes said that a bound copy of the suppressed book, *Ulysses*, was catalogued for sale among the books belonging to the late Lord Birkenhead, the former Lord Chancellor, at 32 Grosvenor Square, in south-west London. Inspector Warner of the CID was put on the job. He established that Hampton's, the auctioneers, were dealing with it and the complaint was reported to the Home Office but nothing further was done. Alfred Noyes was not to be put off. Two days later he telephoned the police again and said that at the suggestion of Lord Darling, he had been trying to contact the Director of Public Prosecutions. He was told to leave it in the hands of Scotland Yard. The next day a reluctant senior Metropolitan Police officer reported:

> I saw the Director of Public Prosecutions and the Home Office. Last evening I saw Lady Birkenhead's private secretary and told her that a complaint was made about the sale of this book, and that there was a possibility of some adverse comment might be made in the press or elsewhere with the result that she will make arrangements to have the lot withdrawn. If Mr Noyes rings again we can say the matter has been 'dealt with' – that is quite enough.

Obviously it was assumed that a former Attorney-General and a Lord Chancellor was not expected to conform to the laws of the land.

Some requests to the Home Office were granted. S. Herbert, a Justice of the Peace, doctor and medical author, wrote in December 1930 asking for permission to have *Ulysses* sent to him for a 'special psychological study'. After checking his entry in the *Medical Directory*, which described him as 'a psycho-therapist who has written widely on sexual matters', the Home Office replied that they had no objection to him obtaining a copy for his private use. The same response was given to E. Haigh, the Director of Education for Eastbourne, who said that he wanted to read the book 'from a critical survey of modern writing point of view'. But the ban was still effective. Harold Nicolson, who had been given some broadcasting work to do, in the form of a series of BBC talks on English Literature, was forbidden by Lord Reith himself to mention *Ulysses*. The row that ensued led to Nicolson's dismissal by the BBC.

In the following year, 1932, the poet and friend of Joyce, T.S. Eliot, tried to suggest that some episodes of *Ulysses* might appear in his magazine, *Criterion*. But Joyce refused, saying that the idiotic state of British censorship made it impossible. He also wanted the book presented intact with its beginning, middle and end. Instead he suggested to Eliot that his publishers, Faber & Faber, might be interested in producing a private, limited edition, which, if highly priced enough, would avoid Home Office action. T.S. Eliot and Faber & Faber took the suggestion seriously enough to arrange a meeting with the Home Office to see if they agreed with Joyce's assessment. The meeting arranged by a future Attorney-General, Sir David Somervell, was held between Eliot, Mr Mosley of Faber & Faber and a senior civil servant, J.F. Henderson of the Home Office. They were not given a firm reassurance that all would be well.

It is clear that by the mid-1930s attitudes were already changing, however, and the new censorship of the 1920s no longer held such sway in the Home Office. The first signs in the *Ulysses* case came in an internal Whitehall debate over a request in January 1934 from Desmond McCarthy, a friend of Harold Nicolson's, who had asked for official permission to import a copy of *Ulysses*. He said that he was to deliver a series of lectures at the Royal Institute in London and wanted to consult the book.

John Lane of the Bodley Head Press had made clear through the newspapers that he was going to finally attempt a British publication of *Ulysses*. The official minutes argue that as the work might finally be published in London 'very shortly' – when the question of its free circulation would have to be decided – that 'it would be impolitic to refuse' Desmond

McCarthy's request in view of the impending events. At least one senior Home Office civil servant did not yet believe the game was up. Mr Henderson wanted to hold the line:

> This is an awkward inquiry at this moment when there have been paragraphs in the press about John Lane's having posted a copy of the book to himself from Paris (he says it got through) and about his intention to publish *Ulysses* here. If Desmond McCarthy were asked at the Royal Institute meeting as to how he got hold of a copy and said that the Home Office had given him leave other people might ask for leave or inquire whether we regarded the book as obscene or not according to its recipient. It is unlikely the inquiry is in the nature of a trap and it is equally unlikely that McCarthy cannot get hold of a copy from somebody of his acquaintance.

The Home Office consulted the DPP, who advised:

> The problem is not easy. The authorities regard a book for the purposes of action as obscene or not according to the use to which it may be put (not perhaps according to its recipient). In practice it is suppression of trade and publicity of obscenities that is aimed at.

In the end the Home Office cut its losses and decided to allow McCarthy his copy: 'See, it shows the Home Office is not as narrow-minded as you thought,' Henderson told the critic.

The pressure for the ban to be lifted was growing. The next major development came from the United States. The Foreign Office papers recording the ruling by a New York judge that *Ulysses* was not legally obscene stirred great interest in the Home Office.

Judge John M. Woolsey accepted the standard US legal definition of obscenity as 'tending to stir the sex impulses or to lead to sexually impure and lustful thoughts'. But he added that it

should be applied to 'the effect on a person with average sex in-
stincts'. He said that *Ulysses* was rather a strong draught to ask
some sensitive, though normal, persons to take but while in
many places its effect on the reader was somewhat emetic,
nowhere did it tend to be an aphrodisiac. Judge Woolsey said the
words that were criticised as dirty were old Anglo-Saxon words
known to almost all men and to many women; as for the fact
that his characters seemed to have sex on their minds nearly all
the time, it had to be remembered that Joyce's 'locale was Celtic
and his season was Spring'. So on these grounds the ban on
Ulysses being imported into the United States was lifted.

The Home Office assessment described *Ulysses* as the 'first
cinematic novel' with its stream of consciousness narrative covering a certain day in 1904 in lower-middle-class Dublin: 'Not
just what the day contained but what they thought about it too.'
The US Court of Appeal ruling in August 1934 upheld the
Woolsey judgment. Although there was obscene matter in the
book, there was such a lot of other material in it that the
obscene part could properly be regarded as swallowed up by the
rest. Henderson noted that this meant the book must be looked
at as a whole and, taken as a whole, *Ulysses* did not promote lust.
Nowhere could be detected the 'sneer of the sensualist'.

T.S. Eliot told the Americans that the most complained of
parts were on pages 451 and 742, which were the 'most remarkable passages in the book'. The first was taken to be a picture of
the general loss of control over one's thoughts in the passage
from ordinary consciousness through a sort of dream or fantasy
stage, to complete loss of control ending in sleep. The second
was the 'famous "interior monologue" of the non-stop variety'.
The lifting of the ban resulted in a hugely successful Random
House unlimited edition. Henderson of the Home Office drily
noted on the file: 'This doesn't help us very much'. As if to drive
the point home, the authorities ensured that convictions in
Britain for sending *Ulysses* through the post continued.

It was to be another two years before *Ulysses* finally breached
the walls of the Home Office. On 21 September 1936, Henderson

informed the Home Secretary: 'An extremely awkward situation has now arisen.' The Metropolitan Police Commissioner had reported that Foyles had indicated that a limited edition was to be published within a few weeks without any indication of who the publisher might be.

> I had a preliminary word with the DPP along the lines that a book costing £6.6.0 or £3.3.0 (£6.30 or £3.15) was not likely to get into the hands of anyone likely to be corrupted by it and that probably the prudent course was to do nothing.
>
> It now appears that the book was published last Saturday by John Lane of the Bodley Head. The *Morning Post* says that John Lane consulted the Home Office first, but there is no record of such consultation on the file and I have never heard of such consultation.
>
> The last time it was discussed in the Home Office was when Mr T.S. Eliot and Mr Mosley of Faber and Faber came to see me in January 1934 being introduced by the present Attorney-General. It was then decided to await developments and see if the book was published here and if there were any protests. It was agreed in 1922 that the Customs and Post Office should seize copies. No doubt many copies got through.

Henderson admitted that the book had for a long time been lectured on at Cambridge, and yet the ban had been kept up. He predicted:

> There are two chapters which will be the battleground if there is a prosecution. They contain many offensive passages. The defence will be that the first is an admirable literary description of the gradual transition from complete consciousness to a state of dream, showing the gradual loss of control over the mind and that the second similarly portrays the 'stream of consciousness'.

It will be argued that it is a Freudian novel form and
that serious adults should not be prevented from reading
a book which may not be suitable for the young. A
limited expensive edition is not likely to get into the
hands of the young but if it goes well there is a risk it
will be followed by a cheaper edition although a cheaper
edition which would be relatively dear.

A Whitehall summit conference between the Home Office, the
Attorney-General and the DPP was suggested to decide on the
fate of *Ulysses*.

A fortnight later on 8 October the *Morning Post* newspaper
reported that 1,000 copies were on sale in London. One
hundred of them were a signed edition costing 6 guineas each
and the rest were 3 guineas. There was a 'brisk demand' for
copies of a work that was advertised by the Bodley Head as the
banned book read by Lord Chancellors and the subject of Cambridge University lectures. On 6 November 1936 the Whitehall
conference finally took place:

Sir David Somervell, the Attorney-General, said the
definition of obscenity in R v Hicklin was inadequate. In
his view the question of intention of the writer has to be
taken into account as in the criminal law generally. The
context or general setting also has to be considered. No
one today would hold that books such as by Havelock-
Ellis on sexual matters or medical books on sexual
aberrations were obscene.

Standards in these matters are constantly changing.
Having applied these tests to *Ulysses* he was of the
opinion that the book was not obscene and having
regard in addition to its established position in literature
he had decided to take no action.

A week later, on 13 November 1936, a confidential note was circulated to the Post Office and Customs cancelling the intercept

warrants allowing them to search any parcel suspected of containing the book. The British ban on James Joyce's *Ulysses* had lasted almost 14 years. Joyce himself proudly told friends that his 20-year war with England was over and that he was the conqueror. The first unlimited edition of *Ulysses* appeared in 1937 but the fears of the Home Office were not to be quickly realised. By the time this unlimited edition appeared, Ulysses had sold barely 30,000 copies during the first 15 years of its existence. Whitehall's assessment of the prospects for the future sales of *Ulysses* did not prove far off the mark. The cover price of the Bodley Head edition meant that its sales rarely reached beyond the intelligentsia. It was not until Penguin produced its cheap paperback edition 30 years later in 1968 that the Joyce classic reached the status of a bestseller. While the negotiations over the paperback rights were going on, Max Reinhart of Bodley Head told Penguin: 'You could easily sell 200,000 copies the first year and certainly 75,000 a year in subsequent years.' In the event Penguin printed 250,000 as a first run. Six months later Penguin printed a second run of 70,000 and then third and fourth runs of 50,000 each. By 1970 the Penguin edition of *Ulysses* had sold more than 420,000 copies. It took time – nearly 50 years – but in the end the ban had helped turn *Ulysses* into one of the biggest-selling books of the twentieth century.

The Well of Loneliness: a phial of prussic acid?

I would rather put a phial of prussic acid in the hands of a healthy boy or girl than this novel. Poison kills the body, but moral poison kills the soul.

James Douglas, editor of the *Sunday Express*[1]

If the complexity of Joycean prose proved no protection from persecution for the sexually explicit language of *Ulysses*, then the complete lack of any graphic detail in Radclyffe Hall's book, *The Well of Loneliness*, was to be even more irrelevant. The most salacious phrases to be found within the 500 pages of the first novel to treat lesbianism seriously are probably 'she kissed her full on the lips' and they slept together one night 'and were not divided'. The condemnation of *The Well of Loneliness* was to prove the low point in the twentieth-century history of British literary censorship. Its effects were to be felt for more than 30 years and ensured that Victorian sexual hypocrisy continues to exert an influence even to this day.

The *Well of Loneliness* case was more dangerous territory for Baldwin's Home Secretary, Sir William Joynson-Hicks, than might at first be assumed. Recently released Whitehall papers show that the Customs, backed by Winston Churchill, then

THE WELL OF LONELINESS

By
RADCLYFFE HALL

" . . . . . nothing extenuate,
Nor set down aught in malice."

with a commentary by
HAVELOCK ELLIS

JONATHAN CAPE
THIRTY BEDFORD SQUARE
LONDON

The Well of Loneliness by Radclyffe Hall, 1928. Title page of the first edition.

Chancellor of the Exchequer and so responsible for Customs and Excise, did not regard the book as obscene and wanted no part in its prosecution.

Churchill's objection meant that Joynson-Hicks, or Jix as he was known, could not simply rely on an executive declaration from the Director of Public Prosecutions that the book was obscene, as he had done in the *Ulysses* case. He would have to persuade the publishers to withdraw the book or (worse still) find a court willing to ban it. The newly released state files show that Jix, the puritanical purge of publishing, was not prepared to leave anything to chance. In the face of Customs' reluctance to ban the book, the Home Secretary resorted to an elaborate 'sting' operation, to prove that the publishers were importing copies from Paris. Then he went on to make sure that the magistrate involved would come to the right decision long before the case ever got anywhere near his court.

The case also marked a major defeat for the literary world of Bloomsbury, which, as Diana Souhami has shown in her biography of Radclyffe Hall, was uneasy in its defence of an openly lesbian author.[2] The effect of the magistrate's decision to exclude all expert evidence of the literary and artistic merits of the work was to shape British censorship for another 30 years. As Leonard Woolf complained at the time in the *Manchester Guardian*:'the existing law has been interpreted in such a way by the police and magistrates, that they can if they so desire, bring practically any book published within its scope.'[3] Others have argued since that the more ridiculous prosecutions of the twentieth century might have been avoided but for the precedent set in this trial.

Radclyffe Hall, already a prize-winning author, was under no illusions about the significance of *The Well of Loneliness*:

> I have put my pen at the service of some of the most
> persecuted and misunderstood people in the world. In a
> word I have written a long and very serious novel
> entirely upon the subject of sexual inversion ... So far as
> I know nothing of the kind has ever been attempted
> before in fiction.[4]

The book was designed to give a voice to British lesbians. In her case, as Diana Souhami documents, it was not necessarily a particularly attractive voice. A wealthy woman who was a cryptofascist and an anti-Semite, and whose claim to be among the most persecuted in the world has to be judged against a lifestyle of fine houses, stylish lovers, inherited incomes, villas in the sun and the rearing of dachshunds. She is not at first sight a natural heroine of the modern-day struggle for lesbian and gay equality.

Una Lady Troubridge and Miss Radclyffe Hall and dachschunds.

Yet the condemnation of the book stirred protests even within the highest levels of government itself in the 1920s, raising questions about just how repressive the British state should be.

The book itself is an explicit portrayal of lesbianism but as many recognised at the time, it was in the tradition of what were then known as the 'Came the Dawn' novels that dealt with romantic love in a sentimental fashion. It is the story of a woman called Stephen Gordon, whose parents had ardently wanted a son, and who became a tomboy as a result, favouring such pastimes as fencing. She falls in love with Angela Crossby, a blonde, blue-eyed American. It has been described as a moving story of ecstatic and unhappy love between women in a hostile society. 'Give us also the right to our existence,' appeals Stephen Gordon at the end of the novel.

This is what Radclyffe Hall's critics were complaining about:

> 'We're both filled with the old peace of Morton, because
> we love each other so deeply – and because we're
> perfect, a perfect thing, you and I – not two separate
> people but one. And our love has lit a great, comforting
> beacon, so that we need never be afraid of the dark any
> more – we can warm ourselves at our love, we can lie
> down together, and my arms will be around you –'
>
> She broke off abruptly, and they stared at each other.
>
> 'Do you know what you're saying?' Angela whispered.
>
> And Stephen answered: 'I know I love you, and that
> nothing else matters in the world.'
>
> Then, perhaps because of that glamorous evening, with
> its spirit of queer, unearthly adventure, with its urge to
> strange, unendurable sweetness, Angela moved a step
> nearer to Stephen, then another, until their hands were
> touching. And all that she was, and all that she had been
> and would be again, perhaps even tomorrow, was fused at
> that moment into one mighty impulse, one imperative
> need, and that need was Stephen. Stephen's need was
> now hers, by sheer force of its blind and
> uncomprehending will to appeasement.
>
> Then Stephen took Angela into her arms, and she
> kissed her full on the lips, as a lover.[5]

It has become regarded as a bible in the literature of lesbianism
as all Radclyffe Hall's contemporaries kept their sexuality firmly
shut in the literary closet.

The Well of Loneliness was well received by the London critics
when Jonathan Cape published it in July 1928 at 15 shillings (75
pence) – more than twice the price of an ordinary novel. Its
publication date had been rushed forward so as to come out
before Compton Mackenzie's novel, *Extraordinary Women*, a
malicious satire on upper-class lesbians, which was to be published two months later in September 1928. L.P. Hartley in the

Saturday Review said the book 'showed what miseries, disabilities, and persecutions women of this type were subjected to in England'.[6] The *Sunday Times* wrote of Radclyffe Hall's courage, honesty and lively sense of characterisation, as did Arnold Bennett. Arnold Dawson in the Labour-supporting *Daily Herald* said that he could find nothing in the book that was pornographic:

> The evil minded will seek in vain in these pages for any
> stimulant to sexual excitement. The lustful sheikhs and
> cavemen and vamps of popular fiction may continue
> their sadistic course unchecked in those pornographic
> novels that are sold by the million, but Miss Radclyffe
> Hall has entirely ignored these crude and violent figures
> of sexual melodrama. She has given to English Literature
> a profound and moving study of a profound and moving
> problem.[7]

In a preface Havelock Ellis said that its 'poignant situations are set forth with a complete absence of offence', while Vera Brittain believed that it was sincere, important, and passionate but was confused on whether Stephen Gordon's 'inversion' was due to nature or nurture. Leonard Woolf was cooler, saying the book was a failure, tendentious and lacking form; Cyril Connolly in the *New Statesman* described it as long, tedious and melodramatic. There was, however, no objection to the lesbianism. The conspiracy of silence had been broken.

The forces of conservatism were quick to counterattack. James Douglas, editor of the *Sunday Express*, politely sent a note to Jonathan Cape saying that he had written a leader for that weekend's paper calling for *The Well of Loneliness* to be suppressed. The terms of the article were less polite: 'This novel forces upon our Society a disagreeable task which it has hitherto shirked,' wrote Mr Douglas:

> The task of cleaning itself from the leprosy of these
> lepers and making the air clean and wholesome once

more. It flings a veil of sentiment over their depravity. It even suggests that their self-made debasement is unavoidable because they cannot save themselves ... If Christianity does not destroy this doctrine, then this doctrine will destroy it, together with the civilisation it has built on the ruins of paganism. These moral derelicts are not cursed from their birth ... They are damned because they choose to be damned, not because they are damned from the beginning.

This bigoted outburst from James Douglas was the most extreme but not untypical example of the kind of moral indignation that the *Sunday Express* was to make its trademark over the next 50 years. When Beaverbrook founded the paper in 1918, he was determined to provide a 'family' alternative to the mass circulation Sunday newspapers, such as the *News of the World* and the *People*, which specialised in sensations, scandals and, by the standards of the time, pornography. It was aimed at the respectable church-going classes who felt themselves above such sleazy sheets. James Douglas, and his successors, provided the kind of fire and brimstone thunderbolts that Beaverbrook cynically believed would appeal to them.[8]

It was enough for the publisher to take fright. Jonathan Cape reacted immediately, without consulting Radclyffe Hall. He sent a copy of the book to the Home Secretary, together with a selection of the reviews, and invited him to pass it on to the Director of Public Prosecutions if he thought it necessary. Cape was trying to test the water in a way that had been legally impossible since the Second World War. The Home Secretary at that time had the power to direct the DPP to prosecute; if Joynson-Hicks decided not to send it to Bodkin, then *The Well of Loneliness* would be in the clear. If he did wish to prosecute, the publisher could withdraw the book before the action went ahead, thus saving a great deal of time and expense for the publisher. Many commentators have since claimed that this was a fatal error of judgment by Jonathan Cape.

The offer to withdraw *The Well of Loneliness* was made in the shape of a letter to James Douglas on the same day as his fulmination had appeared in the *Sunday Express*. Cape said that the book was not intended to be given to boys and girls and had been deliberately published at the high price of 15 shillings to keep it out of the hands of the general novel-reading public. He said that because of the kind of publicity Douglas had given the book, the smut hounds would now be anxious to read it so that they might lift up their hands in indignation that such things could be allowed.

> If it is shown to us that the best interests of the public will be served by withdrawing the book from circulation we will be ready to do this and to accept the full consequences as publishers. We are not however prepared to withdraw it at the behest of the Editor of the *Sunday Express*.

Douglas wasted no time. Monday's *Daily Express* printed the Cape letter and under the headline 'Book to be Banned: Home Secretary's Duty', he underlined the need to tackle this sexual perversity.

Radclyffe Hall's friends were astounded. Cape's naïve assumption that the Home Secretary would clear the book angered them. All the evidence indicated that he would move against a book on lesbianism. Sir William Joynson-Hicks, as president of the National Church League and a fervent evangelical, had already been in the forefront of the fight against such modernist innovations as the Church of England's revised Prayer Book. The Attorney-General, Sir Thomas Inskip, had fought alongside him. Even the Bishop of Durham had called Jix a 'dour fanatic'. He was violently anti-communist as illustrated by his role during the early 1920s and the General Strike; his reputation as Home Secretary was such that it makes Michael Howard look like a model liberal. To this day his name still evokes disgust among senior Home Office civil servants.

Joynson-Hicks got Cape's letter and a copy of the book on the Monday afternoon. He passed it on to the DPP asking for his opinion on whether a jury would convict if Radclyffe Hall were prosecuted for obscene libel under the 1857 Obscene Publications Act. Sir Archibald Bodkin was away. His deputy, Sir Guy Stephenson, replied the next day. The speed with which the opinion was delivered suggests that the book had already been a subject for discussion among the DPP's staff for some days.

Stephenson first noted that the book had been widely and favourably reviewed in the press, with the *Times Literary Supplement* describing it as 'sincere, courageous, high-minded and beautifully expressed'. But the fact remained that the book was a plea not only for toleration but also for the recognition of 'sexual perversion' among women. Stephenson said that under the Hicklin judgment, the fact that Radclyffe Hall did not intend to corrupt her readers was immaterial, given that the test was whether it tended to deprave and corrupt those whose minds were open to such immoral influence, and into whose hands the book was likely to fall.

'In my view this book would tend to corrupt the minds of young persons if it fell into their hands and its sale is undesirable,' said Sir Guy, adding that he thought there was a reasonable prospect that a jury would convict in this case. 'Incidentally it would appear to be clear that the authoress is herself what I believe is known as a homo-sexualist, or as she prefers to describe it, an "invert".'[9]

Amazingly to anyone who cherishes a belief in the independence of the judiciary, the deputy director also made clear that he had taken some 'soundings' as to the likely judgment in the case before it had even reached the courts. As his confidential note to the Home Secretary put it:

> I may state that I have informally consulted the Chief Magistrate upon this matter; he has read the book and tells me that he would have no hesitation in granting process. I should add that before instituting any

> proceedings in this matter I should consider it my duty
> to take the directions of the Attorney-General [Sir
> Thomas Inskip].

However, Stephenson did sound one note of caution. He advised Jix that a prosecution would undoubtedly give the book further publicity and he personally thought it would be better to take up the offer from Jonathan Cape to withdraw the book from circulation.

Jix then had what he described to Stephenson as 'a long private conference with the Lord Chancellor' (then Lord Hailsham, Douglas Hogg's grandfather), after which 'we came to the conclusion that the book is both obscene and indecent and I wrote a letter to the publishers asking for its withdrawal. If they decline proceed at once,' says the note in red ink in Joynson-Hicks's own handwriting.

The letter to Cape pointed out that the book was inherently obscene, it supported a depraved practice, its tendency was to corrupt and it could be suppressed by criminal proceedings. It should be borne in mind that lesbianism is not and was not at this time illegal.[10]

Arnold Bennett makes clear in his journal that Stephenson was not the only one to take informal soundings from Sir Chartres Biron, the Chief Magistrate at the Bow Street police court. He says that on the Thursday after the *Sunday Express* attack, he saw James Douglas and Biron talking to each other in the Garrick Club:

> I set violently on Jimmy at once about his attack on
> Radclyffe Hall's sapphic novel. Jimmy was very quiet and
> restrained but Biron defended Jimmy with real heat.[11]

Cape agreed to withdraw the book. His letter pulling the British publication of *The Well of Loneliness* was printed by *The Times*:

> Sir, We have today received a request from the Home

> Secretary asking us to discontinue publication of Miss
> Radclyffe Hall's novel *The Well of Loneliness*. We have
> already expressed our readiness to fall in with the wishes
> of the Home Office in this matter, we have therefore
> stopped publication.

This was not total surrender by Jonathan Cape, however. He had
already devised Plan B. The publicity had generated a massive
demand for the book with 5,000 copies already in circulation
and a third reprint about to be produced. Cape cancelled this
and told the printer to make moulds of the type. He had learned
one lesson from the *Ulysses* case and intended to send the
moulds secretly to Paris and to print the book there.

The papier-mâché moulds were delivered to Paris by
Jonathan Cape's partner, Wren Howard, who took them as hand
baggage aboard a plane. He delivered them to the offices of the
Pegasus Press, which was owned by John Holroyd-Reece, who
had worked with Cape. Along with the moulds was a list of un-
fulfilled British orders and a mailing list of sympathetic bookshops. A London bookseller, Leopold Hill, of 101 Great Russell
Street, was appointed to act as distributor. There was as yet no
formal ban on British publication, only the 'gentleman's agreement' to withdraw the work between Cape and the Home Secretary, albeit made with the threat of a swift prosecution hanging
over it.

It took the Pegasus Press only three weeks to print this illicit
edition. Circulars were sent to British booksellers advertising
the book at 25 shillings (£1.25) plus postage, making clear that
'not one word has been altered'. Orders were brisk.

Among the first indications received by the Home Office
that something was afoot was a letter from Mrs Anne Stanley,
writing from Harrowhill Copse, Newlands Corner, Guildford,
to a friend of hers, Dr Norris, who worked at the Home Office.
She had seen one of the circulars that had been addressed to her
husband.

Probably the Home Office has already seen it. If they
have not, I do wish it could be brought to the attention
of the proper department – perhaps that is you. To my
mind it is a distinctly medical matter. The book was lent
to me by someone who had acquired it before it was
suppressed, and I read it carefully with a view to seeing
whether there was any harm in it. I must say I came to
the conclusion that these abnormal sexual relations are so
much a matter of *suggestion* that books of this kind do
infinite harm.

I think it is an enormous pity that Cape should have,
as he obviously has, sent the pages to France to
circulation in a way that our medical authorities cannot
touch. The same may be said of Compton MacKenzie's
new book, but fortunately that is so dull that I don't
think many people will read it.

I do think it is an enormous pity that the book should
have been suppressed in consequence of the *Sunday
Express's* hysterical article. The case for non-circulation is
very much stronger than would appear from this
circumstance. I know you are occupied with preventive
health measures and that therefore I am not going
outside the sphere of your work in sending you the
circular.

The first official warning came from the General Post Office
(GPO) on 1 October saying they had detected five copies of the
book sent from Paris and asking the Home Office what action,
if any, was wanted.[12]

Two days after the GPO reported the seizure, a reporter from
the *Daily Sketch* telephoned the Home Office saying that he had
seen the Pegasus Press circular and asking what action the
Home Secretary intended to take against *The Well of Loneliness*.
After being told that the Pegasus Press in Paris had made a fresh
printing and that attempts were being made 'to introduce copies
into this country on a large scale', Joynson-Hicks signed two

new warrants on 5 October. They ordered the seizure of any copies of *The Well of Loneliness* sent through the post or imported through Customs. Any parcel or letter to or from the Pegasus Press, 37 Rue Boulard (14e), Paris, was to be traced and opened. All ports were told that copies found in goods or passengers' baggage were to be seized.

The warrants were issued just in time for the Dover Customs to seize the first consignment of 247 copies addressed to Leopold Hill. The *Daily Express*, which was unhappy about being scooped by its rival, the *Daily Sketch*, on its own witch-hunt, trumpeted the 'revelation' that the Paris firm of publishers was trying to 'nullify the Home Secretary's ban on the book by sending it to England by post'. Once again James Douglas urged swift action: 'The Home Secretary shared our view and did not shirk the issue when his decision was asked.' The Home Office then told a solicitor acting for the Pegasus Press, Harold Rubinstein, that the Dover seizure was a matter for the Board of Customs and Excise, and if he wanted to challenge it, he had to give notice of his intention. Rubinstein wrote a formal letter saying that he was acting for John Holroyd-Reece, who accepted full responsibility and that Leopold Hill was only the London agent. He told Customs they would appear with counsel and witnesses and that he had also been instructed to say that Miss Radclyffe Hall wished to be heard under section 32 of the Customs Act as 'another person'. Under the law as it then stood, the author of a book had no automatic right to appear in any proceedings to ban it.

The stage appeared to be set. There was then a highly unexpected development and one that has remained a secret locked in the basement of the Home Office for more than 70 years. Sir Francis Floud, the Chairman of Customs and Excise and the rest of his Board decided to read some of the copies of the book they had seized and they came to a startlingly different conclusion from that of Sir William Joynson-Hicks: they did not believe it was obscene.

Perhaps Sir Francis Floud was not a member of the Garrick

Club. He certainly did not share Jix's evangelical Christian zeal.
On this occasion at least, he decided that it was time to flex the
independent muscles of Customs and Excise, which is responsible not to the Home Secretary, but to the Chancellor of the
Exchequer, who at this time was Winston Churchill. The documents detailing Floud's request for Churchill's support have only
recently been released. Floud stressed that the powers that
Customs had under the 1876 Act to prevent imports of indecent
or obscene books were independent of the Home Secretary's
powers under the Obscene Publications Act:

> We have therefore had to examine the book and to
> consider whether it is indecent or obscene. If we decide
> that it is indecent or obscene we have to give formal
> notice of seizure, and the owner has a month within
> which he can appeal against seizure.

This is what Rubinstein had been told. What he was never told
was the opinion of the book that the Board of Customs and
Excise reached after reading it: 'Our examination of the book
leaves us in considerable doubt whether the book can properly
be regarded as indecent or obscene,' Floud told Churchill.

> The subject is treated seriously and sincerely, with
> restraint in expression and with great literary skill and
> delicacy. In effect it is an appeal for compassion and
> understanding and the pitiful tragedy of the story does
> not seem calculated to arouse sexual emotion or to
> corrupt morals by encouraging the practice of sexual
> inversion.

That was not all.

> If the subject is one that can permissibly be treated at all
> in a novel, it is difficult to see how it could be treated
> with more restraint. If on the other hand the subject is to

be regarded as inadmissible it will be difficult to know where our censorship is to stop, and questions will at once arise whether similar action must not be taken against other books, particularly Mr Compton Mackenzie's *Extraordinary Women*.

If we were left to ourselves we should have come to the conclusion that, apart from the question of policy whether action on our part would not give the book undesirable publicity and gratuitous advertisement, the book is not one that should be stopped on the ground of indecency or obscenity. We could not point to any particular passages in the book as being indecent or obscene, and we should be very reluctant to be cross-examined as to the grounds on which we could justify the seizure of the book as indecent or obscene.

Floud went on to discount the action taken by Jix so far. Floud said that in

certain literary circles protests were made against the alleged unjustifiable censorship by the Government of a work of literary merit but up until this point no direct action has been taken by any Government department apart from the Home Secretary's personal request to Mr Cape.

This was dynamite. Here was proof that there were sane people at the highest levels of Whitehall even in the 1920s who were prepared to stand up to the moral crusaders. If Sir Francis Floud's advice to ministers had been known to Radclyffe Hall's defence at the time, it would surely have killed stone dead the chance of any jury convicting the book as obscene.

Instead Floud could do no more than make clear that Customs would play no part in the prosecution. They did not want to hold the copies of the book at Dover or testify against it in the High Court. This posed a very big problem for the

Home Office. As Floud himself explained to Churchill: 'If we allowed the consignment to be imported there is no ready or certain means by which the Home Office could take action.' He added that it would also be hugely embarrassing to Jix, as it meant that Customs would be 'flouting the publicly expressed opinion of the Home Secretary, and could hardly fail to prejudice any proceedings he might take subsequently to prevent the sale of the book'.

Floud sat down with Sir John Anderson, the second most senior civil servant at the Home Office, and Sir Archibald Bodkin, the DPP, 'in order to explore the possibility of action being taken by the Home Office rather than by Customs'.

Floud got Churchill's backing for his independent stand. The file simply notes:

> The Chancellor of Exchequer has considered the matter and decided that Customs should not be in a position of having defend this action in court and therefore action under the Customs Laws is ruled out.

Meanwhile Sir John Anderson, the DPP and Sir Thomas Inskip, the Attorney-General, got on with devising an elaborate 'sting' operation so as to prosecute both Cape and the Pegasus Press, if the necessary evidence could be obtained. They excitedly got on with tracking down and interviewing the printers of the original English edition. He told the police that Jonathan Cape had supplied the paper for the printing of the book in Paris and an elaborate operation was devised to tie the publishing company firmly into the scheme.

> It was suggested that the Customs should release the parcel of books detained and they shall inform the consignees that this action has been taken in consultation with the DPP.

This arrangement was confirmed by phone with a reluctant Floud.

> He will arrange for the books to be brought privately to
> London in readiness. It is also suggested that a selection
> of the stopped correspondence should be forwarded and
> a watch kept for letters and parcels to the addresses of
> both the Pegasus Press, Paris, and Pegasus Press, London.

The 'selection of stopped correspondence' was a number of
letters from various people in England to the Pegasus Press in
Paris, ordering copies of the book. Some letters contained
cheques. They were to be sent back to the Post Office to be sealed
up and posted on. The Dover consignment was not only to be released so it could be shadowed all the way to Leopold Hill's
London offices. It was also to be watched to ensure that no books
were removed to any other address. Separately four copies of the
book, ordered by Jonathan Cape and intercepted by the Post
Office, were to be delivered at exactly the same time as the Dover
case. The police were to be waiting at both addresses with search
warrants. The Home Office instructions to the police were clear:

> Hill, when the parcel from Dover has reached him,
> should be informed that the book is identical with that
> withdrawn by Cape, and that if he publishes any copies
> of it, proceedings will be taken against him. He will not
> unlikely adopt the attitude that the book is not indecent,
> whereupon he can be asked to sell a copy to an officer.

Meanwhile Floud was being repeatedly pestered by Rubinstein
as to when the books were going to be released. Floud told the
Home Office:

> The solicitors have written to us three times, and also
> called here, to press for an early decision. It would be
> really impertinent for us to ask them why they are in a
> hurry. It is not our business and we should only expose
> ourselves to a well merited snub. It would be better to
> delay any answer until we can tell them our decision.

The disclosure that Customs and Churchill were firmly opposed to Joynson-Hicks's determination to ban this book may throw extra light on a speech that the Home Secretary gave to the London Diocesan Council of Youth at Central Hall, Westminster, on 15 October 1928. In it Jix revealed what was on his mind:

> The Home Secretary is a man who is exposed to every kind of attack, and gets it pretty often. It may be possible in the near future I shall have to deal with immoral and disgusting books. For instance I have had to deal with immoral and disgusting behaviour in our parks and public places. I have to deal at times with plays and cinemas, though I have no real power in this respect.
>
> I am attacked on the one hand by all those people who put freedom of speech and thought and writing before everything else in the world, as if there were freedom in God's world to pollute the generation growing up. There must be some limit to the freedom on what a man may write or speak in this great country of ours. That freedom, in my view, must be determined by the question as to whether what is written or spoken makes one of the least of these little ones offended.[13]

His proposed test of obscenity – whether it would bring a blush to the cheek of Little Nell – was to dog Jix for his remaining days. A few weeks later he was challenged in the House of Commons by the Liberal MP, Leslie Hore-Belisha, to admit that he was trying to reduce the whole of English literature to a standard that was 'only fit for the least of the little ones'. Jix refused to be drawn, saying that he could not comment while a case was pending. Nevertheless he could not resist claiming that he was not a censor at all and was only carrying out the desires of Parliament – even though he had admitted in his speech that he had banned films and plays without having the formal powers to do so. (Incidentally among the casualties was Eisenstein's classic Russian agitprop film, *Battleship Potemkin*, which was banned from British screens on the orders of Joynson-Hicks in September 1926 four months after the General Strike. It was a ban that was to last until 1954.)

The meticulously planned raids to seize the first lesbian novel were finally carried out on 19 October 1928. The police seized the 247 copies of *The Well of Loneliness* at Hill's and a further six that had been forwarded by the Post Office to Jonathan Cape's offices. It came as no surprise to the Home Office that Sir Chartres Biron granted search warrants to the police for both offices and also issued the summonses 'calling upon both firms to show cause why the books seized should not be destroyed'. The date of the hearing at Bow Street Magistrates' Court was set for 9 November at 10.30 a.m. The court was packed with what the *Evening Standard* called 'many well-known literary figures and fashionably dressed women' when Sir Chartres Biron opened the proceedings.[14] The previous month had not been wasted by either side. They had both been hard at work recruiting potential witnesses.

According to Diana Souhami's account, it had not been an easy task for Radclyffe Hall and Rubinstein. Many were sympathetic but few were willing to go into the witness box. The Archbishop of York foresaw 'practical difficulties'; H.G. Wells had 'gone abroad'; Arthur Conan Doyle 'had left for South Africa'; George Bernard Shaw believed that he was too immoral to have any credibility. Even Bloomsbury itself was having doubts. Virginia Woolf wrote to a friend: 'We have to uphold the morality of that Well of all that's stagnant and lukewarm and neither one thing or the other; *The Well of Loneliness.*'[15] Leonard Woolf told her not to appear in the witness box. There was a real danger that she would 'cast a shadow over Bloomsbury' by saying what they all really thought of the book.

Nevertheless Rubinstein did find 40 distinguished people, including the Prime Minister's own homosexual son, Oliver Baldwin, who were prepared to testify for the principle of literary freedom. Radclyffe Hall recalled: 'We had doctors, male and

female, men of science, educationalists, clergy, journalists, prominent booksellers, and of course a great number of fellow
authors.'[16]

In the courtroom sat the cream of the British literary establishment: James Agate, Arnold Bennett, Vera Brittain, John
Buchan, John Drinkwater, T.S. Eliot, E.M. Forster, Harley
Granville-Barker, Professor Julian Huxley, Rose Macaulay,
Desmond McCarthy, George Bernard Shaw, Lytton Strachey,
and Leonard and Virginia Woolf. Sir Archibald Bodkin sat on the
other side of the court. When Sir Chartres Biron got the proceedings under way, it soon became clear that he was not interested in calling any of the 40 witnesses for the defence. He sent
them all home and his decision meant that it was to be another
30 years before the views of such literary experts would be
heard in any obscenity case held in a British court.

First in the witness box was Chief Inspector Protheroe of
New Scotland Yard, who had carried out the raids on the offices
of Leopold Hill and Jonathan Cape. He testified that the book
had been seized. He told the court that he had experience of a
great deal of obscene literature, and he had read *The Well of Loneliness*: 'The book is indecent, it deals with an indecent subject,'
he said.

Eustace Fulton, appearing for the DPP, said that the case for
the prosecution rested on the fact that the book dealt with
certain relations between women and contended that this was
an obscene theme, and the book should not be published. The
test of what was obscene was that used in the Hicklin case, that
is whether the book tended to deprave and corrupt those whose
minds were open to such immoral influences and into whose
hands such a book might fall.

Norman Birkett, for the publishers, opened the defence by
announcing his intention to call his distinguished witnesses to
testify that the book was not obscene, and those who had passed
the 1857 Obscene Publications Act never intended it to be used
against such a book.

> I want to call medical testimony, I want to call a minister
> of religion, critics, reviewers, authors, authoresses,
> publishers and people from the libraries of London. I
> want to give evidence from every conceivable walk of
> life which bears upon this test as to whether the book
> depraves the mind of the person to read it.[17]

A key witness would be a member of the London Morality
Council and a magistrate. Biron was not impressed:

> I am quite clear. The evidence that is being offered me is
> expert evidence as to whether or not the book is a piece
> of literature. That is not the point. The book may be a
> very fine piece of literature and yet be obscene. Art and
> obscenity are not disassociated. This may be a work of
> art. I agree it has considerable merits, but that does not
> prevent it from being obscene, and I therefore shall not
> admit this expert evidence.[18]

Nevertheless Birkett persevered and sent Desmond McCarthy,
the literary critic of the *New Statesman*, into the witness box.
Birkett asked McCarthy whether, having read the book, did he
think it was obscene? Biron leaped in, saying that he could not
admit such evidence as it was only a matter of opinion. Never
mind that Inspector Protheroe's 'opinion' had been admitted. He
was happy to hear authors testify about whether the book was art
or not but not whether it was obscene. That could not be evidence.

Birkett gave up. He said that the defence contended that the
treatment of the life of the 'invert' could not possibly offend
against the law or good taste but was done with a sense of duty
and with a single and high-minded object.

> This book is a warning, and under no circumstances does
> it corrupt or deprave, because it points out the tragic
> consequences which follow such conduct ... The book
> ought not to be suppressed.

Sir Chartres Biron reserved his decision for a week. When he delivered his verdict the court was packed to hear him make clear that it was lesbianism itself rather than any particular passage in the book that was being condemned.

The 'unnatural offences' that were the subject of the book involved acts which between men would be criminal, and which involved acts of the most horrible, disgusting obscenity. The book failed to treat such vices with the contempt that decent people regarded them. Indeed it was a passionate, almost hysterical, plea for ostracised people. Biron told the court:

> I agree that the book has some literary merits, but the very fact that the book is well written can be no answer to these proceedings, because otherwise we should be in the preposterous position that the most obscene books would be free from stricture. It must appear to everyone of intelligence that the better an obscene book is written, the greater is the public to whom it is likely to appeal.
>
> The more palatable the poison, the more insidious it is.[19]

After an hour of this perverted logic, Radclyffe Hall could contain herself no longer. Despite the efforts of her lawyers for her to be called as 'another person' under the relevant legislation, not even the author was considered to be a witness worth hearing by this Chief Magistrate. She had to sit in the court silently fuming.

Biron started quoting specific extracts from the book to support his case. He was particularly outraged by a passage in which Radclyffe Hall alleged that a 'number of women of position and admirable character' who had driven ambulances at the Front during the war had been 'addicted to this vice'. This was too much for Radclyffe Hall: 'I emphatically protest,' she shouted. Sir Chartres replied: 'I must ask people in court not to interrupt.' Radclyffe Hall: 'I am the author of this book.' Sir

Chartres: 'If you cannot behave yourself in this court I shall have to have you removed.' Radclyffe Hall: 'It is shameful.'[20] Her book was to be condemned and burned as obscene without her voice even being heard in court.

The court order that the book should be destroyed as 'an offence against public decency' was implemented not just in Britain but throughout the rest of the British Empire that relied on the import trade for their books. It meant that *The Well of Loneliness* was effectively banned in Australia, India, South Africa, Canada and New Zealand as well as Britain. But Sir Chartres's ruling caused deep disquiet far beyond Bloomsbury. Even the *Daily Telegraph* railed against it, saying that under this interpretation of the Victorian Hicklin test it would be impossible to defend many of the masterpieces of English literature, from Shakespeare's *Sonnets* to *Tess of the D'Urbevilles*. 'If such a test is to stand then any magistrate can order the destruction of many of the most famous books or of photographs of some of the most famous pictures in our public galleries,' argued the *Telegraph*'s leader-writer.[21]

C.H. Rolph, in his *Books in the Dock* (1969), argued that Fitz-james Stephens, who drafted the 1857 Act, would have been spinning in his grave at Sir Chartres's interpretation of the law.[22] Even in Victorian times Stephens had envisaged there should be a defence of obscenity 'being necessary or advantageous to the pursuit of science, literature, or art'. But it was Sir Chartres's and not Stephens's interpretation that was to stand for the next 20 years.

An appeal was lodged but in some ways it was even more of a farce. Three days before it was to be heard by the Quarter Sessions, Joynson-Hicks made a triumphalist speech to the Authors' Club in London:

> The tone of the Empire comes from you the authors of
> our land. If the tone is pure, the blood will go on
> pulsating through the whole world carrying with it
> purity and safety. If the stream of the blood is impure,

nobody can tell the effect it will have right through our
Empire.[23]

According to the *Daily Telegraph* account, this sentiment was
greeted with cheers; he went on to argue that the police should
be given wider powers to prevent indecent books even being
commissioned by publishers.

On 14 December 1928, the Court of Quarter Sessions met
with 12 magistrates, including two women, on the bench. The
chairman was Sir Robert Wallace KC, aged 78. Before the
hearing Rubinstein wrote to the DPP, Sir Archibald Bodkin,
asking for copies of the book to be released so that the very
large bench of magistrates could read it. Sir Robert Wallace
ruled that it would be neither 'appropriate nor practicable' for
Bodkin to release the book. They were to rule on a work that
they had not even had a chance to read for themselves.

At the appeal, the Attorney-General, Sir Thomas Inskip, one
of Joynson-Hicks's closest political allies, took it upon himself to
conduct the Crown's case. As Attorney-General he had a privi-
lege not available to an ordinary barrister: he could open and
close the case, so making sure that he had both the first and the
last word. Most of the Attorney-General's case consisted of
reading out selected passages from the book, two copies of
which were passed among the magistrates with the offending
passages marked. In summing up his case, Sir Thomas told the
magistrates:

> There are only two references in literature to women
> such as were described. One was in the first chapter of
> the *Epistle to the Romans* and the other was in the sixth
> book of *Juvenal*. It would not be disputed that the vice
> was an unnatural one and that *The Well of Loneliness* was a
> picture of indulgence in it.[24]

Therefore, he argued, the tendency of the book was to deprave
and corrupt the minds of those who were open to such immoral

influences, and that included both young people and those of more advanced years.

This time the government thought that it had better keep an expert or two of its own in reserve in case Sir Robert Wallace was not quite as firm as Sir Chartres Biron on the question of not calling authors as witnesses. At first the Home Secretary suggested to the new Archbishop of Canterbury, Cosmo Lang, that he should ask Hensley Henson, the Bishop of Durham, to testify against the book. The invitation was issued but declined. Instead Jix and Sir Archibald Bodkin turned to Rudyard Kipling, one writer who could be relied upon to ensure that the 'tone of Empire remained pure'. The *Jungle Book* author was a cousin of Stanley Baldwin and, as it happens, a friend of Joynson-Hicks. They persuaded him to make himself available to give evidence, despite the fact that he disliked publicity and rarely criticised any of his contemporaries. Once the defending barrister had said that he did not propose to call witnesses, the Attorney-General spoke to Kipling himself, who then left. He was later to receive a handwritten note from Joynson-Hicks thanking him for attending.

The result was a foregone conclusion. Sir Robert Wallace dismissed the appeal with the words:

> This is a disgusting book. It is an obscene book
> prejudicial to the morals of the community.

Once again the court was packed with supporters of Radclyffe Hall, including this time Dr Marie Stopes. The newspapers reported that Radclyffe Hall wore a loosely fitting grey coat and a wide-brimmed dark blue hat on her closely cropped hair. Outside the court several women took Miss Hall's hand and kissed it. She told reporters:

> I was not surprised at the verdict after what happened in
> the first case. I do not consider that either myself as a
> serious-minded writer or my book as a very serious
> work of fiction has received justice at the hands of the

law. If possible I should continue to appeal from court to court, but I understand it is the end. I would fight on, but I am assured by counsel there is no further appeal possible.[25]

The *Daily Express* also thought that it was 'the end of it' and James Douglas trumpeted the stand the paper had taken 'on this insidious perversion of the English novel … English literature is the gainer and nothing but the gainer,' he wrote.

But there were dissenting voices. Kingsley Martin wrote in the *Manchester Guardian:*

> The Home Secretary says a book ought to be banned if it may cause offence to 'one of the little ones'. Are children's books the only books fit for publication? The law as it now stands can be used for a sweeping censorship and a campaign for purity.[26]

Leonard Woolf also complained in the *Guardian* that the

> existing law has been interpreted in such a way by the police and magistrates, that they can if they so desire, bring practically any book published within its scope.
>
> When they took action against books which would not be bought for pornographic purposes they make the law a serious menace to the freedom of the press. They make the law an engine, not for the suppression of pornographic publications, but for the suppression of any serious work, whether fiction or other, containing views on sexual matters, or dealing with subjects which a magistrate or a judge may happen to think 'disgusting' or even with which he may merely disagree.[27]

No matter how sympathetic the calls in the press for reform of the obscenity laws, none actually mentioned the subject of the book – lesbianism. It remained firmly in the closet.

The same day as Leonard Woolf's plea was published – 20 December 1928 – the Attorney-General of Canada formally banned the book, calling it 'more subtly demoralising, corrupting and corrosive than anything else written'. The next day Radclyffe Hall wrote to the *Daily Herald*, thanking her supporters for the thousands of letters of sympathy and offers to contribute to her legal expenses.

> I particularly want my well wishers to know that their gallant support has brought me both consolation and courage as I have waged a battle for the right to tell what we believe to be the truth and for the honour of decent literary freedom.[28]

The British ban stirred massive interest in the book abroad. Sales were so brisk in Paris that copies of the book went out of the door of Shakespeare and Co. as quickly as they came in. In the United States the book was published at the same time as the appeal was being heard; its reviews took it seriously as a work of art.

It was all too much for John Sumner of the New York Society for the Suppression of Vice, the man who had been responsible in the United States for strangling Joyce's *Ulysses* at birth. With two detectives he had raided the American publisher's offices and seized all copies of *The Well of Loneliness* they could find – some 865. They then went on to Macy's book department and threatened to prosecute Macy's as well if it did not stop selling the book. The shop decided to keep the book on its shelves until the case was heard. The publicity ensured that it was a runaway success. Some 25,000 copies were sold in the United States within a week of the raid.

The trial before Justices Soloman, Healy and McInerney in New York on 8 April 1929 could hardly have been more different from the London proceedings. John Sumner cited 82 of the 500 pages of *The Well of Loneliness* as containing offensive matter. The defence counsel concentrated on the fact that there was not a filthy word or indecent scene within its covers and argued that if the heroine, Stephen, had been a man, the book would be merely a rather over-sentimental bit of Victorian romanticism. The sole objection was to its theme and to suppress it for that reason would lead to the suppression of other works such as *Elizabeth and Essex* by Lytton Strachey, *Swann's Way* by Marcel Proust, *Death in Venice* by Thomas Mann and *The Intermediate Sex* by Edward Carpenter. All were books available to any high-school girl at any New York library. What was more, it could not be absorbed in a single glance like a dirty postcard or perused in a few minutes like a sleazy pamphlet. Any child or seeker after prurient details would be thwarted after 30 pages.

The judges were impressed and after eleven days during which they read the book, they declared *The Well of Loneliness* legal.

> The book in question deals with a delicate social problem which in itself cannot be said to be in violation of the law unless it is written in such a manner as to make it obscene.

Unlike the case of *Ulysses*, the US court ruling did not lead to a reassessment of the British ban. Even as late as 1946, three years after Radclyffe Hall's death, her partner, Lady Troubridge, wrote to the then Labour Home Secretary, John Chuter Ede, asking for permission to publish a memorial edition of her works. The Home Office response was unequivocal. Obscene libel did not change with the times. The official reply was that there was little doubt that if the book appeared again that it would be the subject of proceedings.

Internally the Home Secretary was advised by civil servants whose main responsibilities were in the dangerous drugs branch of the Home Office. They told him that a more lenient view of *The Well of Loneliness* might well lead other and less scrupulous writers than Radclyffe Hall to make use of the same theme with results that could scarcely fail to embarrass all concerned in authority.

In 1949 a hardback edition of the book was finally published with little fanfare and no legal proceedings. Its modern popularity stems from the 1982 paperback edition published by Virago Press, which has rightly celebrated it as a milestone in the development of feminist literature in Britain. The 80,000 sales of this modern Virago edition is testimony that this judgment is shared by the reading public.

4

The heyday of the Scotland Yard guillotine

When little Jix was born, or came alive,
The great Queen ruled and everyone was good,
And England stood, where Mr Gladstone stood,
Since then the times have changed, the clock has
    ticked;
Jix does not think so, Jix was brought up strict.

P.R. Stephenson, *Policeman of the Lord: A Political Satire*, 1929[1]

The moral crusade waged by Sir William Joynson-Hicks – the preposterous Jix as he was endlessly lampooned throughout his five years in office – was inextricably connected with his anti-communism and his terror of social disintegration. Conservative Party historians deny that he was a one-off character in Baldwin's government. They identify his particular brand of social authoritarianism as a product of his background in the Conservative clubs and Orange lodges of Victorian Lancashire and the Presbyterian chapels of north-west England. The moral outlook of such Lancashire Tories was a direct result of the horror they felt when they contemplated what they saw as the feckless Irish Catholic working-class life on nearby Merseyside. For Joynson-Hicks this meant waging a national crusade to arrest the decline in public morality that he believed lay behind the threat of Bolshevism and tainted the purity of the British race. The crusade was not confined to banning books. The police were instructed to take a much closer interest in what was going on behind the bushes in Hyde Park and in the darkened seats of the back rows of the new cinemas. His relentless campaign against after-hours drinking in Soho night-clubs was rather undermined by the police detectives, however, who although disguised in top hats and tails, enjoyed the alcohol rather more than the arrests.

Jix's main target was Kate Meyrick, who owned a string of West End clubs: The 43, the Silver Slipper and the Manhattan among them. The 43 particularly got him going: 'It is a place of the most intense mischief and immorality, even going to the extent of doped women and drunken men. One man was charged 35 shillings for a bottle of champagne. Outrageous,' he told the Metropolitan Police Commissioner.

During one police raid on The 43, Mrs Meyrick was followed out by shouting, laughing groups in the company of policemen: 'They were variously attired. Some were in evening clothes, some in fancy dress, and others were even in Plus Fours,' read the Scotland Yard report.

> They shouted to one another as they were pushed into vans: 'The never-stop railway to Vine Street,' shouted one. 'All aboard the Bow-Street Express,' retorted another.
> One van drove away with the occupants singing: 'It ain't goin' to raid no more.' Another group started the refrain: 'We won't get home till morning.'

Although dubbed the night-club queen of London who won and lost £500,000, Mrs Meyrick was arrested so often that the prison terms were eventually to kill her.

Other foolish campaigns waged by Joynson-Hicks or the 'policeman of the Lord', as his critics dubbed him, had equally serious consequences for those who were his targets. More than any other English Conservative of his time, he saw a Red under every bed. In the run-up to the General Strike he succeeded in having the twelve-strong leadership of the British Communist Party put on trial at the Old Bailey and jailed for incitement to mutiny. It is now regarded as one of the few genuine political show trials to be staged in Britain in the twentieth century. In the strike itself he waged relentless war against the Communists with daily police raids on the party's London headquarters. Two years later he found himself a national laughing stock after he sent in 200 police officers to raid the offices of Arcos, the Soviet trading organisation in London, but they could not find a single scrap of evidence to incriminate the British Communists.

Evelyn Waugh caught the sense of derision which greeted 'the preposterous' Jix's literary crusade in *Vile Bodies*, when he described Adam Symes's encounter with a Customs officer who when going through his suitcases tells him:

> Particularly against books the Home Secretary is. If we can't stamp out literature in the country, we can at least stop it being brought in from outside. That's what he said in Parliament the other day … 'Well, see here,' he said. 'You can take these books on architecture and the dictionary, and I don't mind stretching a point for once and letting you have the history books, too. But this book on Economics comes under Subversive Propaganda. That you leaves behind. And this here Purgatorio doesn't look right to me, so that stays behind pending inquiries. But as for this autobiography (pointing at Adam Symes's own manuscript), that's just downright dirt, and we burns that straight away, see.
>
> 'But, good heavens, there isn't a word in the book – you must be misinterpreting it.'
>
> 'Not so much of it. I knows dirt when I sees it or I shouldn't be where I am today.' 'But do you realise that my whole livelihood depends on this book?' 'And *my* livelihood depends on stopping works like this coming

into the country. Now 'ook it quick if you don't want a
police-court case.' 'Adam, angel, don't fuss or we shall
miss the train,' says Symes's girlfriend ending the
encounter.[2]

In this atmosphere, banning a book or two was a duty to prevent
the pollution of the next generation. After *The Well of Loneliness*
victory, his Conservative colleagues in Parliament and social
moralists were to deluge him with demands to send many more
books to the furnaces. One of the casualties was a novel, *Sleeveless Errand*, by Norah James, the publicity manager at Jonathan
Cape. Its crime was the inclusion of a few expressions such as
'bloody', 'balls' and 'poor little bugger'. It was published in the
United States with the deletion of only three words but has
never been republished in Britain. There was some poetic justice
in the decision to ban Shane Leslie's *The Cantab*, which offended the Roman Catholic church. Leslie had been prominent
among those who had attacked *Ulysses* but the floodgates had
been opened by *The Well of Loneliness* decision. Wallace Smith's
Bessie Cotter, the *Satyricon* of Petronius and Huysmans' *La Bas*
were among those sent to the furnaces.

As Sir Francis Floud, the chairman of Customs, had warned
when he opposed the decision to prosecute Radclyffe Hall, if
lesbianism – or sexual inversion as he preferred to call it – was
to be regarded as a banned subject, then it would be difficult to
know where the censorship would stop. He rightly predicted
that Compton Mackenzie's *Extraordinary Women* would be the
next in the frame. The official complaint came from James
Hope, a fellow Conservative MP but a Catholic: 'My dear Jix,'
he opened before describing Compton Mackenzie's book as 'on
the same delectable subject' as *The Well of Loneliness*.

I am particular incensed against this particular
pornographer because I am told he is supposed to be of
my persuasion. At this rate we shall have stories about
bestiality next.

**SLEEVELESS
ERRAND**

A NOVEL

BY

NORAH C. JAMES

THE SCHOLARTIS PRESS
30 MUSEUM STREET, LONDON
1929

Sleeveless Errand
by Norah James,
the publicity
manager at
Jonathan Cape.
Banned in 1929 its
crime was the
inclusion of a few
expressions such as
'bloody', 'balls' and
'poor little bugger'.
It was published in
America with the
deletion of only
three words but has
never been
republished in
Britain.

Jix immediately ordered a Home Office report on *Extraordinary Women*. It concluded:

> This is an obnoxious book. It is principally a narrative of
> a number of nasty, idle, wealthy, women in an Island not
> far from Naples and modelled on Capri. There they
> drink, quarrel, make love to each other and exhibit
> jealousy and with completely amoral ideas.

It also dealt, the Home Office censors said, with 'this most un-
savoury subject' – lesbianism. Compton Mackenzie's book was,

in fact, in a very different class from *The Well of Loneliness*. It was actually a malicious satire on Radclyffe Hall and her upper-class lesbian friends. One Home Office civil servant described it as

> a tedious book which lacks the earnestness of *Well of Loneliness*, and while it may therefore be less dangerous, there seems less excuse for its ever having been written.

Jix decided to consult the Lord Chancellor, Lord Hailsham, about what he should do this time. The Lord Chancellor struggled through it:

> I spent a miserable afternoon reading your vile book. I have come to the conclusion that in your place I should not attempt to stop it.

Lord Hailsham said that since the publishers were unlikely to withdraw it from sale, as Jonathan Cape had done, it was therefore prosecution or nothing. The Lord Chancellor agreed that 'the whole subject is a beastly one'. But he said that he could not find any description of obscene practices and he did not think that the fact that all the characters were disgusting people brought the book within the criminal law. What was different about *The Well of Loneliness* was that the whole purpose of that book was to excite sympathy for the disgusting practices involved.

For Sir Archibald Bodkin, the Director of Public Prosecutions, the fact that it was a malicious attack on lesbianism also caused a bit of a problem. Once again he decided that it would be a good idea to have an informal word with the Chief Magistrate – Sir Chartres Biron – to see if he was minded to ban it. Sir Chartres read the book, not once, but twice, and told Bodkin that he thought it was very cleverly written, though perhaps not as good a piece of literary work as some of Mackenzie's other books. Although there were many passages that he regarded as indecent, he found it difficult to come to the conclusion that it was likely to corrupt anybody.

Sir Chartres told Bodkin that as the book had been written as a satire on the 'lesbian cult', a certain amount of latitude had to be allowed in describing the obnoxious practices that it involved. He doubted whether a prosecution for indecent libel would succeed, as the book did not advocate lesbianism. Bodkin wrote to Joynson-Hicks:

> *The Well of Loneliness* rather extols or at least finds excuses for indulgence in vice, whereas *Extraordinary Women* draws a most distasteful and detestable picture of practitioners in vice and the degraded condition into which they ultimately fall. There have therefore been rather divers opinions formed as to *Extraordinary Women* by critics and by lawyers, and perhaps it would be wiser to leave the book alone.

The DPP did see one argument for prosecuting Compton Mackenzie, however, as it would indicate that 'the Authorities intend to purge so far as the law permits English literature from such specimens as these two books provide'.

Bodkin's admission that what was going on was an official purge against lesbianism is all the more remarkable as their refusal to take action against Compton Mackenzie. The Home Office concluded that the book had been written only as a 'bestseller' and its publication coincided with the furore over Radclyffe Hall. Mackenzie, who was later to receive a knighthood, was said to be dismayed by Jix's refusal to ban his book and that he had been planning to defend himself from the witness box. It sold only 2,000 copies. While condemning lesbianism was not to be a criminal act, when it came to any other form of sexual activity, the author's alleged disapproval was to be no barrier to prosecution.

The next book to come across Joynson-Hicks's desk, *Sleeveless Errand* by Norah James, was to mark the beginning of an era in which books were defended on the grounds that they condemned the obscenity they portrayed. *Sleeveless Errand* was a

novel of frank dialogue between a couple talking about adultery
and promiscuity. Jix sent it straight to Bodkin, who got one of
Sir Chartres's colleagues at Bow Street Magistrates' Court,
Rollo Graham Campbell, to issue an order for its destruction. At
the hearing on 4 March 1929, the prosecution was particularly
upset that one of the characters was quoted saying: 'For Christ's
sake give me a drink.' The publishers, Scholartis Press, defended
the book on the grounds that it had intended to 'portray and
condemn the mode of life and language of a certain section of
the community'.

The same year saw a manuscript of a collection of D.H.
Lawrence's poems, *Pansies*, intercepted and seized by the police
on its way to his publishers, Martin Secker. Although Jix claimed
in the Commons in the face of protests that the poems had been
discovered in the 'open book post' which, he said, was sometimes investigated as a matter of Post Office routine, few MPs
believed him. The DPP suggested to the publishers that the collection be published without the offending verses. Martin
Secker complied.

In July 1929 it was the depiction of pubic hair in an exhibition of Lawrence's paintings that led to a police raid on the
Warren Galleries in London in July 1929. Although pubic hair
was to be tolerated in a Modigliani or a Matisse, the very name
of D.H. Lawrence by this time was sufficient for the paintings to
be seized and threatened with destruction. Only an undertaking
to the court to withdraw the pictures and close down the exhibition saved them from the furnace.

This wave of prosecutions did not stop there. The Home
Office files fairly bulge with complaints from MPs, the public
and particularly from an organisation called the London Morality Council. It was formed in 1899 by the Bishop of London,
Winnington-Ingram, who was to be its moving force and president for 25 years. The council campaigned against all sorts of
'vice' including contraception. It tried to suppress indecent publications, close down disorderly houses and night-clubs, prevent
semi-nudity on the stage and improper conduct in London's

open spaces. Its committee included most of the suffragen
bishops of London, the Salvation Army and the Dowager Lady
Nunburnholme. It lasted up to and beyond the Second World
War, by which time it had gone national as the Public Morality
Council. Known as 'prudes on the prowl', it was an organisation
whose aims were close to the heart of Sir William Joynson-
Hicks.

By the end of 1928 it was routinely sending book after book
to the Home Secretary asking for them to be banned. Letters to
Jix from Howard Tyrer, the Public Morality Council's secretary,
were to become a regular feature of Home Office life. It was a
letter from Tyrer that led to the Warren Galleries raid. The Public
Morality Council demanded action over the *Confessions of Aleis-
ter Crowley* and over *Bohemian Glass*, a book that was apparently
a 'thoroughly pagan work'. They even wanted to ban an Aldous
Huxley novel: 'Is it possible for you to suppress Aldous Huxley's
novel, *Point Counter Point*?' Tyrer asked the Home Secretary.

> It came to me from the Times Book Club, published by
> Chatto and Windus, and is therefore likely to fall into
> anyone's hands, yet a more degenerate and disgusting
> book it would be difficult to find. I ask you if in some
> quiet way if you can get the Libraries to refuse it.

In this case the Home Office appears to have persuaded the
Home Secretary that it was not worth taking on both Aldous
Huxley and the Times Book Club. *Point Counter Point* was left
unmolested.

About a fortnight later the London Public Morality Council
had discovered an even more degenerate and disgusting book
that demanded to be banned. It is clear from the confidential
Home Office files that some of the civil servants were less impressed than Joynson-Hicks by the credentials of this self-
appointed watch committee. In preparing for a deputation from
the council to the Home Secretary, one senior official pointed
out that it could do with a few more distinguished names on its

executive committee and rather fewer people that some might regard as cranks. In many cases the requests went round the circuit from the Home Secretary to the DPP, to an informal word with the Chief Magistrate. Under Jix it became a routine and regular dance each ending more often than not with the banning of the book in question.

There was one further variation. The plea from the London Public Morality Council to have a quiet word with the libraries was not as fanciful as it sounds. The circulating libraries alongside the public libraries were the main source of serious reading matter for the vast bulk of the population before the war. The circulating libraries had long organised their own censorship, so restricting the circulation of books such as *Jude the Obscure* and *Veronica* among many others. So an appeal to Jix could have a major impact.

The Home Office files show that in the case of the dancer Isadora Duncan's autobiography published by Gollancz, this is exactly what Joyson-Hicks did and with some success. This initiative came from another Conservative MP, Lt.-Colonel Sir Alan Burgoyne, a director of Mudie's Library. He sent his 'Dear Jix … ' letter in May 1928, saying that the directors of Mudie's had decided not to circulate this book as it was highly objectionable and asked Jix to take action against it. Burgoyne, however, stressed that his request had to remain secret for fear of commercial retribution by the other libraries should they get to hear of it.

The book was essentially a very early form of 'kiss and tell'. The famous dancer described her 'amours' with various men. In one passage she described spending the night with Craig, the son of the actress Ellen Terry, in Berlin:

> Here stood before me brilliant youth, beauty, genius; and, all inflamed with sudden love, I flew into his arms with all the magnetic willingness of a temperament which had for two years lain dormant, but waiting to spring forth. Here I found an answering temperament worthy of my

metal. In him I had met the flesh of my flesh, the blood of my blood...

Hardly were my eyes ravished by his beauty than I was drawn towards him, entwined, melted. As flame met flame, we burned in one bright fire. Here, at last, was my mate; my love; my self – for we were not two, but one, that one amazing being of whom Plato tells in the Phaedrus, two halves of the same soul.

This was not a young man making love to a girl. This was the meeting of twin souls. The light covering of flesh was so transmuted with ecstasy that earthly passion became a heavenly embrace of white fiery, flame. There are joys so complete, so all perfect, that one should not survive them. Ah, why did not my burning soul find exit that night, and fly, like Blake's angel, through the clouds of our earth to another sphere?

His love was young, fresh, and strong, and he had neither the nerves nor nature of a voluptuary, but preferred to turn from lovemaking before satiety set in, and to translate the fiery energy of his youth to the magic of his Art.

In his studio was no couch, no easy chair, and no dinner. We slept on the floor that night. He was penniless and I didn't dare go home for money. I slept there for two weeks ... My poor mother went around to all the police stations and embassies saying that some vile seducer had run off with her daughter; while my impresario was wild with anxiety at my sudden disappearance. Vast audiences had been turned away.[3]

As the Home Office report put it: 'The descriptions are full of passion and sensuousness if not sensuality.' The civil servant once again presumably failed to find any actual sex.

So off went Isadora Duncan's *Life* to Sir Archibald Bodkin. He agreed that it was not a desirable book but said that it was not against the law. He suggested to Jix that he urge the libraries themselves to ban such books so as to 'set a higher standard to a good deal of modern literature'.

The idea appealed to Joynson-Hicks. He wrote back to Burgoyne: 'My own view is that circulation is very undesirable. It may cause harm especially to the inexperienced and the young.' He put to him Bodkin's suggestion that concerted action might be taken among the publishers and the circulating libraries to stop books of an offensive character that, like Isadora Duncan's autobiography, failed the legal test of being indecent or obscene. 'The initiative must come from the trade itself. It would improve the tone and raise the standard of current literature.' Mudie's wrote back assuring Jix that Isadora Duncan's book would not be pushed by the circulating libraries.

Not surprisingly this crusade by Joynson-Hicks provoked a fierce reaction. Most of the literary world was in ferment over what Arnold Bennett called the 'new censorship'. Bennett's attacks appear so regularly in the official files that civil servants started dismissing them as 'the usual mischievous stuff from Arnold Bennett'.

But he was not alone. There was a particularly devastating critique by Rebecca West in *Time and Tide*: 'Thanks to Sir William Joynson-Hicks there are now few children old enough to read who are not in full possession of the essential facts regarding homosexuality.'[4] It went on in similar vein. Victor Gollancz, the publisher, tried to grapple with the problem of a new definition of pornography, saying that the Hicklin rule amounted to arguing no more than that a beautiful poem is defined as a poem which appears beautiful to the minds capable of thinking it beautiful. He said that there were some things everybody recognised as pornographic, such as what was

> offered by the evil-smelling touts in the streets of Port Said, or the illustrated books which in the two or three years after the War were displayed on every kiosk in Paris and are still to be found in some of the fine bookshops in the aristocratic quarters of that City.[5]

Gollancz was also uneasy about Norah James, saying a jury might well conclude that she had 'behaved badly' in printing a few swear words. But the difficulty lay in other categories. The suggestion that pornography was any book or picture that excited sexual passion would not do as it would catch *Tristan and Isolde* and even *Parsifal*. Instead Gollancz wanted pornography to cover only those books written with the intention of exciting lust. In his scheme there were to be exceptions for works of scientific or artistic interest such as *Madame Bovary* or the works of Dr Sigmund Freud. Gollancz believed that this would result in a clean sweep of the filthy photographs and books that were displayed in bookshop after bookshop of central London but would prevent the stigmatising of decent authors and decent books. He also wanted to see juries rather than magistrates alone deciding the fate of a book, but then rather spoilt his argument by insisting that only those with a sense of the history and meaning both of art and morals should be allowed to serve as jurors. Gollancz concluded:

> That Miss Radclyffe Hall should be branded the author
> of an immoral book, while any boy with a shilling or so
> to spend may freely gorge himself on filthy garbage, is
> one of those anomalies which, like wars and starving
> miners, make me mildly wonder why the Almighty has
> endured us so long.

The Home Office was not prepared to endure Gollancz's views even for a moment. When he suggested that the suppression of any manuscript or book before its printed date was tantamount to censorship, the civil service's private response was: 'But publishers are the worst offenders in this respect: they suppress many manuscripts.'

Towards the end of Jix's five years as Home Secretary he got the Home Office to draw up a balance sheet of his activity in suppressing books. One measure cited by the civil servants was the number of warrants in force each year against 'foreign dealers in indecency'. These gave the Post Office the power to open any letters sent from Britain to the dealers and to inspect any parcels they sent back. Even Jix described this as a justified 'violation of the secrecy of His Majesty's mail'. The figures show that in 1924 there were 100 such warrants in force, 125 in 1925, 131 in 1926, 104 in 1927 and 115 in 1928. The vast bulk were against dealers in France; during Jix's period in office there were 73 criminal prosecutions for importing indecent material. A further 271 people were warned about bringing indecent books into Britain. The Home Office noted:

> Among the persons warned have been a number of
> students at universities and public schools. Their orders
> have been stopped in the post. The DPP has written to
> the head of the university and the public school
> concerned who has dealt with the offender, often in a
> drastic manner.

The crackdown against French dealers became so active that in 1927 the French government actually lodged an official complaint about the interference with parcels sent to customers in England of legitimate French businesses. Indeed this crackdown also produced a shameful moment in the history of British publishing when in 1928 the Associated Booksellers of Great Britain and Ireland repeatedly lobbied Joynson-Hicks to produce a Home Office list of banned books so that they could protect themselves from prosecution. The association's secretary regretted that the old standards of the book trade which had ensured that indecent books were not published had gone into decline. He blamed the need for the list on new firms such as Jonathan Cape, which were prepared to publish anything if there was a profit in it.

In March 1929 Joynson-Hicks congratulated himself that the traffic in obscene publications had declined in the previous two years, but so obsessed was he with his anti-vice drive that he was even prepared to enlist the help of Mussolini in suppressing

English novelists, including D.H. Lawrence. Jix wrote on 5 March 1929:

> Recently two very obscene books written by well
> known English writers now resident in Italy … were
> intercepted in the post. Copies have been sent to the
> Italian central authorities and an interim reply which has
> been received from Rome indicates that the Fascist
> government will take effective action.

After he had left office and been ennobled as Viscount Brentford, Jix wrote a small pamphlet, *Do We Need a Censor?*, in which he outlined his justification for what others described as censorship but he maintained was just the administration of the existing law:

> The law is founded upon public morality; it will be a bad
> day for this country when we cease in our legislation and
> administration to found ourselves on morality and allow
> any and every form of filth to pollute the minds of the
> young unchecked … I suppose nothing contributed
> more to the degradation of the Roman Empire than the
> stream of pernicious literature which flowed like an open
> sewer through that great city. It may be difficult to
> restrain the stream; it may be difficult to say which books
> or which pictures are on one side or the other of a line
> not easy to draw. But … if the law is administered with
> courage … the administrator may well disregard the
> attacks made upon him and rely on the support of the
> masses of his fellow countrymen.[6]

Joynson-Hicks said that censorship would become unnecessary only when the people learned to detest all forms of indecency and they had attained through religion 'that cleanness of heart which alone can ensure cleanness of thought and action'.[7]

In the 1929 general election the Conservatives were thrown

out of office and were replaced by the short-lived first Labour
government. Joynson-Hicks went to the House of Lords but his
working day of 12–15 hours in the Home Office had taken their
toll and seriously damaged his health. He died only three years
later.

The exact fate of the books that were seized became a matter
of public speculation after Joynson-Hicks left the Home Office.
The *New Statesman* in December 1929 even claimed that confiscated copies were being sold by Scotland Yard police officers for
their own profit. The Home Office demanded to know if this
charge was true:

> One cannot help seeing the potential of temptation
> especially in cases such as *Well of Loneliness* and *Sleeveless
> Errand*, when they are holding large quantities of
> something for which it would be easy to get high prices
> in certain markets.

The Home Office asked the Metropolitan Police Commissioner for details of the safeguards taken to prevent such pilfer-
age and also demanded a detailed account of what had
happened to the books in the two cases. Scotland Yard was less
concerned about the *New Statesman*: 'That paper is always very
hostile to the police, and need not much be attended to,' replied
an Assistant Chief Constable dismissing the allegation.

> When the bulk to be destroyed is small, it is burned in a
> furnace [at New Scotland Yard], but with large
> consignments other methods have to be used. I find, e.g.,
> that in the case of *The Well of Loneliness* 253 copies were
> seized. Of these three were retained for reference here,
> and the remainder were destroyed by means of a
> guillotine machine in the Printers Department, and
> disposed as waste paper.

In the case of *Sleeveless Errand*, 785 of the 799 seized copies were

sent to the guillotine. Of the remaining copies, three went to the
solicitors involved, two to the DPP, two to the Home Office,
one to the British Museum, one to the Bodleian Library,
Oxford, one to Cambridge University Library, one to the National Library of Scotland and one to Trinity College, Dublin.
The City of London police had one copy and the Metropolitan
Police kept the other 'for reference'. The Chief Constable
assured the Home Office: 'I do not think there is any cause for
uneasiness here.'

The practice of sending a copy of each banned book to the
British Museum and the other national libraries began in July
1916. It started after the Keeper of the Department of Printed
Books at the British Museum, G.F. Barwick, wrote to the Director of Public Prosecutions, pointing out: 'It constantly
happens that the copies which escape seizure become rare and
are of considerable literary merit or historical interest', adding
that it would be better simply to send him a seized copy

> so that public money might not have to be subsequently
> spent in the acquisition of a copy. Books condemned are
> at once withdrawn from the general catalogue and placed
> in special cases not available for general use.

Access to books in these closed cabinets at the British Library
(BL) is still available only under supervision. Books with a PC
(private case) shelfmark are kept in a strong room in the basement of the new British Library building at St Pancras and can
be read only in the Rare Books reading room at designated
desks under the personal supervision of BL staff. Among the
books still kept in the PC cases at St Pancras are John Cleland's
Fanny Hill, the Marquis de Sade's *Juliette* and an extensive collection of erotica donated to the British Museum by Henry
Spencer Ashbee in the 1870s.

Jix's publishing purge cast a shadow for more than a decade
over the book trade in the British Empire. The Bodley Head
waited until 1937 before it felt it was safe to publish *Ulysses* in

Britain. But even in the late 1930s the legacy of Joynson-Hicks was still making itself felt and the Public Morality Council was still sending books to the Home Office asking for their suppression. George Routledge & Sons withdrew an autobiography of a prostitute, *To Beg I am Ashamed*, in 1938 after a complaint from the Public Morality Council led to two police officers calling at their offices on the instructions of the Home Secretary and the DPP. Their representations also led to a destruction order being issued against a sex instruction manual, *The Sex Impulse* by Edward Charles, despite support from Sir Julian Huxley and many other leading medical figures. But somehow subsequent Home Secretaries never quite carried out the task with the same degree of commitment and passion that Joynson-Hicks had shown.

Pulped fiction

The legal authorities of this country can be relied upon
to mishandle any issue touching the censorship of books.
Unfortunately this record of ineptitude does not make
them fight shy of this subject.

Roy Jenkins, November 1963

The second great British literary purge of the twentieth century
took place during the austerity years after the end of the Second
World War. Despite the threat of Nazi invasion, the police and
the courts still found time for the prosecution of obscene or indecent books. The desire to present a good face to the US forces
when they arrived in Britain in the summer of 1942 has been
put down as the real reason behind two high-profile obscenity
trials in the middle of the war.

The first involved Dr Eustace Chesser, who published his
book, *Love Without Fear,* with the aim of providing a popular
advice book for married couples based on the works of Havelock Ellis, Kraft-Ebbing and Marie Stopes. Among the subjects
it covered were oral sex, lesbianism and flagellation. In June
1942 Dr Chesser put up a brave fight at the Old Bailey to save
his book. His obvious sincerity in the witness box and a neutral
summing up from the judge led the jury to acquit him after
only an hour's consideration.

The second wartime trial did not have such a happy outcome. The case concerned a Cornish mail order company, the Economy Educator Services, which specialised in sex instruction books. The police raided the company in 1942 and seized 12 titles, including the *Encyclopedia of Sexual Knowledge*, which had been edited by a well-known physician, Norman Haire. Some 50,000 copies had been sold since it was published in 1934 and reviewed in the *New Statesman* and *The Listener*. Thousands of people had dealt in the book. The judge at Bodmin Assizes was not impressed, however, and sentenced the company's managing director to six months. The severity of the sentence caused a national outcry and the Home Secretary, Herbert Morrison, remitted his sentence in August 1943, but not until he was almost due for release anyway.

The advent of the 1945 Labour government looked as though it might create a more liberal atmosphere when in a landmark decision the DPP and the Attorney-General refused to ban Norman Mailer's *The Naked and the Dead* in the face of a *Sunday Times* campaign claiming that it was obscene. The book's publishers, Alan Wingate Ltd, defended it on the grounds that it portrayed a true picture of the way that soldiers had talked and behaved during the war. American critics compared its merits with Stendhal and Tolstoy. The Labour Attorney-General, Sir Hartley Shawcross, who had been a prosecutor at the Nuremberg war crimes trials, thought that there was much in 'this most tedious and lengthy book' that was foul, lewd and revolting. But he said that looking at Mailer's book as a whole, he did not think that its *intention* was to deprave or corrupt or that it was likely to lead to any result other than disgust.

On these wise grounds Shawcross refused, despite the popular pressure, to send it to the courts to be condemned. But first he secured an undertaking from the publishers that they would remove its prolific four-letter words and replace them with dashes and capital Fs. Norman Mailer was allowed to use the word 'Fu' a few times, prompting Tallulah Bankhead to remark when she met him: 'Are you the young man who can't spell fuck?'

This more relaxed attitude did not last any longer than the 1945 Labour government, however, and under Winston Churchill's 1951 Conservative government there was an explosion in the number of destruction orders issued by magistrates. This reached a peak in 1954, when an astonishing 167,000 volumes were sent to the guillotine or used to stoke the furnaces of Scotland Yard. Sir Stephen Tumim, the former Chief Inspector of Prisons and a circuit judge for many years, has said that this postwar wave of obscenity prosecutions was largely due to the Jix-like anti-vice enthusiasm of Churchill's Home Secretary, Sir David Maxwell-Fyfe. Some commentators point to a meeting of the International Criminal Police Commission in Oslo in 1953 which discussed the apparent ineffectiveness of an international convention on the Suppression of Traffic in Obscene Literature. The British police delegates were especially interested to learn of Interpol's belief in a link between crime, particularly sexual offences, and the reading of pornography. The evidence for such a direct link is still being hotly debated, but the senior police officers returned to London with a new crusading zeal pulsating through their veins.

Sir David Maxwell-Fyfe and the police were determined to act with a new resolve. Home Office figures show that that was exactly what they did. There were 132 separate prosecutions under the Victorian Obscene Publications Act – then nearly a century old – in 1954 compared with only 39 in 1935. In 1954 111 people were found guilty of publishing obscene libels compared with only 39 in 1935. The total of 167,000 books and magazines that were destroyed by Scotland Yard in 1954 was more than the totals for the previous four years put together, compared with only 900 volumes destroyed in 1935.

The sentences were also getting heavier, with those imprisoned at the height of the 1954 purge being sent down for an average of three to eighteen months compared with sentences of between six weeks and twelve months which were handed out in 1935. By any standard 1954 was truly a vintage year for the censors.

This drive against pornography was only one part of Maxwell-Fyfe's anti-vice crusade, which also saw a witch-hunt against homosexuals and a crackdown on prostitution. It was a reassertion of the kind of stifling lower-middle-class strait-laced morality that John Osborne, Joe Orton and Arnold Wesker and other radical playwrights were to revolt against later in the 1950s.

One indication of the zeal with which the purge was carried out was that when the ordinary British family went on holiday, it discovered that it was not even allowed to enjoy the cheeky seaside postcards that were on sale. Seaside sweetshops and newsagents all faced prosecutions for indecency. In the summer of 1953 shopkeepers in Bournemouth, Cleethorpes, Folkestone, Llandudno, Margate, Poole, Ramsgate, Swanage, Weymouth and Ryde (Isle of Wight), all found themselves branded criminals for selling postcards with the kinds of vulgar jokes and puns the British had been swapping in school playgrounds for decades. Only the Blackpool and Isle of Man censorship committees were not prepared to swim with the tide and said that they would put up with the now celebrated work of Donald McGill and David Millar. This was a serious crackdown. In the second week of September 1953 the Lincolnshire police, acting under orders from the Director of Public Prosecutions, raided 16 stationer's shops in Cleethorpes alone. Some 5,405 postcards were seized – most of them had been on sale all summer – along with 15 rubber dolls which were described in the official correspondence as 'obscene representations' or simply 'the novelties'.

More than 165 versions of the cards were condemned, including 30 by McGill himself. Six companies were charged with unlawfully publishing obscene postcards, including R.D. Constance Ltd, in which Donald McGill was the sole artist and partner. The crown court trial involving McGill's company ended with the firm being fined £50 and the directors £10 each plus £25 costs. McGill told the court he had been in the business since 1930 and had his first card published when he was 16. Another of the companies involved, Bamforths, was outraged

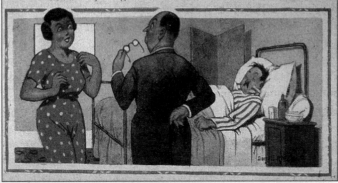

Two Donald McGill postcards that were declared obscene in 1954 at Grimsby. 'If you were a doctor' (number 58), 'Gentleman's requisites?' (number 108).

at being charged. It had been in business for 50 years and protested to the DPP that it thoroughly deplored the smut that had come into the business in recent years; all its cards were vetted by the Blackpool censorship committee. As president of the Postcard Publishers' Association, Mr Bamforth's plea was not ignored. He was acquitted of the charges.

McGill's cards were undoubtedly vulgar but have been celebrated by George Orwell and others as traditional examples of English humour. A typical example had the caption:

> 'I want you to put this notice of the birth of my son in your paper.' 'Yes, sir. How many insertions?' 'Mind your own business.'

Another of the cards for which McGill was charged by the Cleethorpes police on 12 September 1953 with 'publishing an obscene postcard' showed a male customer talking to an attractive shop girl: 'Gentleman's Requisites? Yes, Sir, go right through "Ladies' Underwear"!' Another showed a woman sitting on the lap of a man on a sofa with the caption of her saying: 'Don't worry, Dear, we'll straighten that out when we're married.' One with the caption 'The further you're in, the nicer it feels' attracted a £5 fine alone. Defence counsel argued:

> They may be things that are extremely vulgar, but they are not obscene. Some of these, I suggest, are of the traditional English music hall vulgarity which has stood the test of many years.[1]

But the prosecution was not prepared to accept that Max Miller had been cracking even bluer jokes on the boards for years: 'The postcards are displayed for public sale indiscriminately, to be seen by all, particularly at holiday resorts,' they complained before sending them off to the furnaces to be burned with the books.

The Home Office files show that a total of 1,772 different

paperback titles and 2,200 different editions of magazines were condemned in the four years between 1950 and 1953. Many were American pulp fiction books which had been shipped over to Britain to be sold in bulk as a more profitable alternative to being machine-pulped in those puritanical US states which had already banned them. These 'trash' novels included such titles as *Don't Mourn Me Toots*, *No Pay Off for Blondie*, *Reefer Rhapsody* and *Road Floozie* by 'Darcy Glinto'. The titles were all listed in a secret *Blue Book* that was issued to chief constables by the Home Office in the early 1950s. Its existence was kept secret from MPs at the time and has been ever since. The files show that civil servants were even prepared later to lie to a parliamentary committee to keep this blacklist secret. Home Office briefing papers for hearings before the special select committee on Roy Jenkins's Obscene Publications Bill show that senior civil servants and ministers were advised to avoid all mention of this secret *Blue Book* to the point of being prepared to deny its existence.

The 4,000 titles named in its 42 closely printed pages in its 1954 edition included crime fiction books by authors such as James Hadley Chase – his famous *No Orchids for Miss Blandish* was among the banned – and Mickey Spillane and Edgar Lustgarten. A second James Hadley Chase, *Miss Callaghan Comes to Grief*, had been banned as a result of an Old Bailey trial in 1942 with a £100 fine levied on the importers for their trouble. A quick scan through its pages reveals that the most hated book in Britain in the early 1950s was Hans Vogel's *Love from Las Vegas*, which attracted 77 separate magistrates' orders for its destruction in just four years. A close second was Hank Janson's *Baby Don't Dare Squeal*, with 76 destruction orders.

Chief constables were told that if they 'find any of the listed novels or magazines being in your area you should arrange for copies to be purchased and forwarded to the DPP'. It goes on to list each of the 4,000 titles with its author, publisher and number of destruction orders. It starts with *Abandoned* by Henri Lamonte and ends with *Zowie Bedtime Stories* by Paged

IPN 22/1/3

3

CONFIDENTIAL

Novels in respect of which orders for destruction have been made by various Magistrates Courts in the years 1950, 1951, 1952 and 1953.

Note.—Details are included of all successful proceedings taken in respect of the titles named. The lists enclosed with Home Office letters dated 20th April 1951, 26th June 1952, and 2nd July 1953, should now be destroyed.

Title	Author	Publisher	Destruction Orders
Abandoned . . .	Henri Lamonte	Phoenix Press . . .	22
Accused . . .	Hank Janson . .	New Fiction Press . . .	27
	Fine imposed for selling, Douglas, Isle of Man, 7/8/53.		
Affaire in Montmartre .	Don Hugo .	Hamilton & Co. (Stafford) Ltd. .	7
Afterwards . . .	Paul Renin .	R. & L. Locker . . .	4
Alcatraz Break .	Steve Markham .	Art Publicity	38
All That Glitters .	Paul Renin .	R. & L. Locker . . .	13
All The Things You Ain't	Nat Karta .	Muir-Watson Ltd. . . .	36
Allouma . . .	Guy de Maupassant	Camden Publishing Co. Ltd. .	3
Always a Dame .	Brett Vane .	Curtis Warren Ltd. . .	9
Amok . . .	Hank Janson .	New Fiction Press . .	13
Amorous Adventuress .	Roland Vane .	Archer Press Ltd. . . .	11
*Amorous Moments .	Jacque Braza .	Modern Fiction Ltd. . .	1
*Amorous Nights .	Ramon Lacroix .	Barnardo Amalgamated Industries Ltd.	2
Amorous Nymph .	Ramon Lacroix .	Barnardo Amalgamated Industries Ltd.	3
Amours of Marie, The .	D. L'Arnaud .	1. H. & J. Edmands . . 2. M.C. Publications Ltd. . }	28
	£100 fine imposed for publishing, Sheffield, 5/3/53.		
And The Body Came Too	Leonard Boden	Hamilton & Co. (Stafford) Ltd. .	7
And Worms Have Eaten Them.	William J. Elliott .	1. Gerald G. Swan Ltd. . . 2. Harborough Publishing Co. Ltd. }	25
Angel of Desire .	Henri Lamonte	Phoenix Press . . .	5
Angel Shoot to Kill	Hank Janson	1. S. D. Frances . . . 2. New Fiction Press . . }	49
	£5 fine imposed for publishing, Blackburn, 30/5/52.		
Angel Without Wings .	Frank Norman	Hamilton & Co. (Stafford) Ltd. .	27
Angela Darling .	Gordon Grinstead .	Rylee Ltd.	4
Angels Are So Few	Earl Ellison .	John Spencer & Co.. . .	25
Angels Bruise Easy	Larry O'Brien .	World Distributors (Manchester) Ltd.	35
*Angels Shoot to Kill	—	Hamilton & Co. (Stafford) Ltd. .	1
Angels Sleep in Bed .	Nat Karta .	Muir-Watson Ltd. . . .	30
Any Minute Now .	Al Bocca .	Scion Ltd.	9
Anyone's Grief .	Ricky Drayton .	Scion Ltd.	11
Ape-Man's Offering .	H. Kaner .	Kaner Publishing Co. . .	2
Arabian Passion .	Paul Reville .	R. & L. Locker and Archer Press Ltd.	5
	Fine imposed for selling, Douglas, Isle of Man, 7/8/53.		
*Armchair in Hell .	Henry Kane .	T. V. Boardman & Co. . .	3
Arrest Ace Lannigan .	Leslie Halward .	Bear, Hudson Ltd. . . .	1

The secret Home Office Blue Book for 1954 sent to all chief constables.

Productions Ltd. Occasionally an entry will show that a fine was also imposed on the publisher. For example, *Make Mine a Corpse* by Michael Storme, published by Archer Press Ltd, was fined £650 at Stoke-on-Trent on 19 September 1951. Also on the secret list were more serious works including Jean Paul-Sartre's *Intimacy*, Upton Sinclair's *Damaged Goods*, Daniel Defoe's *Moll Flanders* and even Gustave Flaubert's *Madame Bovary*. *Scandal at School*, a crime whodunit co-authored by the Oxford historian and Fellow of All Souls, G.D.H. Cole, was not spared: it was the target of destruction orders by three separate benches of magistrates.

The existence of this blacklist, including the blanket ban on several of the major classics, was kept secret from the general public. What was to stir up the movement for obscenity law reform most was the succession of five separate Old Bailey prosecutions and, in each case, the books that were in the dock were not the kind of soft-porn pulp fiction that made up the bulk of that blacklist. What shocked the literary world was that all five cases involved a respectable British publisher. The five prosecutions came after a less celebrated pulp fiction case in which Reiter Books was put in the dock for publishing the works of Hank Janson, who was the alleged author of such works as *Accused*, *The Jane with Green Eyes* and *Kill Her If You Can*. The official explanation of how the five books and some of the leading figures of the publishing world found themselves in the dock at the Old Bailey was given by the DPP, Sir Theobald ('Toby') Mathew, in evidence to a Commons select committee in 1957. He told Lord Lambton:

> One of them had been found by a court in the Isle of Man to be obscene, and was referred to me. I referred it to the Treasury Counsel, and he advised me that there was a *prima facie* case to be put before the Court. That was *The Philanderer*. It was acquitted. The other three cases arose in this way. We were prosecuting in a case called *Reiter Books* which, if I may say so, I don't think

anybody could have argued were not pornographic. The defence in that case sought to put in a number of novels, including these three, which they said were as bad as, if not worse than, the ones which were being prosecuted, to show that public taste had changed. They were not allowed to put the books in, but an intimation was given, both in the court below and in the Court of Criminal Appeal, that these books might be looked at. That is not an intimation which I can ignore.

The three books that the Lord Chief Justice, Lord Goddard, had suggested in the Court of Appeal ought to be looked into were *The Image and the Search* by Walter Baxter (Heinemann), *September in Quinze* by Vivian Connell (Hutchinson), and *The Man in Control* by Charles McGraw (Barker). The DPP sent them to the Treasury Counsel, who said he thought that they were obscene.

The obscenity trials of the two original books under attack – *The Philanderer* by the American author, Stanley Kauffman (Secker and Warburg), and *Julia* by Margot Bland (T. Werner Laurie) – were heard separately. *Julia* had also been condemned in the Isle of Man, where Boots the Chemist's circulating library was fined £2 for 'lending on hire' by the Douglas magistrates. In all five cases, unusually for such trials, it was the publishers themselves who were to be found sitting in the defendant's dock in Number 2 criminal court. In two of the trials they were found guilty and fined. The juries acquitted the publishers in two of the other cases and the jury was split in the fifth. The sight of publishers sitting in the dock at the Old Bailey – it was Katherine Webb, a director of Hutchinson's, in the case of *September in Quinze* and Frederic Warburg for *The Philanderer* – alarmed the entire literary world.

What really got things going was Mr Justice Stable's summing up in the case of *The Philanderer*, one of the two books to be acquitted. In his landmark decision, the judge ruled that although a book may be unsuitable for adolescents, it did not mean that publishers were guilty of a criminal offence for putting it on sale to the general public.

The prosecution counsel, Mervyn Griffith-Jones, who was later to play a crucial role in the *Lady Chatterley* case, putting the case for the Crown, told the Old Bailey that 6,000 copies of the book had been sold during the 15 months since its publication. He asked the jury, as his colleagues had done on numerous occasions, to use the hundred-year-old Hicklin test of obscenity to decide whether the book had a tendency to deprave and corrupt. To the surprise of all, and to the pleasure of the literary world in particular, Mr Justice Stable made clear that he did not regard this test of Victorian prudery to be good enough any longer. He told the jury:

> I remember a most serious discussion between my mother and father, whether my mother could possibly go and see Mr Shaw's play *Pygmalion*. When the lady in the play said: 'Not bloody likely' it was the biggest social shock I can remember. If I had used the word when I was 21, I would have been ordered out of any respectable house in England.
>
> Remember the charge is a charge that the tendency of the book is to corrupt and deprave. The charge is not that the tendency of the book is to shock or disgust. That is not a criminal offence.

He told the jury to take the book home and read it. 'Read it as a book,' he stressed.

> Don't pick out the highlights. Read it through as a whole. And then we'll all come back here on Friday and proceed with the case.[2]

Here was a senior judge in courtroom Number 2 at the Old Bailey using the word 'bloody' and implying that it was all right to do so. This must have made some kind of impact on the jury.

It was no doubt compounded when he went on to ask them whether the act of sexual passion really was 'sheer filth' and if unmarried women in New York (the setting for the book) believed that babies were (1) brought by the storks? (2) found in cabbage plots? (3) found under gooseberry bushes? He finished his summing up by asking the jury

> if we drive the criminal law too far, in our desire to stamp out the 'bawdy muck' isn't there a risk that there will be a revolt, a demand for a change in the law, so that the pendulum may swing too far the other way and allow to creep in things that at the moment we can keep out?[3]

The jury duly found the publishers 'not guilty'. C.H. Rolph in his *Books in the Dock* (1969) believed that it signalled a change in the direction of the prevailing wind, even if some reformers observed that legally all Mr Justice Stable had actually done was to restate the 1867 Hicklin test but in more modern language.

Warning bells were now going off inside the Home Office. The Home Secretary, Sir David Maxwell-Fyfe, was happy to see this anti-vice campaign in full flood, as was the still active Public Morality Council. But some senior Home Office civil servants were less than happy, as the newly released Whitehall files testify. Their anxiety was only increased when they realised that magistrates around Britain were following the lead set by the Home Secretary and the DPP and adopting a noticeably tougher line on indecent publications. Unsuccessful attempts were made to ban the American *Kinsey Report on Sexual Behaviour* in Doncaster and elsewhere. But it was the action of the Swindon magistrates in ordering the destruction of the Renaissance classic Boccaccio's *Decameron*, but at the same hearing sparing a clutch of the hated pulp fiction books such as Hank Janson's *Don't Mourn Me Toots*, that most alarmed the Home Office. The national press had a field day blaming Sir David Maxwell-Fyfe and pointing out that the bench at Swindon did not seem to know the difference between a literary classic and a bit of cheap trash. The case for the magistrates was not helped by the fact that Boccaccio's *Decameron* was at the time openly available on the shelves of the town's public reference library. Swindon's reputation has yet to recover.

A Home Office inquiry was launched into the Swindon decision to ban the *Decameron* mainly on the grounds that it had led to embarrassing criticism of the Home Secretary in the press. An internal Home Office report recognised that the book was 'not merely a world classic, but one which has been widely read for centuries'. A senior civil servant, J.H. Walker, reported:

> The ridicule provoked by the incident reacts most
> unfairly on the Home Office, since the public and press
> are very ready to assume that the Home Office directs
> proceedings of this kind. This assumption is completely
> unjustified – in this particular instance we had not even
> heard of the proceedings, let alone directed them, until
> they were reported in the press – but experience suggests
> that it is hopeless to try to correct this mistaken
> impression.

Walker's report says that well over 1,500 novels had been banned between 1950 and 1953, including three classics of the first rank. He named them as Flaubert's *Madame Bovary*, the works of Rabelais and Daniel Defoe's *Moll Flanders*. He said that all had erotic content but both the Flaubert and the Rabelais were recognised as world classics; while Moll Flanders might not be in the same class, it was undoubtedly a classic of English literature.

Mr Walker conceded that there were some minor classics among the other books condemned during the period, like Balzac's *Droll Stories*, the works of Maupassant and Alphonse Daudet's *Sapho*, but he argued that their destruction had not provoked the kind of public indignation that the banning of the *Decameron* had. He suggested that the way to spare any more of the Home Secretary's blushes would be to ensure that books that were more than 100 years old and were also recognised as classics were not banned. His idea was taken up by the permanent secretary of the Home Office, Sir Frank Newsam, who called a meeting with the Director of Public Prosecutions, Sir Toby Mathew. Newsam told him that the unfavourable press reaction to the Swindon banning of the *Decameron* 'places the Home Secretary in a most invidious position', despite the fact that he had nothing to do with the decision. Sir Frank, the most senior Home Office civil servant, said that the 'condemnation of a classic which for some hundreds of years has been widely recognised in many countries as a masterpiece of European literature, is very difficult to defend'. He went on to warn the DPP that the kind of public derision they now faced would only fuel the demand for reform of the law at a time when neither of them wanted legislation or a full-scale inquiry.

Instead he told Sir Toby that what he had in mind was a second secret circular to the police of a short list of recognised classics which, although their text might well be regarded as obscene by many people, should not be seized unless there were exceptional circumstances. Exceptional in this sense might include an edition that used grossly obscene illustrations.

Sir Frank said he appreciated that other books, such as those by Marie Stopes and Havelock-Ellis on birth control, also raised problems but said he was less worried about them as public opinion regarded the practices they advocated as undesirable. They would have to continue to take their chances at the magistrates' court alongside the collected works of Darcy Glinto and Hans Vogel.

The DPP agreed and it was decided to consult the police and the Lord Chief Justice before this secret 'white list' was issued. The scheme ran into difficulty, however, when the Whitehall chiefs decided that they could not trust the magistrates with such sensitive information. The official minutes of their meeting stated:

> It was agreed that it would be undesirable to send copies
> of the circular to Clerks to Justices, since it was desirable
> that the circular should be kept confidential and clerks
> would be bound to show it to their Benches.

The minutes fail to explain how the white list would operate if
the courts were not to be told of its existence.

Whitehall's contempt for local magistrates was on display
again when the Home Office sent the DPP its proposed list. Sir
Toby Mathew did not think that the idea would necessarily
work. He told the Home Office:

> Although the police and I can and do try to stop the
> courts making fools of themselves, this service has
> obvious limitations, and the courts that are apt to be
> foolish, are, generally speaking, the most likely to stand
> on their dignity and be reluctant to accept advice.

The list of works whose seizure was now officially regarded as
likely to bring the law into disrepute included: a translation of
any work by Aristophanes, Aristotle, Boccaccio, Catullus,
Juvenal, Ovid and Rabelais; *The Golden Ass* by Apuleius, *The
Heptameron* by Margaret, Queen of Navarre, *Satyricon* by Petronius, *The Arabian Nights* and *One Thousand and One Nights*, plus
Daniel Defoe's *Moll Flanders*. The appearance of Aristotle on the
list is thought to be in connection with a popular anonymous
seventeenth-century guide to gynaecology, which was known as
Aristotle's *Masterpiece*. It was a list that could fairly be said to
reflect the tastes of public-school-educated Oxbridge classicists,
who were to be found in some numbers in the upper reaches of
government and the Whitehall civil service in the 1950s.

The police were not happy either and their opposition killed
the idea off completely. The Central Council of Chief Constables – the forerunner of the present-day Association of Chief
Police Officers – debated the matter in secret in November
1954. They concluded that if the existence of an approved list of

classics became known, it would lead to considerable embarrassment and undesirable repercussions. They told the Home Office
that they had to insist that they should keep their discretion to
seize whatever books they liked – old Roman authors included.

It was not an auspicious start to the Home Office's campaign
to head off what it had recognised as the beginning of a political groundswell to reform the law. The Society of Authors, led
by Sir Alan Herbert with Roy Jenkins, H.E. Bates, Michael Foot
and Norman St John Stevas by his side, was in the vanguard of
the reform movement. At Christmas 1955 the Society presented
the Home Secretary with its draft Obscene Publications Bill. It
proposed scrapping the Hicklin test of obscenity. In its place it
said the court would need to consider the dominant effect of
the book, to listen to expert evidence on its artistic and literary
merit, and to extend the definition of obscenity to include violence, horror and cruelty, not just sexual conduct. There were to
be no prosecutions without the consent of the Attorney-
General.

A Whitehall council of war was formed to consider how to
handle this bill, which was first introduced by Roy Jenkins into
the Commons under the ten-minute rule in March 1955. It had
no chance then of becoming law but the Home Office, the Lord
Chancellor's Department and the DPP got together to consider
how to respond. They decided that as it was such a controversial
issue, there was no justification for government legislation and
there was no need for an immediate amendment to the law.
They looked at the figures and agreed that there had been an
explosion in the number of destruction orders in the early
1950s. But they attributed this increase not to any great moral
crusade by the Home Secretary and the police, but to three
other completely different factors. The first and most important
factor to their minds was the flood of cheap paperback novels,
many of them American, dealing with sordid subjects, coming
on to the market. They thought that the second was the re-
quirement placed on chief constables in 1946 to report all cases
to the DPP, which led to a more energetic enforcement of the

law. Thirdly, and most bizarrely, was the increased sale of those vulgar postcards at seaside resorts. The finest minds of Whitehall were prepared to admit, however, that it was open to question whether many of the cheeky works of Donald McGill were actually obscene, despite the fondness of local magistrates to burn them by the thousand.

This cosy civil service cabal tut-tutted over the Jenkins bill before deciding that it was fundamentally flawed and would need drastic amendment to make it work. They doubted the value of literary experts, arguing that a work could have artistic merit yet still be pornographic. They also congratulated themselves that the law as it stood was not aimed 'at setting up in each locality a censor morum with the duty of compiling on the principles of Mrs Grundy an index expurgatorius of the literary and artistic productions of all the ages'.[4] We now know why there was no need for such a system of local censors. As the files now show, it was a job that they secretly did every year in Whitehall in the form of the 42-page confidential *Blue Book* issued each year by the Home Office. Roy Jenkins's draft obscenity bill did have some impact on the Home Office. In the face of a storm of newspaper protest about the alleged effects of imported American horror comics on the nation's youth, the government introduced legislation to ban them. The 1955 Children and Young Persons (Harmful Publications) Act banned comics that were likely to fall into the hands of young children and which portrayed acts of violence or cruelty, the commission of crimes or incidents of a repulsive or horrible nature. To qualify as a comic, the magazine had to 'consist wholly or mainly of stories told in pictures'. Although at first sight this piece of legislation would have banned a cartoon version of any Sherlock Holmes story, it did acknowledge one of the Herbert committee's demands that offensive material should not just be defined in terms of sex.

However, this particular law seems to have been as much use as another notorious piece of knee-jerk legislation – the dangerous dogs law of the late 1980s. Seven years after the harmful publications law hit the statute book, the Home Office had received only 12 complaints against particular comics and the Attorney-General had refused to act on five of them. Forty-five years on, this piece of legislation has yet to make its debut in court. It is easy to see why from the nature of the complaint made in 1962, when a certain Lady Snow demanded that two comics aimed at young teenagers entitled *Horror Monsters* and *Creatures* be banned. They both used film stills from Hollywood horror B-movies, including pictures from such classics as Lon Chaney as Frankenstein, *The Creature from the Black Lagoon* and Anthony Quinn as the French Fried Fiend. Despite Lady Snow's pleading, the Attorney-General failed to find a picture of Lon Chaney in full make-up sufficiently frightening to persuade him to prosecute the comics. This law is still on the statute book.

A year later it was not American horror comics or pulp fiction that were worrying the nation's custodians of public morals, but the arrival of a far more potent force from across the Atlantic – rock and roll. The Conservative moral crusader, Sir David Maxwell-Fyfe, was no longer in charge at the Home Office. To the disappointment of some sections of the Conservative Party and some newspapers which were getting very worked up about the dangers to Britain's youth, the official reaction to the arrival of Bill Haley and Little Richard was in the language of Whitehall 'seriously relaxed'.

The Home Office files are quite clear on what the civil servants at the time thought of the alleged 'riots' which accompanied the screening of *Rock Around the Clock* in 1956.

The official file says that there were complaints about behaviour at 25 of the 400 cinemas that showed this U-film. One newspaper's claim that the inside of a cinema had been wrecked by the rioting audience turned out to amount to no more than damage to three light fittings. In another incident a press photographer had set a group of young people dancing in the street to get pictures of this rock 'n' roll hysteria.

Some 80 local authorities banned the film, which featured Bill Haley and the Comets. The Home Office reported: 'It appeared to the cinema owners that they had done so on the advice of chief constables without a due sense of responsibility.' Most banned it without seeing it and those that did see it tended to feel that the film was innocuous and lifted the ban. The managers' reports on the most highly publicised incidents give the lie to the 'moral panic' which some newspapers tried to generate. For example, the *Daily Express*, the biggest-selling daily newspaper at the time, claimed that the rock 'n' roll crazed audience at the Avon Theatre in Glasgow had smashed glass display panels at the cinema's entrance. Photo stills showing scenes from the film had been ripped out and carried away as the crowd made for side streets. The cinema manager reported wearily: 'The only damage done at the theatre was to one glass display panel which is smashed an average of once a week by local hooligans – irrespective of the film.'

At the Gaumont, Saltaire, the *Yorkshire Post* reported: 'Rock N' Rollers Brawl at Shipley, Vanload of police in action ... fight broke out between a large group of Teddy Boys at the rear of the cinema.' The manager stated:

> Nothing happened at the theatre that could be remotely described as a brawl. The vanload of police was in fact three constables standing by the side of a small commercial van just in case they were needed. There was no fight.

Although attitudes were beginning to change inside the Home Office, the Board of Customs and Excise seemed to be going in the opposite direction. The shameful decision by Customs to impound two volumes of Jean Genet's complete works in French in the autumn of 1956 betrayed the liberal legacy of Sir Francis Floud's secret stand over Radclyffe Hall's lesbianism. The Jean Genet affair also demonstrated that the demand for reform of the obscenity laws went far beyond the chattering classes of London's literary circles and was well understood in the rest of Britain. The Genet decision sparked a wave of angry protests in the Birmingham newspapers. 'MP Probes Into Mystery "Blue Pencil" Man' and 'Law Made At Time Of Ark', shouted the *Birmingham Evening Mail*. 'The Novel You Must Not Read', screamed the *Sunday Mercury*. The more sedate *Birmingham Post* warned that 'the power to withhold books is more widely spread than the public imagines … it must be justified in the eyes of reasonable people. Society can be grievously harmed by overzealous protectors.' The paper added that if the affair did anything to draw attention to the untidy state of the laws on obscenity, it would have been worth it. The *Birmingham Evening Mail* was more direct. Under the headline 'Rock 'N Read', it grumbled:

> Our City elders, it seems, are competent to decide if local youngsters shall be allowed to Rock 'n roll, but not whether they may, so to speak, Rock 'n read. Weighty decisions of that sort appear to rest with the Lords Commissioners of the Treasury.[5]

It was to lead to a fierce debate on the floor of the Commons between Enoch Powell and Denis Howell, who was later to make his name as the first Minister for Sport, and more famously in the summer of 1976 as the Minister for Drought.

Birmingham Central Lending Library had ordered from Paris the three volumes of Genet's collected works in the original French, after the chief librarian, Victor Woods, had read a favourable review in the *Times Literary Supplement*. Blackwell's, the Oxford booksellers, imported them from France, but when they reached England they were impounded under the 1876 Customs Consolidation Act. Woods explained his decision to order the books:

> I have not myself read any of the books in the collection, but a review about two years ago in the *Times Literary Supplement* said that in the opinion of Sartre, who is a man of some standing, and in the opinion of many

French critics, Genet was reckoned to be among the greatest of his contemporaries.[6]

The councillors of Birmingham Libraries committee at first defended their chief librarian all the way down the line. The outraged chairman, Meyrick Rees, told the *Birmingham Post:*

> I suppose Customs were carrying out the letter of the law, which was made at the time of the Ark. We should try to press for the return of these books. We have got representatives of the Church and men of high literary standing on our committee. I do not believe they would allow an obscene book into our libraries. This is an insult to them. We are living in 1956, and to impound a book which is freely read in France seems, to say the least, old-fashioned.[7]

But just to cover their backs, the councillors reassured any anxious ratepayers worried about the arrival of French filth in their city that the books would be kept only in the reference library and would not be loaned out to any casual readers. A vigilant eye would be kept on anybody who asked to see them.

Even so the Genet seizure sparked a passionate debate in Birmingham and Denis Howell, then Labour MP for All Saints, Birmingham, took up the cudgels on behalf of the city council's right to order its own library books. He said:

> I never knew that we had a censorship of literature like this. It must mean that somebody unknown to the general public is sitting down, reading books and deciding whether they are fit for the country. We ought to know who it is and what factors are taken into consideration.[8]

The Birmingham press joined in the fight, with editorials demanding to know what explanation the Chancellor of the

Exchequer, as the minister responsible for Customs, had for the seizure of their library books. The press warned that the untidy state of the obscenity laws in the hands of such over-zealous protectors could do grievous harm.

Mr Howell was not the only MP to protest. The Labour MP for Brierley Hill, C.J. Simmonds, himself a former chairman of Birmingham Libraries committee, said that prejudice was being stirred up and 'there was no way of knowing where this censorship caper would end'.

The official position was set out in a memo from Rose of Customs to Burley of the Home Office:

> The seized books are volumes two and three of the
> complete works of Genet. Volume one, which is a critical
> study of Genet by Sartre, was not seized. The two
> volumes had already come to the notice of Customs in
> 1953 in respect of the French text and in 1952 in relation
> to an English translation of one of the novels in volume
> two. Homosexuality is the predominant theme of both
> volumes. Each of which contains a number of grossly
> obscene descriptive passages. The works were ruled to be
> obscene.

While the Birmingham Libraries committee was all for fighting the case all the way through the courts, the law provided no means to do so. The 1876 Customs Consolidation Act, unlike the Obscene Publications legislation, allowed only the importer to challenge a seizure in the courts. Those who had originally ordered the books had no rights at all. Blackwell's was told that it had a month in which to mount a legal challenge and to attempt to prove that the book was not obscene. But for its own feeble reasons the booksellers decided not to act.

In the absence of any legal challenge, Customs decided to take the initiative and indulge in what these days would be described as a bit of Whitehall selective briefing or spin doctoring. The day before a Commons debate on the Genet affair was to be held, Customs invited Meyrick Rees, Victor Woods and the Birmingham Town Clerk, John Gregg, down to London for a meeting with the deputy chairman of the board of Customs and Excise, A.D. Owen. Customs helpfully provided them with all the dirty bits translated into English, so they could see just what it was they were arguing about. There was no need under the Customs legislation to do anything boring like 'taking the book as a whole' or judging it on its literary merits. Meyrick Rees professed to be shocked by the acts of gay sex which the carefully selected extracts described:

> When I had the opportunity of reading the translated passages for page after page I felt sick to the foundations of my being. The theme was homosexuality. I am satisfied that the Customs and Excise has rendered a public service.[9]

But Mr Rees's sudden attack of literary nausea did not silence Denis Howell. A fortnight later he said that this 'solemn procession' sent down to London by the Birmingham city fathers was something straight out of a Gilbert and Sullivan opera. Mr Howell told the Commons:

> One could almost hear them singing Gilbert's famous song: 'I have a little list.' It is like the old story of the Mayor and the Town Clerk who watched a film three times before deciding it was unfit for public exhibition.

There were others in Birmingham who were not impressed by Councillor Meyrick Rees's sudden change of tune. Geoffrey Allen, a former Birmingham councillor, observed that standing on one's head might be a suitable occupation for a circus clown but it was hardly fitting for a civic leader like Mr Rees. Allen believed that the reason the works of Genet were available to the tiniest literate child in France but banned in England was because he was illegitimate, a convicted thief and an admitted homosexual. He argued that if all authors with sexual or mental abnormalities were to be banned, Birmingham's library shelves would be left bare. Even Shakespeare had written poems to a young man.

Mr Howell was also to prove an equally staunch defender of Genet in the Commons. He told MPs that it was a farce that the French-speaking public of Birmingham was to be denied access to the books by Genet when they were already available in the British Museum and Reading University library. 'Some think him mediocre. Others a genius. But I am assured that he must be read to get any opinion of contemporary French literature.' Mr Howell claimed that the Customs action under a Victorian statute amounted to a particular 'insidious form of censorship and an abuse of power'. He demanded to know whether some kind of secret index of undesirable books was in use saying all of Genet's books were being banned regardless of whether they were obscene or not. Mr Howell added that it was high time the public were treated as adults capable of censoring their own literary works.[10]

It was left to Enoch Powell, as the Treasury minister responsible for Customs, to defend the ban in the Commons. This he did on the grounds that it was a legitimate interpretation of the law by the Customs officers. He referred often and fully to the conversion of Meyrick Rees and pointed out that the failure by Blackwell's to challenge the ban meant that legally it was now accepted that the books were obscene. Birmingham City councillors confirmed after legal advice that they had no other option but to give up the fight and so banned Genet from their shelves.

Although he had not managed to save Genet for Birmingham, Mr Howell had (without realising it) come very close to unearthing another of the great censorship secrets of Whitehall. During the late night Commons debate between Denis Howell and Enoch Powell over the fate of the two volumes of Jean Genet, the Birmingham MP had demanded to know whether a pre-censorship list of banned books was operating in Britain. Mr Howell told the Economic Secretary to the Treasury:

> I am told upon inquiries from some booksellers that they
> have now reached the position that they find it
> impossible to get any of this author's work into the
> country, whether it is pornographic or not. Is that true?
> If it is true, it means that in respect of this author there is
> an index system at work. This is a very serious matter, far
> beyond anything we have previously heard. It means that
> this author's works are not to be judged on their
> individual merits, but that the fact that he has written
> anything stops its importation.[11]

Enoch Powell refused to answer the direct question about the
existence of the confidential index of banned books but insisted
that each book was examined separately:

> He asked whether this action means that this author's
> works will automatically be regarded as obscene, and the
> answer to that is 'No'. Each case must be taken on its
> merits. If other works – for example, the hon. Member
> referred to Volume I, which was reviewed in *The Times* –
> are sought to be imported into this country, then an
> opinion on their merit will have to be formed, and there
> will again be an opportunity to the importer of having
> the matter properly settled in the courts.[12]

But Enoch Powell – a lifetime advocate of parliamentary sovereignty – was clearly being disingenuous here in failing to disclose the existence of the separate Customs list of banned
books. As the Customs files now show, the list did exist at the
time and had done so for a number of years. It did include the
second and third volumes of Genet's *Oeuvres Complètes* (including its component parts such as *Miracle de la Rose*) as well as the
English-language version of one of the books, *Our Lady of the
Flowers*.

The public confirmation that Powell had misled MPs about
this emerged a year later when Rose of Customs admitted to

the House of Commons Home Affairs Committee that the separate Customs blacklist did exist and that there were about 60
books on it. However, he refused to give any details and it was
only with the release of confidential Customs files at the Public
Record Office in 1998 that it was made public. The Customs list
was known as Appendix C and was much shorter than the
Home Office *Blue Book*'s titles because it contained only those
books that had been prosecuted in a crown court before a jury.
The more comprehensive Home Office list also included all the
material that had been subject to destruction orders in the magistrates' courts. The list was updated and revised all the time.

The Customs files give a few examples, and show that in the
Genet case, even they were anxious about banning the two
volumes of his collected works. In one case the seizure of several
books from a South African first-class passenger, A. Bowman, at
Heathrow Airport when he arrived in London in August 1953
for a week's visit prompted a revision of the list. 'He protested
that they were not intended for this country but for a friend in
South Africa,' recorded A.J. Gully, a preventative officer. The
books seized were the *Memoirs of Fanny Hill* (Obelisk Press), *The
Bedroom Philosophers* by D.A.F. de Sade and *Amorous Exploits of a
Young Rakehell* by Guillaume Apollinaire, both published by the
Olympia Press, Paris.

'*The Memoirs of Fanny Hill* is included in List 1 in Appendix
C, Customs Code, Vol 1, part 4. In view of the offensive letter-
press of the other two, I beg to submit them for the [Customs]
Board's directions,' wrote Gully. This note disclosing that all
Olympia Press books were seized regardless of their titles simply
on the basis of its 'offensive letterpress' blows apart Enoch
Powell's later claim that all such seizures were done on individ-
ual cases dependent on the merits of the book.

Mr Bellew of the Board wrote back to Gully asking for the
de Sade to be sent to him in a sealed envelope:

> You may not be aware of the *Bedroom Philosophers* which
> is new to us. Incidentally the *Amorous Exploits of a Young*

Rakehell is becoming popular – Channel Ports and
mainly Northolt. The books retained locally should now
be destroyed by burning and a certificate of destruction
sent to me.

The two Olympia Press books were added to Appendix C after
this seizure. Around the same time the Genet books were blacklisted:

I suggest we include Volumes II and III of *Oeuvres
Complètes* by Jean Genet which are becoming popular.
But it may be risky to add such a comprehensive title
and more preferable to list the works which are
comprised in the various 'Tomes' of Genet's complete
works.

The Customs files make clear that the list was not intended to
be comprehensive but was 'confined to those which for special
reasons are brought (or come) to notice from time to time'.
These excluded the 'cheap continental types which can be
recognised immediately as obscene', which explains why it contains only works of literature. The Customs Board also felt that
if it was made comprehensive then it would have the effect of
'stimulating special vigilance in looking out for such books and
might lead officers to think that the books on the list are the
only ones to be detained'.

It was certainly an imperfect process. The list was not revised
at all between 1930 and the early 1950s, which meant that both
Ulysses and *The Well of Loneliness* was still on Appendix C long
after their publication had been approved in Britain. By 1956 the
list also included J.P. Donleavy's *The Ginger Man* and Samuel
Beckett's *Molloy*. The Customs documents show that the great
bulk of what was detained at Britain's ports was in addition to
the Appendix C listed works. The daily haul seized by Customs
consisted mainly of books, dirty postcards, photographs and
films for the trade in porn. In one typical month, August 1956,

the Customs seized from private individuals 96 photographs, 20 magazines, 100 prints, 14 separate Olympia Press books, two books of limericks, a copy of *Lady Chatterley's Lover*, Frank Harris's *My Life and Loves* and ten other miscellaneous obscene books.

Both Customs and the Home Office were very concerned that the Commons Select Committee looking into obscenity should not find out about the existence of their banned book lists. Secret correspondence before they were both due to give evidence shows civil servants trying to agree what explanation they should give if any MP should challenge them about their existence. The Home Office wrote to Customs in May 1957 to agree the preparations for the hearing. They had decided to omit all references to the list of banned books in their evidence and added: 'We will deal with it orally if it is to be referred to at all.' They pressed Customs to delete all references to their list in their evidence to the Select Committee.

The July 1954 version of the list of 'Books which are to be seized as indecent or obscene' runs to more than 50 titles. It covers mostly those works regarded as borderline by Customs. Most officers operated on the basis that 'like the elephant, you knew it when you saw it' and the routine output of the pornographic trade was easy to recognise. This list was compiled at the peak of the second great British literary purge and covers quite a few books now regarded as classics of twentieth-century literature. Here it is published for the first time. The country indicates the place of publication.

List I: Books which are to be seized as indecent or obscene

Amorous Adventures of a Gentleman of Quality, The, Fernand
    Kolney, France;
Amorous Adventures of a Lady of Quality, The, M.L. Laurent-
    Tailhade, France;

Amorous Exploits of a Young Rakehell, Guillaume Apollinaire, France;

Ananga Ranga, France;

Bedroom Philosophers, D.A.F. (Marquis) de Sade, France;

Black Spring, Henry Miller, France;

Boy, James Hanley, France;

Children for Shame, Rowena Ripston, France;

Courtesans, Princesses, Lesbians, M.L. Laurent-Tailhade, France;

Dialogues of Luisa Sigea, Nicolas Chorier, France;

Fanny Hill, The Memoirs of, John Cleland, France;

Fleshy Prelude, The, Robert Semaise, France;

Gamiani (French text), Alcide, Baron de M, France;

Guide to the Science of Caresses, Claude and François Gerland, Belgium;

I Shall Spit on Your Graves, Vernon Sullivan, France;

Joujou (French text), Liane Delorys, France;

Justine (French text), Marquis de Sade, USA;

Kama Sutra of Vatsyayana, unknown, France;

Lady Chatterley's Lover, D.H. Lawrence, France, Italy, Germany, Sweden;

Lady Take Heed, Cecil Barr, France;

La Trilogie Erotique (French text), Paul Verdaine, Belgium;

Le Roman de Mon Alcove, Gustave Colline, France;

Love Counts Ten, Theodor Zay, France;

Love Orchid, The, Eric Wensleydale, France;

Max and the White Phagocytes, Henry Miller, France;

My Life and Loves (Vols I–IV), Frank Harris, France;

Nadja, M. Kerrels, France

Oeuvres Complètes (French text), Jean Genet, France;

Tome II comprising: Notre Dame des Fleurs, La Condamnée à Mort, Miracle de la Rose, Un Chant d'Amour

Tome III comprising: Pompes Funèbres, Le Pêcheur du Suquet, Quenelle du Brest

Our Lady of the Flowers, Jean Genet, France;

Perfumed Garden, The, Sheik Nefzawi, France;

Romance of Lust, Paul Somtrevil, France;

Rosy Crucifixion – Sexus (5 vols), Henry Miller, France;
Secret Love, Dr Jaf, France;
To Sin I Was Constrained, Marjorie North, France;
Tropic of Cancer, Henry Miller, France;
Tropic of Capricorn, Henry Miller, France;
Veuve Amoreuse, La (French text), unknown, France;
Voyage au Bout de la Nuit (French text), Louis Ferdinand
     Celine, Belgium;
Where Love is Fear, André Foucalt, France.

The new items on the July 1954 issue of the list included a
Swedish edition of *Lady Chatterley's Lover*, the Apollinaire book,
the complete works of Jean Genet and Marjorie North's novel.
The list was included in the instructions issued to local Customs
officers and books that appeared on it could be seized without
any reference to headquarters. Books that were not on the list
were not necessarily immune from seizure. They could also be
confiscated at the discretion of an individual Customs officer
but the decision to do so had to be referred upwards before it
was confirmed. The confidential Customs documents show the
civil servants congratulating themselves on the list and telling
each other they must have got it about right because the
Customs Commissioners' rulings had been challenged in the
courts only twice in the previous 20 years and both attempts had
failed.

   They firmly resisted all suggestions from ministers and others
that the list should be published so that reputable booksellers
could avoid importing these banned works. That would never
do, they said. Such a list would have to be extremely long if it
were to be a comprehensive catalogue of all the obscene titles
and would only have the effect of advertising them.

   Four years later the most senior Customs official (Mr Rose)
finally admitted the existence of the blacklist but refused to
allow it to be published. He also confirmed that it had grown by
then to 60 books and included unexpurgated versions of Pepys'
Diaries and of *Tristram Shandy*. The instructions to Customs

officers also warned them that there were two classes of Rabelais and Boccaccio to be alert for. The first was intended for 'men of letters' and should be admitted, but the second was 'for apprentices and ought to be stopped'. One MP on the select committee, Mr Strachey, the MP for Dundee East, observed:

> The customs officers had not been given any definition of obscenity – like the elephant they are left to recognise it. They are the most unguided missiles in the business.

MPs were particularly outraged to discover that the 1958 Customs list banned J.P. Donleavy's *The Ginger Man*, when it was then on sale at every bookshop in Britain. When it also emerged that practically the whole of Jean Genet's works were also on the list even though they were in French, the *New Statesman* launched a vitriolic attack on the Customs for being a bunch of philistines. The political weekly also pointed out that the books were banned entirely at the whim of Customs and that there were books on the list that no court had ever pronounced upon.

The attack stung the deputy chairman of Customs and Excise, who wanted to reply directly to the *New Statesman*. He regarded the criticism as unfair, saying that it was the usual 'acidities which pass for humour in the long-haired weeklies'. He wanted to point out that there were two versions of *The Ginger Man*. Donleavy's book was described officially as 'a study of drift, of desperation, of don't careism, of youth upon the world as on a strange planet'. The expurgated edition on sale in Britain omitted one whole chapter and had 30 other differences of text from the 'very dirty' unexpurgated version on sale abroad. It was this filthy foreign version that Customs were trying to keep out. The deputy chairman, having vented his anger on an internal memorandum, decided that it would be wiser to treat the *New Statesman* 'with disdain' and not worth an official public response.

The crass decision to ban Birmingham from reading Genet

gave an important new impetus to the campaign to reform the Obscene Publications Act. It provided a clear example of why the Society of Authors was saying that an exception had to be made for literary merit. It also fuelled the demands for all seizures to be referred to the courts instead of it being left in the hands of individual Customs or police officers to make the decision that something was obscene.

Roy Jenkins and A.P. Herbert's committee waged a relentless and ultimately successful battle in Parliament. After the Birmingham affair, the Society of Authors' private members' bill was reintroduced into the Commons by Lord Lambton but failed to get the government backing needed to make progress. Nevertheless, Roy Jenkins did manage to get the bill, which was drafted by the future Conservative Cabinet minister, Norman St John Stevas, referred to a select committee, whose evidence (as we have seen) served only to strengthen the hands of the reformers. Sir Alan Herbert put the case in his evidence to the House of Commons Select Committee on the Obscene Publications Bill:

> We do say that the dominant effect is the thing that matters. You may get a phrase which may shock some old lady and may surprise some young girl, but unless the whole purpose of the thing is to make people randy, or the author goes so far that it is against common decency, then we say that man ought to be left alone.[13]

The government realised that the game was almost over. Sir David Maxwell-Fyfe, together with his anti-vice crusade, was long gone from the office of Home Secretary. Instead of opposition the Home Office tried to smother the measure with 'helpful amendments' – a process which Sir Alan described as a long game of snakes and ladders. The bill avoided being killed completely at the end of the 1956/57 parliamentary session by the cunning device of making a formal report to Parliament. At the start of the 1957/58 session it was resurrected with a remit to 'consider whether it is desirable to amend and consolidate the law relating to obscene publications'. The MPs continued to take evidence from the police, authors, publishers, printers and the Public Morality Council. T.S. Eliot and E.M. Forster both gave evidence. It finished its work in the summer of 1958.

Everyone expected that the government would include a bill to reform the obscene publications laws in the Queen's Speech that autumn. Nothing, however, was announced. The campaigners were stunned, especially when Roy Jenkins reintroduced the Society of Authors' measure as a private member's bill and it failed to get a second reading. Sir Alan Herbert decided that it was time to take matters into his own hands. For 15 years he had been the Independent MP for Oxford University – a sort of Martin Bell of his time – but was deprived of his seat in 1950 when the university franchise was abolished. This popular figure now threatened to stand again against the Conservative candidate as an independent. It proved a potent threat and the prospect finally sparked the government into action, to find parliamentary time for the bill. The text of the bill became a real battleground between the reformers and the Attorney-General. Roy Jenkins had to make compromises, especially over the question of the author's intention; the Obscene Publications Act finally reached the statute book on 29 August 1959.

The new test, which replaced the Hicklin judgment, said that an article was deemed to be obscene if its effect, if taken as a whole, tended to deprave and corrupt persons who were likely, having regard to all the relevant circumstances, to read, see or hear the matter contained or embodied in it. It embodied the spirit of Mr Justice Stable's ruling in the *Philanderer* case five years before. But the new Act went further and introduced a defence of 'for the public good'. This meant that although a book might be found to have a tendency to deprave and corrupt, the case would fail if it could be demonstrated that its publication was in the interests of science, literature, art or learning.

The legislation placed a time limit on prosecutions for the

first time – no more than a year after publication for magistrates' court cases and two years for cases to be brought before a judge and jury. Booksellers were given a defence of 'innocent dissemination'. It gave authors and publishers the right to appear in magistrates' courts and be heard before their books were ordered to be guillotined or burned. It also protected the private collector's library from being thumbed over by the police. At the same time the police were given much stronger powers to act against 'genuine filth'.

The Act did not contain any new guarantee of a jury trial, however, and left intact the powers of Customs officers and magistrates to issue destruction orders. There were other problems with the new legislation, which were to become clearer as the 1960s got into their stride.

One indication of the change in moral atmosphere even before the legislation reached the statute book was seen in the case of Vladimir Nabokov's Lolita, which was recently the subject of fierce criticism when the film version triggered a new debate about its sympathetic depiction of child abuse. It was not the paedophiliac theme that worried the authorities about the 1950s Lolita. Nabokov's work had entered the British consciousness at Christmas 1955 when Graham Greene told the Sunday Times that he thought it one of the best books of the year. The Olympia Press (successors to Jack Kahane's Obelisk Press) then published it in Paris. Four US publishers had turned it down and the French edition was not doing well. Sales were extremely slow. Nobody wanted to know about a book whose theme of an older man's obsession with a 12-year-old girl was seen as an allegory for the ageing culture of Europe trying to revive itself by debauching the seductive young culture of America.

John Gordon of the Sunday Express, who had taken over the role of vice watchdog for the nation practised by his predecessor, James Douglas, had noticed Graham Greene's endorsement and got hold of a copy from Paris. 'It is the filthiest book I have ever read,' he announced in the finest Douglas tradition in January 1956. 'It is sheer unrestrained pornography. Anyone who

published or sold it here would certainly go to prison.'[14] The
Home Office read its copy of the *Sunday Express* and persuaded
the French to ban the sale in Paris of an English edition of *Lolita*
book under the International Convention for the Suppression
of Obscene Publications first drawn up in Geneva in 1923. (This
ban provoked little reaction among the French public, although
there was an outcry in December 1956 when the Olympia Press
in Paris was raided as a result of British pressure under this
Geneva convention.)

Around the rest of the world, publishers saw the British
outcry over *Lolita* as a major commercial opportunity and
Nabokov's book was saved. Six European countries immediately
published it. Even Japan decided to do the same. Publishers of
the Israeli edition said that their original publication had been
met with complete silence; the second printing of the book
would never have met with such success 'had not the John
Gordons of this world scared American publishers into rejecting
it in the first place'. Weidenfeld and Nicolson then thought
again about producing a British edition. They approached Sir
Toby Mathew, the Director of Public Prosecutions, asking
whether he would prosecute. Despite the fact that he did not
want to be seen as a censor, he assured the publishers that the
book would not be the subject of legal action. This decision may
have owed more to the fact that the bill was then going through
Parliament than the merits of the book. A prosecution at that
moment might have risked protests at the government's support
for the new legislation.

The authorities were finally beginning to learn that banning
things sometimes only made them appear even more desirable.
Only a year later Tony Hancock was getting a big laugh on BBC
Television by going into East Cheam Public Library and saying:
'There's not much choice in here, is there? I suppose *Lolita*'s still
out?' Stanley Kubrick's 1962 film version was regarded as acceptable at the time once the girl's age had been raised from 12
to 14. It is an interesting comment on our changing attitudes
towards child abuse that the recent film version of *Lolita* faced

much greater difficulties than Kubrick's because of the 1996 US Federal law banning the depiction of sexually suggestive scenes with children. In fact as *Time* magazine pointed out, there was nothing in Adrian Lyne's 1990s version that the viewing public needed to be protected from. Lyne had previously directed *Indecent Proposal* and *Fatal Attraction*. Both film versions of *Lolita* departed from the book in order to get on to the screen. In both cases the age of the girl was raised to 14 and all passages which would have stimulated or enticed would-be paedophiles were excised. In both films, unlike the book, the older man, Humbert Humbert, is punished for his 'nymphetomania' as it is portrayed.

Kubrick had a minor hit with an Academy Award nomination for Nabokov's script, but the American distributors refused to handle Adrian Lyne's version for two years after its release; humiliatingly for a $50-million movie it was released straight to cable. Jeremy Irons, its leading actor, claimed that Hollywood was frightened of the subject matter. Lyne complained: 'The atmosphere in America has become very moralistic in the last three years, similar to the way it was in the 1950s.' Well, not quite. In the 1950s the United States was a lot less bothered about the depiction of child abuse on the screen than it is now.

The hounding of D.H. Lawrence and the hunt for the missing witnesses

> Pornography and obscenity. What they are depends, as
> usual, entirely on the individual. What is pornography to
> one man is the laughter of genius to another.
>
> D.H. Lawrence, 1929[1]

David Herbert Lawrence, the son of a miner and a teacher and known to his family as Bert, grew up in the Nottinghamshire coal field at the turn of the twentieth century, and won his literary reputation with his second novel, *Sons and Lovers*. The explosive mixture of the themes of sexual fulfilment and social class in his novels was to make him the most hounded British author of the past hundred years.

The full extent of the relentless and secret war that was waged against D.H. Lawrence by those he dubbed the 'grey elderly ones' of Whitehall has only recently become clear with the final release of the official papers. It lasted from the burning of his novel, *The Rainbow*, in 1915 through to the famous trial of *Lady Chatterley's Lover* in 1960. Home Office files and papers belonging to the Director of Public Prosecutions, which were due

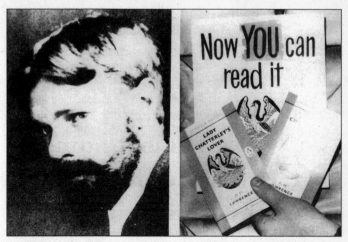

D. H. Lawrence and a bookshop window display of the Penguin edition of Lady Chatterley's Lover *on the day of its first British publication in 1960 some 32 years after it was first privately printed in Florence in 1928.*

to be kept secret until 2030 under the hundred-year rule but have been released earlier by ministerial discretion, at last reveal the full extent of an official vendetta that continued long after Lawrence's death.

It began in the middle of the First World War when the publication of *The Rainbow* was greeted with a storm of newspaper criticism about its open discussion of the subject of sex. The fact that Lawrence thought it primarily an anti-war novel, and an anti-Boer war novel at that, did not trouble his tormentors. Spurred by a complaint from an anonymous private citizen, the police bought a copy and read it. They wasted no time in taking it to the Bow Street magistrate, Sir John Dickinson, who helpfully issued a warrant under the 1857 Act for the seizure of all the copies to be found in the possession of the publishers, Methuen. When the police raided the publishers they confiscated all 1,011 copies on the premises. The police solicitor said that the obscenity in the book 'was wrapped up in language which I suppose will be regarded in some quarters as artistic and intellectual effort. I am at a loss, Sir, to understand how Messrs Methuen came to lend their name to its publication,' he told Sir John Dickinson.

Methuen was not happy. The publishers had twice tried to get Lawrence to moderate the manuscript and he had twice refused. But after taking legal advice they had gone ahead with the publication. Sir John Dickinson had no hesitation in agreeing with the police: 'I am sorry that a firm of such high repute should have allowed their reputation to be soiled as it has been by the publication of this work,' he said. This suppression of *The Rainbow* led to a general vilification of Lawrence. There were unpleasant accusations that he and his wife, Frieda von Richthofen, the cousin of the German air ace and the divorced wife of a Nottingham professor, were German spies. If this were not enough to poison Lawrence's reputation in the minds of the British public, the vendetta against the author intensified when Sir William Joynson-Hicks became Home Secretary. His period in this high office was to see what amounted to an official campaign against Lawrence and his works. It began when copies of the first edition of *Lady Chatterley's Lover*, which had to be printed in Florence, were seized by British Customs.

It continued in February 1929 when a volume of his poems, *Pansies*, was condemned in the House of Commons by Joynson-Hicks. The authorities had gone to the lengths of staging a covert surveillance operation so that they could intercept the manuscript when it was sent by Lawrence, who was living in Italy, to his London literary agent, Curtis Brown. It did not end there. Months later in July 1929, Scotland Yard raided an exhibition of Lawrence's paintings at the Warren Galleries in London. The police took away 13 of the pictures, including some depicting pubic hair, as well as a selection of anti-militarist cartoons by the German artist George Grosz. This vindictive and relentless campaign to suppress Lawrence's work did not even end after his early death from tuberculosis at the age of 45 in March 1930.

Jix, who always denied that he operated as a literary censor,

personally ordered the seizure of this volume of poems, *Pansies*,
by the Post Office after 'information had been conveyed to him'
that the book was about to be published. The Postmaster-
General had got hold of the manuscript after intercepting and
opening all of Lawrence's post sent to Britain from Italy. The
Home Secretary tried to cover up the existence of this surveillance operation when in February 1929 the redoubtable Labour
MP, Ellen Wilkinson, accused him straight out in the Commons
of censoring the post. He denied it and said that the GPO had
come across the Lawrence manuscript during what they
claimed was a routine examination of what was being sent
through the 'open book post'. The postal workers had been so
disturbed by these 'indecent' poems that they decided to send
them to the Home Office. Few MPs appeared to have believed
his claim that no public servant had opened a sealed packet
while in the care of the GPO in this case. Items sent in the
cheaper 'open book post' were supposed not to be sealed so they
could be inspected. But the incident shows that in fact all of
Lawrence's post to his London agent, Curtis Brown, was being
monitored and opened.

Joynson-Hicks said that he had been advised that the poems
included in the volume were 'grossly indecent matter' and there
was 'no question of literary merit at all'. The books were to be
detained for two months while the Director of Public Prosecutions considered whether it should be banned and to give the
importer the chance to mount a legal challenge to the seizure.
But the DPP in question – the same man who seven years previously had banned James Joyce's *Ulysses* after reading just 42 of
its 732 pages – was not prepared to follow Jix all the way in this
case. Sir Archibald Bodkin suggested to the publishers that if the
offending verses were omitted, he would not press on with a
prosecution. This advice, combined with the Home Secretary's
attack on Lawrence in the House of Commons, was enough to
scare off the publishers, Martin Secker. A new edition of *Pansies*
was produced in July 1929 but without the 12 controversial
poems. *Pansies* (1929) is not the same book as *Pansies* (1928). In

a foreword printed in a 1939 edition but written at the time, Lawrence gave his own account of the affair:

> Some of the poems are perforce omitted – about a dozen from the bunch. When Scotland Yard seized the manuscript in the post, at the order of the Home Secretary, no doubt there was a rush of detectives, postmen and Home Office clerks and heads to pick out the most lurid blossoms.
>
> They must have been disappointed. When I now read down the list of omitted poems, and recall the dozen not terribly important bits of *Pansies* which have had to stay out of print for fear a policeman might put his foot on them, I can only grin once more to think of the nanny-goat, nanny-goat-in-a-white-petticoat silliness of it all.
>
> It is like listening to a Mrs Caudle's curtain lecture in the next house, and wondering whether Mrs Caudle is funnier or Mr Caudle; or whether they aren't both of them merely stale and tedious.[2]

But Lawrence did not give up. In August 1929, 500 copies of the first edition of *Pansies*, including the offending blooms, numbered and signed by the author, were put on sale in London. On its last page the book announced: 'This edition of five hundred copies is privately printed for subscribers only by T.R. Stevenson of Museum Street, London, WC1.' A *Daily Express* reporter interviewed Mr Stevenson, who said:

> I have printed a limited edition of 500 copies of the book. These have all left these premises, and are in the hands of bona-fide collectors and those who have satisfied me that in subscribing two guineas for the book are doing so out of genuine interest in the work of D.H. Lawrence. In the event of any action being taken, which I do not consider likely, it would have to be proved that the book was likely to fall into the hands of people who

were liable to be morally influenced by it. It has not been published; merely, as I say, printed in a strictly limited edition.[3]

It was at this point that Bodkin decided that he should part company with Jix in his vendetta. He refused to prosecute Stevenson. Bodkin told Jix in a secret Whitehall memorandum to the Home Office:

> *Pansies* is a very mixed production, and so far as I have read it there are eleven so-called poems only, to which exception could be taken, and they are of the nauseous and disgusting kind rather than of the corrupting and immoral kind.
>
>   The book has recently been extolled in a review, and if it be correct that the present edition was for private circulation to subscribers the case stands differently from a book which is on every bookstall for indiscriminate publication. Probably by this time a good many 'subscribers' have had their copies, and much good may they do them!

Sir Archibald argued that it was better 'to keep a strict look-out' for copies imported in the posts and seize them under the Post Office regulations than apply to a magistrates' court for them to be banned 'with the consequential advertisement'. Anyway he was not entirely confident that a magistrate would consider the publication of a book by private subscription to be a misde-meanour and 'proper to be prosecuted as such'.

The Home Secretary never actually told the Commons that his view that the poems were 'grossly indecent' was not shared by the DPP. Instead Jix demanded that Scotland Yard track down the dozens of copies of the privately printed edition of *Pansies* that had been sent abroad by Stevenson, the London bookseller. Detective Inspector Crapper was instructed to cable the 'central authorities' in the United States, Canada, New Zealand and

Argentina, where parcels of books had been sent, and to ask that they be traced, seized and destroyed. So although no court ever ruled the dozen offending blooms to be obscene, the uproar was enough for Lawrence's London publishers, Martin Secker, to run scared and omit them from the British edition published in 1929.

By the time that the police raided D.H. Lawrence's exhibition of paintings in July 1929, it seemed that his very name was enough to ensure that official action was taken to suppress his art. There were 25 pictures on show at the Warren Galleries in London at the opening of the exhibition. The police seized 13 of the paintings along with four books of reproductions and a copy of *Ecce Homo* by the German savage cartoonist and forerunner of Steve Bell, George Grosz. A constable also seized a book of the pictures of William Blake. But the officer in charge of the raid, an Inspector Hester, appears to have heard of this English visionary poet and thought better of it. Police interest was first roused a fortnight before the exhibition opened when the Mandrake Press started advertising their book of reproductions of Lawrence's paintings. The publishers had produced 500 copies of a limited edition to be sold at 10 guineas (£10.50) a time and a further ten signed copies on Japanese vellum at £52 10 shillings (£52.50). The books included 26 large plates in colour. The seized pictures, which had titles such as *Fight with an Amazon*, *A Boccaccio Story* and *Spring*, 'portrayed the human frame in its most intimate details', that is pubic hair was clearly visible in several of the paintings.

At Great Marlborough Street magistrates' court, Mr St John Hutchinson, appearing on behalf of Lawrence, argued that the raid amounted to a new form of censorship. 'I have not been able to find any case in which serious paintings have been brought into a police court and a magistrate has been asked to decide whether they were obscene,' he told the court.[4] At the back of the courtroom sat Augustus John, Sir William Rothenstein and other luminaries of the artistic establishment but the magistrate, Frederick Mead, waved them away without being heard. He offered to dismiss the summons on payment of 5 guineas (£5.25) costs as long as the exhibition was closed. St John Hutchinson accepted the offer, to Lawrence's lifelong humiliation. It was the first obscenity hearing to involving works of art but it was not to be the last. Seven years later two paintings were banned from appearing in an International Surrealist Exhibition to be staged in London.

The raid on Lawrence's paintings hurt him deeply despite the fact that some 13,000 people saw the exhibition before the police closed it down. In his pamphlet, *Pornography and Obscenity*, he wrote:

> When the police raided my picture show, they did not in the least know what to take. So they took every picture where the smallest bit of the sex organ of either man or women showed. Quite regardless of subject or meaning or anything else: they would allow anything, these dainty policemen in a picture show, except the actual sight of a fragment of the human pudenda. This was the police test. The dabbing on of a postage stamp – especially a green one that could be called a leaf – would in most cases have been quite sufficient to satisfy this 'public opinion'.

He railed against the 'grey elderly ones' and claimed that the vast majority of young people at that time had, among themselves, come out into the open about sex, even if in public they were still under the shadow of the older generation.

> The grey elderly ones belong to the last century, the eunuch century, the century of the mealy-mouthed lie, the century that has tried to destroy humanity, the nineteenth century ... the century of purity and the dirty little secret.[5]

After the banning of his bunch of *Pansies*, Lawrence published a new volume bemoaning the desire of the British censors to neuter all public mention of sex. He called it *Nettles*. This is among its poems:

> *Editorial Office:*
> *Applicant for the post as literary critic: Here are my credentials,*
>   *Sir! -*
> *Editor: Er-quite. But-er-biologically! Have you been fixed? -*
>   *arranged - you understand what I mean?*
> *Applicant: I'm afraid I don't.*
> *Editor (sternly): Have you been made safe for the great British*
>   *Public? Has everything objectionable been removed from you?*
> *Applicant: In what way, quite?*
> *Editor: By surgical operation. Did your parents have you*
>   *sterilised?*
> *Applicant: I don't think so, Sir. I'm afraid not.*
> *Editor: Good morning! Don't trouble to call again. We have the*
>   *welfare of the British Public at heart.*[6]

By the time that the police went to the Warren Galleries, the Customs officers had already started seizing copies of *Lady Chatterley's Lover*. It had been published six months before in an edition of 1,000 copies by an Italian publisher, Giuseppo Oriolo, who was based near Lawrence's Florentine home under the author's personal supervision. Lawrence told his literary agent, Nancy Pearn of Curtis Brown:

> It is what the world would call very improper. But you know it is not really improper - I always labour at the same thing to make the sex relations valid and precious, instead of shameful. And this novel is the furthest that I have gone.

In fact one of the women typists refused to complete the man-uscript, saying it was distasteful, and Maria Huxley, wife of Aldous, finished the task. A second edition of 3,000 copies of *Lady Chatterley* was published in Paris, which now, thanks to

Joynson-Hicks, was the home of a lucrative English-language book trade. This edition was produced by Edward Titus, the husband of the cosmetics magnate, Helena Rubenstein.

Lawrence had initially sent his book to Jack Kahane, the legendary Mancunian 'booklegger' who had set up in Paris in 1931 with the object of bringing out works that were banned in England. His Obelisk Press had published editions of *The Well of Loneliness*, *Sleeveless Errand*, Cyril Connolly's *The Rock Pool*, Lawrence Durrell's *Black Book* and eventually Henry Miller's famous autobiographical *Tropic of Cancer* and *Tropic of Capricorn*. All were books that British publishers declined to publish either because they had been banned or because the publishers feared prosecution. These English-language books published by the Obelisk Press were aimed purely at the British and American tourist trade and were a constant target for Customs officers searching the bags of passengers returning from Paris. As the Customs papers show, the company was regarded as 'being noted for printing indecent literature' and the authorities constantly tried to find new ways of persuading the French to remove this thorn in their flesh. Kahane died in 1939 but the publishing company was revived after the war by his son, Maurice, first trading as Obelisk and later under the name of Olympia Press. Maurice published Samuel Beckett, Vladimir Nabokov, Henry Miller, Jean Genet and J.P. Donleavy.

Jack Kahane turned down *Lady Chatterley* because of the financial problems that the Obelisk Press was going through. Lawrence was bitterly disappointed and mistakenly believed that even Kahane thought it was too indecent. This all contributed to Lawrence's anxieties about the British censors. His fears were justified. *Lady Chatterley* went straight on to the Customs secret banned list without any reference to the courts or indeed any great fuss in the newspapers. A bowdlerised edition was published in Britain after Lawrence's death in 1930 but there was nothing in the book to tell the reader that it was not 'the full Monty' that the author had intended. Indeed it was to be another 30 years before his novel, complete with those passages which had been praised by George Bernard Shaw as essential reading for every marriageable daughter, was to see the light of day.

It is important to remember just how vilified Lawrence was by the authorities during his lifetime to understand the magnitude of victory that his eventual acquittal at the Old Bailey some 30 years after his death represented. The official vendetta against him began with the burning of 1,000 copies of his anti-war novel, *The Rainbow*, in 1915. It rose to a peak in 1929 – the year before his death – when the authorities ensured that *Lady Chatterley* did not find a British publisher, his poems were seized and his paintings were withdrawn from public view. He felt the persecution keenly and his reputation as an author of 'dirty books' lingered long.

The story of the trial of *Lady Chatterley's Lover* has been told many times before but never with the benefit of the Director of Public Prosecutions' own papers. The official files provide an answer to some of the key questions in this landmark trial, which, in the words of Sir Stephen Tumim, introduced the 1960s as an age of permissiveness in British minds and manners. The DPP's papers show that the Crown had bungled the case before it had started. The case was lost even before the prosecution counsel, Mervyn Griffith-Jones, had the chance to get on his feet to patronise the jury with his famous gaffe when he asked them whether *Lady Chatterley* was a book which they would wish their wives or servants to read. The files also reveal the ultimately unsuccessful strategy that the DPP adopted to try to discredit the 35 witnesses who were called as experts in defence of Lawrence.

At the time the Attorney-General explained the famous failure of the Crown to match the defence 'bishop for bishop and don for don' on the grounds that such witnesses would have been out of order. The official files paint a different picture and show that despite strenuous efforts by the authorities, not a single leading literary figure of the day could be found who was prepared to give evidence against Lawrence. Not even Rudyard

Kipling was able to help them out this time. The files also show that the claims after the trial by the Director of Public Prosecutions that he had not consulted the Home Secretary or the Home Office before taking the decision to put *Lady Chatterley* into the Old Bailey dock were a complete lie.

The ill-fated attempt to block the British publication of an unexpurgated edition of *Lady Chatterley's Lover* began was not the first trial under the new Obscene Publications Act. That honour fell to a publication called the *Ladies' Directory* , which was a contact book for prostitutes in central London. It contained paid advertisements from prostitutes, which listed their phone numbers, and in some cases their photographs and the sexual tastes they were prepared to indulge. Its Soho publisher was tried at the Old Bailey in December 1960 and found guilty of conspiracy to corrupt public morals, living on the earnings of prostitutes and of publishing an obscene article. To the surprise of no one, the *Ladies Directory* failed to qualify as an exempted work under the new literary or artistic merit test of the Obscene Publications Act. The publisher was sentenced to nine months' imprisonment.

Officially the first that the authorities knew of the decision of Sir Allen Lane, the founder of Penguin Books, to publish a British edition – four-letter words and all – of *Lady Chatterley's Lover* was in March 1960. The Chief Constable of Peterborough, F.G. Markin, sent the Director of Public Prosecutions a copy of 'what appeared to be an unexpurgated edition' of *Lady Chatterley* published by Penguin Books. This sudden appearance of a book which had been on Whitehall's secret blacklists for 30 years should not have been too much of surprise. Penguin's decision had obviously been influenced by the new Obscene Publications Act but it had also taken into account a US court judgment the year before. In this case the Federal Judge Frederick Bryan ruled that the US Postmaster-General had been wrong to regard the book as obscene, saying there was no doubt as to its literary merit. Judge Bryan said that the book described sexual intercourse in great detail with complete candour and realism and four-letter Anglo-Saxon words were used frequently; while this might shock the sensitive-minded, these passages were relevant to the plot and to the development of the characters.

Nevertheless the letter from the Chief Constable of Peterborough sent Whitehall into a spin. As the letter reached Maurice Crump, the deputy director of Public Prosecutions, the New York Court of Appeals was upholding Judge Bryan's ruling. Chief Justice Charles Clark said that D.H. Lawrence wrote with power and 'with a tenderness that was compelling once our age-long inhibitions against sex revelations had been overcome'. Maurice Crump wrote back to the Chief Constable of Peterborough asking for further information about the circumstances surrounding the publication of the book. In particular he wanted to know whether it had fallen into the hands of somebody who if they read it was likely to be depraved and corrupted by it – the key test in the new legislation.

Markin, the Chief Constable, replied saying he knew that the book had been banned in the past and no reputable company had published it for a number of years:

> It was therefore a surprise to me to find that the Penguin publishing company have printed a new edition which includes all the passages to which the Courts have taken exception in the past. As this is going to be offered for sale by such reputable firms as W.H. Smith and Sons I thought it possible that some more recent decision had caused a broader view to be taken and it was in order to clarify this position that I wrote to you. I would be obliged for your observations on this matter and would be grateful if you would return the book to me.

But Crump was not willing to rush into a blanket condemnation of *Lady Chatterley* for this pushy policeman, however senior he might be. He wrote back again in a couple of days, repeating his request for further details and patiently explaining that each sale of a book had now to be considered in detail:

> If the book is hawked around school children, that is one
> thing. If it is offered by responsible people for sale only
> to responsible people that is another. I am not prepared
> to say that a book by so distinguished an author is
> necessarily in all circumstances obscene though clearly in
> some it might well be.

Crump's initial caution is admirable. What a shame he did not
stick with it. The single copy that was offered by the Peterborough policeman was not enough for the DPP to act. It needed
evidence of publication and so far that did not exist. It was not
to be long coming.

The Peterborough police were not the only ones looking for
guidance in this new permissive world. In April 1960 Customs
and Excise wrote to Sir Austin Strutt at the Home Office, saying
that they had always seized copies of *Lady Chatterley* under the
powers in their well-worn 1876 Act. Indeed only recently they
had issued a writ against the importers of 20 copies of the unexpurgated edition in French and the case was pending. They
wanted to know what to do about it. This was a serious business.
In 1960 alone there had already been 24 forfeiture orders against
various book importers for bringing in banned works. Some
had indeed been sent to prison.

Customs wanted to know what position they would be in
once Penguin went ahead with an English edition, as there
would be no justification for continuing to seize copies coming
through the ports. They had done the same in the *Lolita* case, but
they did not want to act without Home Office guidance. Whatever they did would be taken 'as an indication of the Government's attitude towards the publication of the unexpurgated
English text. It occurs to me that this might be embarrassing
from your point of view,' said Mr Owen, the head of Customs.

Strutt asked Sir Toby Mathew, the DPP, what to do: 'I agree
it would be unfortunate if different departments were to appear
to be taking different views of the same publication,' replied
Mathew.

I understood in the case of *Lolita* it was because I decided not to prosecute the recent publication that the Customs withdrew the embargo on importation.

Should there be a domestic publication of the unexpurgated edition of *Lady Chatterley's Lover* I should have to consider whether to prosecute, in the light of the circumstances at the time of publication, and clearly one of the important considerations would be the fact that condemnation proceedings were pending. Indeed it may well be that it is the existence of such proceedings that has caused Penguin to abandon their projected publication for the present, and it may also deter others from publishing until the result is known. But should there be a prior publication I would certainly consult all interested parties before deciding not to institute proceedings.

So now Sir Toby not only had the Chief Constable of Peterborough pressing for prosecution but also was facing pressure from Customs and Excise for similar action as they did not want their own attempts at legal suppression to be jeopardised. Sir Toby promised to consult them before any final decisions were made.

In May 1960, Penguin Books announced its intention of publishing the unexpurgated text of *Lady Chatterley's Lover* in an ordinary cheap Penguin paperback format. It immediately ran into trouble. In the Commons the Attorney-General, Sir Reginald ('Reggie') Manningham-Buller, was challenged as to whether or not he would prosecute Penguin. He said that it was not a question for him to answer but one for the DPP. The printers that Penguin normally used took fright at these exchanges and refused to print the book; matters were delayed while new printers were found.

The next month Strutt of the Home Office wrote back to the DPP telling him that Penguin had found new printers and that the publication date had been announced for 25 August 1960. The book would be published at 3s. 6d. (17.5p) so it would get a wide circulation On 17 June 1960, Strutt wrote:

In fact the Home Secretary has had a letter from Isaac J. Pitman MP to the effect that the Western Printing Services, who are a subsidiary of Sir Isaac Pitman and Sons, are undertaking the printing, and are doing so as a matter of principle.

Strutt made clear that the Home Office view was that a decision on whether or not to prosecute would have to be taken before the Penguin edition was published. He was worried that the promised consultations around Whitehall would take some time. They could not wait until they knew the circumstances surrounding its publication.

It would seem to be important that if a prosecution is to take place, proceedings should be instituted immediately following if only for the reason that a delay will result in a large number of copies being sold, and the damage – if the court eventually holds the book to be obscene – will already have been done.

If any more evidence is needed that far from acting alone, the DPP had the full backing of the Home Office, and by implication of the then Home Secretary, R.A. Butler, then the following memo from Sir Toby Mathew to the Home Office would appear to end all speculation:

June 21 1960: Dear Strutt, I agree it would be desirable that we should now decide our line of action in the event of publication of an unexpurgated edition by Penguin books. As a start I am consulting the Treasury Counsel and when I have received his opinion we might meet with Customs and Excise and discuss the situation. Yours sincerely, Theobald Mathew.

Three weeks later Mathew's deputy, Maurice Crump, wrote to Mervyn Griffith-Jones in his chambers at the Temple, saying that it was getting near the moment when they needed to come to a decision on *Lady Chatterley*.

The DPP wrote on 17 August to the Home Office to confirm officially that on the advice of Mervyn Griffith-Jones, the decision to prosecute had been taken, that the summonses were being applied for, and that Customs had also been told of the decision. The files contain no minutes of the repeatedly promised consultations before the decision to prosecute was taken. But it is clear that the whole process went ahead with plenty of opportunity for the Home Office to make clear their opposition and to stop the prosecution if they thought it unwise. At no time did they raise any objection. Let us look at the evidence. They had already 'decided our line of action' and the decision to go for a pre-publication prosecution was to be 'percolated to the publishers through the Home Office'.

On the second point Crump explained what it meant to Mallows of Customs: 'The publication was by arrangement to provide the basis of a test case,' he said, referring to the decision that the act of 'publication' should take the form of Penguin handing over a copy to a police officer.

When Crump sent Griffith-Jones the official letter asking for his counsel's opinion on 13 July 1960, he admitted that it would look bad if it got out that they were acting as pre-publication censors. Crump wrote:

> When a new book is to be published, it seems obviously right that we should refuse to act as censors and should delay our decision until after publication when the reaction of the public, whose servants we are, can be felt. But in the case of an old timer like *Lady Chatterley's Lover* the situation is different and it seems only fair to come to a decision before publication. This we would not actually announce (for fear of creating a precedent and thereby becoming censors) but it could be percolated to the publishers through the Home Office.

He added a postscript, saying that if Mervyn wanted to discuss the book to let him know but he thought it best to refrain from expressing, as yet, his own views. Griffith-Jones delivered his legal opinion within a fortnight. It arrived in the DPP's offices on 27 July 1960 and was short and to the point:

> In my opinion the unexpurgated version of *Lady Chatterley's Lover* – a proof copy of which I have read – is obscene and a prosecution for publishing an obscene libel would be justified. Indeed if no action is taken in respect of this publication it will make proceedings against any other novel very difficult.

Sir Toby Mathew accepted the Senior Treasury Counsel's opinion but there remains a minor mystery as to where the proof copy he read came from. It was suggested at the time that the police had bought a copy in London's Charing Cross Road, then regarded officially as Britain's Port Said. But this explanation does not answer the question of how Crump got hold of a proof copy a month before publication. It might have been the mysterious copy supplied by the Chief Constable of Peterborough but there is no further reference to it in the files. Normally the police would have obtained a search warrant and seized a copy, but this time they were going to act before it was published. Nor could they send a police officer over to Paris to buy a copy or use one of a batch seized by Customs, as Penguin had not published the book abroad.

The truth may have been that the book was simply handed over by Penguin so that a decision on whether to prosecute could go ahead. Indeed it would have been wholly in keeping with much else that happened in this 'test case by arrangement'. It would be a further indication that the *Lady Chatterley* trial was perhaps one of the last great examples of a courtroom battle played out within the gentlemanly rules of English public-school life. For this was, in essence, an act of voluntary censorship by Penguin who, in an *Alice in Wonderland* way, really wanted to know the jury's verdict before they committed the crime. As the note on the DPP's file put it:

> In view of the nature and extent of the proposed
> publication, the Director [of Public Prosecutions]
> instructed the police to see the company and ascertain
> the position.

Detective Inspector Charles Monahan went to see Sir Allen Lane of Penguin on 4 August. Lane told him that 200,000 copies had been printed to be sold at 3 shillings each. They were to be distributed to agents for release on 25 August. Monahan suggested to Penguin that there should be

> a limited publication so that the issue might be decided
> before full publication. Accordingly 12 copies of the
> work were published to Inspector Monahan on August
> 16.

In other words Monahan collected 12 copies from Hans Schmoller, the Penguin art director, at the offices in High Holborn. In fact the police first suggested that the 12 copies be sent to a bookseller so that the police could buy them, but Penguin did not want to implicate some innocent third party in the business and so handed over the books to the police officer. Another court was later to rule that this was not sufficient to amount to publication because a police officer was not considered somebody capable of being corrupted or depraved.

One of the 12 copies was quickly dispatched to the Attorney-General, Sir Reginald Manningham-Buller, whose task was to read *Lady Chatterley's Lover* and say whether he agreed with the DPP's decision. He appears to have tried to do this while riding on the boat train from London to Southampton to catch a liner, the *Caronia*. The Attorney-General delivered his opinion in a hastily scribbled handwritten note on House of Commons notepaper, marked 'On the train to Southampton'. He said that he had read only the first four chapters, 'but if the remainder of the book is of the same character I have no doubt you were right to start proceedings – and I hope you get a conviction.' The Attorney-General said that he would be away for two weeks and warned Sir Toby Mathew to 'watch out for contempt of court in relation to *Lady Chatterley*' and not say anything in public or to potential witnesses that might prejudice the case as he prepared for the trial.

Although Manningham-Buller had left Britain he did ask the Solicitor-General, Sir Jack Simon, to read the book as well on his behalf, which he did. Not only did the Solicitor-General make no objection to the prosecution, but also the records show that he actually asked the DPP 'perhaps we could have a word about tactics if you are free sometime next week'. This contrasts sharply with Sir Toby Mathew's statements after the trial that the Attorney-General gave no directions in connection with the prosecution.

Armed with this unambiguous endorsement from both the government's law officers, the DPP and his deputy, Crump, set about preparing their case. The summonses had been issued and the date of the trial set down for 27 October 1960 at the London Central Criminal Court, the Old Bailey. *Lady Chatterley's Lover* already had a lengthy criminal record. The ban on the book in Britain had been rigorously enforced. In the decade between 1950 and 1960 alone, 19 different printings of the book had been referred to the DPP and different courts had granted 17 separate orders that the copies of the book be destroyed. Customs had repeatedly seized copies sent from abroad to private individuals. In December 1955 a Soho bookseller was sent to prison for two months for selling *Lady Chatterley*. He was released only when the court reduced his punishment to a £50 fine on appeal.

The first task facing the prosecuting authorities was to find some witnesses. Sir Toby Mathew was later to insist that there had been no need to put up any prosecution witnesses to match the squad of literary experts fielded by the defence because the

Crown conceded that the book had literary merit. Its case was that the book was obscene and although it had literary merit, that did not justify its publication. The newly opened files clearly show that this was far from the situation. Indeed it appears that an almost frantic search went on for prosecution witnesses who would be prepared to go into the dock and assault Lawrence's literary reputation. The all-important invitation to potential witnesses went through several drafts before the DPP was happy that it could be sent out without compromising the Crown's case.

Sir Toby's invitation read:

> I am most anxious to obtain the advice of persons of literary standing as to the literary merit of the book. Your name has been suggested to me as someone who might be prepared to give me this advice.
>
> I would therefore be most grateful for your opinion as to the literary structure of *Lady Chatterley's Lover* bearing in mind particularly that it is to be published at a price of 3/6 and sold from countless bookstalls and therefore will be readily available to anyone who may choose to buy it. I can also send you a copy of the Penguin edition should you wish to read it.

One of the young staff in the DPP's office who had read modern history at Oxford was asked for a list of suitable names of academics to be approached. He suggested Professor Neville Coghill at Merton, Professor Lord David Cecil at Merton, John Brayson of Balliol, J.B. Leishman at St Johns and Roger Minns. At Cambridge he thought that Dr E.M.W. Tillyard, a personal friend of his, and Dr David Daiches, who was an English don, a Director of Studies and an expert on the modern novel, might do. Other staff prepared a complete survey of the literature on Lawrence, not only to spot potential witnesses but also to show 'there was a considerable divergence of expert opinion as to the literary merit of this particular work'. Off they went to the

British Museum to look up the references. They were all to be
sent to Mervyn Griffith-Jones to help him prepare the case.

Dark Sun, by Graham Hough, an English lecturer and a
Fellow of Christ's College, Cambridge, was thought to be most
useful; the DPP's report comments:

> He says that *Lady Chatterley* is a good novel but it
> contains a number of undesirable irrelevancies, i.e. the
> continuous use of four-letter words. If this is so then it
> does add strength to the argument that the expurgated
> edition contains all that is important in the book.

J. Middleton Murry's *Son of Woman* was regarded as 'useful for
general information about Lawrence but you may also consider
that literary criticism such as this will be well above the heads of
the average member of the jury'.

T.S. Eliot, *The Two Articles*: 'These are written by the author
who is probably the greatest lay critic (as opposed to academic)
of the day. But T. S. was a staunch upholder of the Establishment
of which Lawrence was a violent antagonist and that therefore
this author is biased.'

E.T.'s D.H. Lawrence : 'You may find this useful as E. T. is a
pseudonym for Jessie Chambers, a boyhood friend of
Lawrence's. She is the prototype for Miriam in *Sons and Lovers*
and the first girlfriend described by Mellors in *Lady Chatterley*
on page 208.'

F.R. Leavis's *D.H. Lawrence, Novelist*: 'It is noted that the
author is still alive and that this is the standard work from a critical point of view and was published in 1955. See page 70 –
Leavis does not appear to approve of the book. See page 292 –
he says this use of obscenity is an offence against taste.' The file
does not tell us if the DPP was foolhardy enough to send Dr
Leavis an invitation to enter the witness box. It would have been
a delicious irony, given the attitude of the authorities to this legendary Cambridge critic 40 years before. But he did turn down
a request to appear for the defence. After the acquittal, Leavis,

the man who did more than most to create Lawrence's literary
reputation, was to denounce the publication of the novel and
the Old Bailey trial that it provoked, saying that it could only
harm the author as *Lady Chatterley* was such an unrepresentative
novel of his work. He thought that Penguin had invited the
prosecution only to make some money.

H.T. Moore's *The Life and Works of D.H. Lawrence* was regarded as 'The standard biography of Lawrence. No good for us
but essential.'

The DPP's staff was excited to discover that Lord David
Cecil in his 1932 book described Lawrence as a 'guttersnipe' and
an 'uncontrollable egoist'. A note on the DPP's file from a Frank
W. Turner, who was night editor at the influential Press Association, was about the only clear-cut critic they had, saying he
'cannot see any justification for the utter frankness about sex'
but he lacked the necessary qualifications to be regarded as a literary expert.

Within a few days the invitations started to go out. One was
sent to Noel Annan, the Provost of King's College, Cambridge,
and on the same day, 23 August, an invitation went to Helen
Gardner, Reader in Renaissance English Literature at St Hilda's
College, Oxford, and a member of the BBC 'Critics' panel.

The final version mentioned the 'public good' defence in the
new Act and said that experts might be called to give evidence
by either side on this point, which looked likely to happen for
the first time in this case. Sir Toby asked if they could help and
said he would be happy to send someone to discuss the matter.
Helen Gardner's reply came back by return of post:

> I am strongly in favour of the completion of the Penguin
> edition of the works of D.H. Lawrence by the
> publication of the full text of *Lady Chatterley's Lover*. I
> should therefore be unwilling to give any assistance to
> those who are desirous of suppressing the work.
>
> I do not consider the literary merit of this particular
> work is an important, or indeed relevant, consideration. It

is, in my view, a serious work of literature which merits serious consideration. Its merits and defects as a work of literature present a critical problem to which I am not prepared to give a hasty answer. I am not willing to discuss what is I think a purely literary problem with anyone who does not accept as a premise to the discussion that *Lady Chatterley's Lover*, whatever its merits or defects, is the work of a writer of genius and complete integrity.

Yours sincerely, Helen Gardner.

And this was from a potential witness who they had reason to believe might be persuaded to back the Crown's case. It must have been a big disappointment.

Noel Annan also replied the next day. He was brief and to the point:

I approve the action of Penguin Books in publishing an unexpurgated edition of *Lady Chatterley's Lover*. I would of course be happy to receive your representative, but you may feel, in view of this statement, that it would not be a profitable journey.

Sir Toby sent this to Crump. His only comment was a note on the envelope saying simply: 'Snub no 2'. Still the DPP's approach did produce a response. Both academics appeared in the witness box at the Old Bailey – to give evidence on behalf of Lawrence. Miss Gardner even testified that Lawrence was among the five or six greatest writers in English literature in the twentieth century.

The DPP did not give up. An article in the January 1960 edition of *Encounter* by an American short-story writer, Katherine Anne Porter, sounded promising. In the piece she described how when she had read *Lady Chatterley's Lover* some 30 years before, she had found it 'a dreary, sad performance with some passages of unintentional, hilarious, low comedy, one scene at least simply beyond belief in a book written with inflamed apostolic solemnity'. It was enough for the DPP and his staff to consider the possibility of flying Katherine Anne Porter over from the United States to testify at the trial. A letter to the US Embassy in London asking if it could help find her was of little use. The reply from assistant legal attaché, Alden McCray, merely underlined how much everyone was licking their lips over the prospect of this contest. 'I shall be looking forward to the trial in Old Bailey and, if possible, would very much like to attend,' asks McCray, without providing any means of finding the witness.

The DPP gave up on bringing Katherine Anne Porter to London. They decided instead to ask Mervyn Griffith-Jones to lean heavily on quotations from her *Encounter* article when cross-examining defence witnesses such as Graham Hough.

There was one last hope. J. Holroyd-Reece was the founder and managing director of the Paris-based Pegasus Press, which had published the banned Radclyffe Hall and now brought out the works of Aldous Huxley and Thomas Carlyle. He had turned down the chance to publish *Lady Chatterley*. The DPP's men rushed off to interview him. According to their report, he had said he regarded *Lady Chatterley* as a 'bad book'. Holroyd-Reece was a friend of the Lawrences but he also considered himself a candid one. He believed that the book was bad because Lawrence had failed in his purpose, which the literary minority had hoped he would fulfil, that of portraying sexual intercourse in simple language and show that unsuccessful sexual relationships could be a reason for a marriage to end in tragedy. He also believed that the dialogue and description were not up to standard. The four-letter words were, in his opinion, completely unnecessary. Indeed they were distasteful and Holroyd-Reece believed they had been included only to annoy Frieda (Lawrence's wife), who disliked their use. The civil servant who interviewed him reported:

> While Holroyd-Reece is an extremely interesting and

knowledgeable person to talk to, he makes it almost impossible to get a word in edgeways, and as a result it was impossible to keep him to the points on which we require information. I asked if he was prepared to go into the witness box and say it was a bad book. He said he would need notice of that question. My own opinion is that he will go into the witness box and say it is a bad book by literary standards but only if he is allowed to express the view to the jury that he regards the prosecution as unwarranted. I personally think that might be a good idea.

Griffith-Jones did not share the view that there would be some point in putting into the witness box a prosecution witness who did not think that the prosecution should go ahead. The DPP was now ready to throw in the towel on the question of witnesses. He wrote to Griffith-Jones:

It had been thought advisable to endeavour to obtain some expert evidence to the effect that the book's literary merit is so outweighed by its obscenity as to make publication of a 3/6 Penguin unjustifiable. With this end in view two dons – one at Oxford and one at Cambridge – have been approached and other lines of enquiry have been pursued without success.

While there is plainly a considerable divergence of literary opinion as to Lawrence's standing in general, as an author and the literary merit of *Lady Chatterley's Lover* in particular, there is a general feeling in the literary world that this prosecution is in principle repressive and unwarranted and in these circumstances people, whatever their views on the book may be, are not prepared to assist.

Counsel has herewith certain copies of books and articles which are adverse to Lawrence and to *Lady Chatterley's Lover*. In particular, he will note those of two eminent authors, T.S. Eliot and Lord David Cecil.

> Although attempts are being made to obtain an
> introduction with a view to sounding them out as to the
> possibility of their giving evidence for the prosecution so
> far no progress has been made.

In fact the attempts to contact T.S. Eliot and Lord David Cecil
seemed less than wholehearted. A director of Faber & Faber was
asked for an introduction to Eliot and the *Spectator* received a
request for a copy of a review by Lord David Cecil more than a
quarter of a century old. At the trial Eliot gave evidence, but
only in writing and for the defence.

> Counsel is therefore asked to advise as to what evidence
> should be called for the prosecution, who should be
> approached to give it and in what ways he considers such
> an approach could be made.

This despairing letter from the DPP is surely an indication that
he realised he was on course for disaster. He had the power to
stop this prosecution even at this stage and yet he still pressed
on. Mervyn Griffith-Jones wrote back asking for the number of
four-letter words in the book to be added up.

The hopelessness of the position was unwittingly underlined
in a diary item in the *Observer* on 18 September 1960 which,
after listing the glittering array of literary talent available to the
defence, added:

> The prosecution also has its closely guarded list of
> possibles. It is rumoured they will include Sir Basil
> Blackwell who declined to stock *Lolita* at his Oxford
> bookshop and that a number of Roman Catholic
> personalities will be asked to give evidence.

Sir Toby Mathew must have been only too aware that he did not
even have Sir Basil Blackwell.

The DPP and Crump sat down and tried to carry on. They

drew up a plan of action so that Griffith-Jones could deal with
the growing number of witnesses who were to be called by the
defence. The confidential files contain a 'trial tactics' notebook
and under the heading 'Possible points for XXD' (cross-examining defence) sets out the DPP's secret advice to Griffith-Jones,
the senior Treasury Counsel:

1. If we can't debunk the book we must debunk the
   expert.
   a. Ask if the expert holds himself out as being
      familiar with the works and life of D H Lawrence.
      i. If he says 'no' but holds himself out as an expert
         literary critic then the point is made.
      ii. If he says 'yes' try a few searching questions, i.e.
          see if he can place and identify a person
          described as 'cast out to play a superior role in
          the God-damn bourgeoisie.'
      iii. If he comes through that test all right I suggest
           there are two possible lines of attack. Ask him to
           identify and compare a rather obscure but good
           piece of writing, e.g. A Fragment of Stained Glass
           with a fairly well known bit of *Lady Chatterley*.
      iv. If he can try to identify an extract of D H
          Lawrence and something that is not.
      iii Also goes to the point of *Lady Chatterley's Lover* is bad
      D H Lawrence and iv also goes to the point that the
      expert is giving evidence because it is a book by D H
      Lawrence that is the subject of the proceedings.

A summary of the plot was prepared for Griffith-Jones as well as
a commentary on it. The book was described in the following
terms:

Lady Chatterley is a young woman, whose husband was
wounded in the First World War. They were married at
the beginning of the war; he comes back wounded so

that he is crippled and paralysed from the waist downwards and unable to have sexual intercourse. The book describes how that woman, deprived of sex from her husband, satisfies her sexual desires – a sex starved girl – with a particularly sensual man who happens to be her husband's gamekeeper. There are thirteen episodes of sexual intercourse, which are all described in the greatest detail, except for the first.

As Mr Griffith-Jones was to tell the jury: 'The curtain is never drawn.' This mutual sexual attraction leads to 'real love'.

The DPP's commentary on the book was scathing about its literary merits. It admitted that while it may be doubted that physical love was a suitable subject for a novel, it was rather difficult to see how it could be written about without dealing with the subject in considerable detail. But while conceding that Lawrence's description of the sexual act was writing of the highest calibre, the same could not be said for the rest of the book, which is dismissed as a 'trashy novelette'. Among the examples cited is the description of Chatterley's tie as 'careful' and the objection: 'Drive a careful car might be a good slogan for Mr Marples [then Transport Minister] but it would hardly earn him a prize for literature.' Worse, there was no depth to the character of Mellors, the gamekeeper. The DPP's men wanted to know: 'In India did he shoot? Did he drink? Did he have affairs?' The book was no more than a tract on the disappointments and benefits that can follow from the sexual act.

It is little wonder then that with this kind of poor-quality briefing, Griffith-Jones, in the face of 35 witnesses, who included most of the leading literary figures in England of the day, such as Dame Rebecca West, Richard Hoggart, E.M. Forster, Helen Gardner, Raymond Williams, C. Day Lewis, C.V. Wedgwood and Graham Hough, soon gave up all attempts at debunking the expert despite his instructions. Perhaps he might have done better if he had made more of the DPP's criticisms of Lawrence for treating Connie as 'little more than a female body

into whose acts of love making we are invited to pry'. Germaine
Greer launched a robust assault on *Lady Chatterley* on these
grounds, saying that students in the 1990s were more likely to
object to the 'co-opting and annihilation of a female character
as a sex object' than anything to do with smut or any alleged
radicalism.[7]

The 1960s feminist author and literary critic Kate Millett
chose to quote the following passage in her landmark work,
Sexual Politics (1970), to demonstrate that Lawrence's claim to
celebrate sexual passion was no more than a celebration of the
penis and that he was an evangelist for 'phallic consciousness':

'Let me see you!'

He dropped the shirt and stood still, looking towards
her. The sun through the low window sent in a beam
that lit up his thighs and slim belly and the erect phallus
rising darkish and hot-looking from the little cloud of
vivid gold-red hair. She was startled and afraid.

'How strange!' she said slowly. 'How strange he stands
there! So big! And so dark and cocksure! Is he like that?'

The man looked down the front of his slender white
body, and laughed. Between the slim breasts the hair was
dark, almost black. But at the root of the belly, where the
phallus rose thick and arching, it was gold-red, vivid in a
little cloud.

'So proud!' she murmured, uneasy. 'And so lordly!
Now I know why men are so overbearing. But he's
lovely, *really*. Like another being! A bit terrifying! But
lovely really! And he comes to *me*! –' She caught her
lower lip between her teeth, in fear and excitement.

The man looked down in silence at the tense phallus,
that did not change … 'Cunt, that's what tha're after. Tell
lady Jane tha' wants cunt. John Thomas, an' th' cunt o'
lady Jane! –'

'Oh, don't tease him,' said Connie, crawling on her
knees on the bed towards him and putting her arms

round his white slender loins, and drawing him to her so
that her hanging, swinging breasts touched the top of the
stirring, erect phallus, and caught the drop of moisture.
She held the man fast.

'Lie down!' he said. 'Lie down! Let me come!'

He was in a hurry now.[8]

Griffith-Jones did, however, concentrate on the 'dirty words'.
The DPP's staff had sat down and carried out a page-by-page
analysis of *Lady Chatterley*. A typical extract ran: 'pp 177–185.
Connie goes to the hut the same day after tea. Intercourse un-
satisfactory to Connie to start with but all right the second time
(full details and four-letter words).' Note in pencil: 'This language has everything. The presumption of the man thinking that
it takes him to fly in the face of convention. If this is not to
shock for shocking's sake. What is? Just letting out his own mis-
erable ego,' scribbled the DPP's man.

Under the heading: 'Gratuitous filth', the DPP's office had
tried to keep a running count of the offending words. It notes
on page 204 a 'bitch goddess of Success (coined by Henry
James)', a fucking, a shit, 'best bit of cunt left on earth', balls
(three times). On page 232 is found an arse (twice), arsed, slits
(twice), and so the file goes on. At the trial Griffith-Jones told
the jury that the word 'fuck' or 'fucking' appeared no fewer than
30 times; 'cunt' 14 times; 'balls' 13 times; 'shit' and 'arse' six times
apiece; 'cock' four times; and 'piss' three times. 'No doubt they
will be said to be good old Anglo-Saxon four-letter words, and
no doubt they are, but they appear again and again.' He then
managed to raise a laugh from the jury when he told them: 'For
those of you who have forgotten your Greek, phallus means the
image of a man's penis.'

We can safely assume that while it is highly unlikely that
many, if any, of the Old Bailey jury had ever learned ancient
Greek, they all knew the meaning of the word phallus. The
failed hunt for witnesses also led to some other rather more desperate measures being explored. Someone inside the DPP's

office was given the task of investigating Lawrence's family background to see if he could come up with any skeletons. It was established that Lawrence's father, Arthur, was unpopular with the pit owners because of his gambling and was portrayed in *Sons and Lovers* as a brutalised drunkard. His grandfather, George Beardsal, was an evangelist who sang hymns and clashed with the family of Jesse Boot (of the chemists) over the governorship of a Wesleyan chapel at Snerton, just outside Nottingham. His mother was Lydia Beardsal, who came from an old Nottinghamshire family which had lost money, and was a disappointment as a miner's wife. General Booth, the founder of the Salvation Army, who was born at Snerton, had also clashed with the Beardsals. Lawrence's great-grandfather, John Newton, was a famous hymn writer who wrote 'Sovereignty', one of the most popular of Victorian chapel hymns. From all this evangelical family history, the DPP's office concluded that all the 'getting back to nature' in *Lady Chatterley* had been inspired by Lawrence's memory of his 'roistering father'. It is an analysis that does not appear to have recommended itself to Griffith-Jones as a legal line of attack.

There were other problems. Crump got involved in a protracted misunderstanding with Her Majesty's Stationery Office (HMSO) when he tried to get it to produce some more copies of *Lady Chatterley* for the jury to use. He did not want it to copy the Penguin edition but the expurgated version that had been circulating in Europe since 1929, however, he failed to make this distinction clear to HMSO. He wrote only a few weeks before the trial was due to start to the HMSO controller, telling him that so far he had only one copy and more were needed for use as exhibits for the court and jury. No question of copyright arose in the circumstances. Crump was desperate: 'Counsel are anxious to read it. So far they have not had the opportunity,' he said.

But HMSO was not happy and was anxious about the moral danger: J.R. Simpson, HMSO Controller, told Crump:

We are reluctant to take on the job unless there is no alternative. It would involve a considerable amount of work at a time when we are very hard pressed with a great many urgent jobs for various government departments. Another reason is that the copying process would have to be undertaken by a staff mainly composed of young girls. Although I have not read the unexpurgated edition of the book, from all I hear there might be serious objections to our putting it into the hands of these young members of staff.

Simpson suggested to Crump that he approach Penguin to get some more copies:

Normally one would not expect the publisher to volunteer any assistance to the prosecution but one gets the impression in this particular case that the publishers have invited, or at least welcomed, these proceedings to be instituted.

Crump exploded. Through clenched teeth, he replied:

I fully sympathise with your feelings. Your reluctance does highlight the importance of this trial for if the prosecution fails, the obscene version will be offered openly and persuasively to every child or teenager who has 3/6 in his or her pocket. This is a fearsome thought.

He went on to explain that it was copies of the first of the three versions written by Lawrence that he needed, not the Penguin edition. This first expurgated *Lady Chatterley* had been published in Switzerland. 'The jury will need to read both versions,' he explained. In the event a dozen copies of the continental expurgated version had to be flown in especially from Switzerland in time for the trial.

There was one further tricky problem facing Sir Toby

Mathew and his colleagues. A request by a *Daily Telegraph* journalist, Con Coughlin, had been made to Penguin's solicitors on
behalf of Old Bailey journalists, also asking for copies of the
book (the full version this time). 'We feel we need copies of the
book in the interests of accuracy as no doubt extracts of it will
be referred to during the trial,' wrote Coughlin, who promised
that they would be returned if there was a guilty verdict.

C.G.H. Leaf of the DPP's office consulted Sir Toby Mathew
and told Penguin's solicitor, Michael Rubinstein, 'off the record'
that it was a sensible request but they could not possibly give
their consent. He said nobody would say that the press could be
corrupted and depraved by the book, but the judge might see
them turning the pages as they sat in the press box listening to
the evidence and ask why they had been given copies. The
DPP's office told Rubinstein that it was up to him. He replied
that he might give the press copies but put them inside the
covers taken from *Sons and Lovers* so as not to alarm the judge.

The trial finally got under way on 27 October and was over
in just five days. The Old Bailey heard 35 witnesses for the
defence. The prosecution called only one witness – Detective
Inspector Charles Monahan – whose evidence was simply to
prove that the book had been published. Mr Griffith-Jones first
provided huge amusement for the national press by asking the
jury of nine men and three women, which included a radio
dealer, a cabinet maker, a teacher and a dock labourer:

> You may think that one of the ways in which you can
> read this book, and test it from the most liberal outlook,
> is to ask yourselves the question, when you have read it
> through, would you approve of your young sons, young
> daughters – because girls can read as well as boys –
> reading this book. Is it a book that you would have lying
> around the house? Is it a book you would even wish
> your wife or servants to read?[9]

It even raised a laugh from the jury, which was reported to be nine to three in favour of an acquittal from the beginning. The jury men and women would have been lucky to have run to a 'daily' cleaner, let alone a footman or a chambermaid.

When Griffith-Jones announced that he was to call no further witnesses – other than Monahan – there was an audible gasp in the courtroom. The defence said that they had another 35 witnesses lined up ready to go into the witness box to support *Lady Chatterley*. It would have meant 70 literary and other experts being called in total.

On 2 November the jury, after a retirement lasting three hours, returned a verdict of not guilty. The judge refused to make an order for costs and left Penguin with a legal bill of £13,000; they soon recouped this as the publicity surrounding the trial ensured that *Lady Chatterley* became a bestseller that even outsold the Bible. Within a year *Lady Chatterley* had sold more than 2 million copies, catapulting the cheap paperback novel out of the pulp-fiction world of Hank Janson's *Lola Brought Her Wreath* into the bright lights of 1960s mass popular culture.

At the time the star of the 35 literary experts on parade at the Old Bailey was not any of the distinguished Oxbridge scholars but Richard Hoggart, a Leicester University lecturer and a genuine son of the working class, whose passionate defence of Lawrence impressed all who heard him. He had sincerely given evidence as to Lawrence's reverential attitude towards sex and insisted that the author was actually very puritanical in his approach. The Bishop of Woolwich may have received more column inches for his assertion that *Lady Chatterley*'s adultery with the gamekeeper was an act of Holy Communion but it was Hoggart, the working-class critic, who highlighted the gap in generations and class between Griffith-Jones and the jury.

After the trial, Roy Jenkins criticised the judge's summing up, saying that it concentrated more on the question of adultery than it did on obscenity and wondered whether a decree nisi for Sir Clifford Chatterley might have been more in order than an acquittal. But he hoped that the trial would mean no more comparable nonsense from the Director of Public Prosecutions for at least a few years.

The recriminations against the bungled prosecution from those who felt that the protection of public morals had been dealt a savage blow began almost at once. The *Sunday Express*, *Daily Telegraph* and *Evening Standard* – all were outraged by the verdict. *The Times* ran an editorial, 'A Decent Reticence', demanding to know why the prosecution had not been ready to match the defence witness for witness. The saving grace of the whole affair had been that Lawrence had been concerned only with 'normal copulation' and had not described any 'unnatural practices or perverted vices'. However, Constance Chatterley had been unchaste both before and during her marriage and had lain with man after man until she had found satisfaction. Surely such a book could only be harmful to adolescent morals, said *The Times*. The *Spectator* attacked the Home Secretary, R.A. Butler, placing responsibility for the trial's failure firmly on his shoulders. In the same magazine, Bernard Levin, in 'The Lady's Not For Burning', got nearer the truth when he argued that if the prosecution could find nothing worse to say against the book than a few dirty words, then they could not have had much of a case. The Archbishop of Canterbury turned on the Bishop of Woolwich for being mistaken in the belief he could take part in the trial 'without becoming a stumbling block and a cause of offence to many Christians'. But Barbara Barr, Lawrence's step daughter, was to prove closer to the public mood when she said: 'I feel as if a window has been opened and fresh air has blown right through England.'

In the Commons, MPs from both sides of the House queued up to demand to know why steps had not been taken to find literary experts to testify on behalf of the prosecution. Fourteen Tory MPs put down an amendment to the Queen's Speech demanding the repeal of the Obscene Publications Act and called for the *Guardian* to be prosecuted for printing one of the four-letter words mentioned during the trial. All the Attorney-General, Sir Reginald Manningham-Buller, could do was hide behind the bland formula that it was not the practice to disclose the preparations made for a prosecution. He declined to take action against the *Guardian*.

In the House of Lords a special debate was held, which was no more than an attempt to overturn the verdict of the Old Bailey jury. In the face of an onslaught from the only members of the British public who feared that their gamekeepers might actually read *Lady Chatterley*, the Lord Chancellor, Lord Hailsham, wisely told them that he regarded putting four-letter words into print as bad taste but he recognised that they were generally known to everybody above a certain age. His real objection was that the book had been published as a paperback selling at 3s. 6d. He would have far rather it had been sold as a hardback 'in boards at 12s. 6d.' and so presumably kept out of the hands of impressionable youngsters and gamekeepers everywhere.

A note from Sir Toby Mathew to Lord Hailsham for his preparations for the debate tried to answer the criticism that it was the government who had fouled up over the prosecution. Despite the evidence of the files he tried to claim that the decision was his alone and nothing to do with the rest of the government. Sir Toby said that the Attorney-General, who had read *Lady Chatterley* on the boat train down to Southampton, had given no directions about the case and had not been consulted about the decision to prosecute. He must have forgotten those notes from the Solicitor-General asking for a quick chat about tactics. 'Neither the Attorney-General, nor the DPP consulted, or received any representations from the Home Secretary or the Home Office.' So much for all those letters from Sir Austin Strutt then.

Sir Toby went even further. He claimed that the reason the prosecution did not match the defence witness for witness was because the Crown conceded that the book had literary merit. Instead the prosecution case was that these merits did not outweigh its obscenity. Sir Toby told Lord Hailsham:

The question of whether a book is obscene, and the

questions of whether publication is justified, are both matters for the jury and no evidence is admissible on either of them. The evidence on the merits, other than literary merits of the book, did not appear to the prosecution to call for any rebutting evidence.

It was indeed a sham argument. They had lost the case before the trial started but did not have the guts to stop what they had started and admit what had gone wrong afterwards.

It took a while for the true significance of the verdict to sink in. Maurice Crump told his opposite number in New South Wales, Australia, not to get too excited about *Lady Chatterley* when he wrote asking for further details:

> Do not read too much into the verdict of this case. Under the 1959 Act it is a defence to establish that a book is of such literary, scientific, artistic or educational merit that its publication was passed for public good. Accordingly the jury's verdict of Not Guilty could equally well mean that they thought the book was not obscene or that they thought it was obscene but of outstanding literary merit or that some thought the former and others the latter.

However, this reasoning was irrelevant as the jury had only one choice: guilty or not guilty. No longer could a British jury be relied upon to convict in an obscenity case.

For the next year Sir Toby Mathew and Maurice Crump were to be on the receiving end of letters from Methodists, Scottish Presbyterians, Evangelists and Catholics asking why no effective witnesses had been called for the prosecution and if there had been none available, why the case had gone ahead. It was criticism that stung and to which they had no answer.

The Home Office was rooting for the hippies: unreasonable Grundyism at bay

> Sexual intercourse began,
> In nineteen sixty-three,
> (Which was rather late for me),
> Between the end of the Chatterley ban,
> And the Beatles' first LP.
>
> Philip Larkin, 'Annus Mirabilis'[1]

John Calder, an anti-establishment Scot, who published the plays of Samuel Beckett and Ionesco, as well as the poetry and prose of American 'beats' such as William Burroughs, felt emboldened enough by the *Lady Chatterley* decision to attempt a British publication of Henry Miller's *Tropic of Cancer* in early 1963. This was another piece of unfinished prewar business. *Tropic of Cancer* was first published in 1934 in France and is one of Miller's autobiographical series set in the seedy Paris of the Left Bank in the 1920s and early 1930s. Miller himself said that *Tropic of Cancer* was promptly banned in all the Anglo-Saxon countries but continued to sell steadily under the counter. He said in 1948:

> The only effect which censorship has had upon its circulation is to drive it underground, thus limiting the sales but at the same time insuring for it the best of all publicity – word of mouth recommendation ... The book is living proof that censorship defeats itself.[2]

It was to be another decade or so before that simple truth was realised in London and it was not until the early and middle 1960s that *Tropic of Cancer, Tropic of Capricorn, Plexus, Nexus* and *Sexus* were all finally published in Britain. Their common theme is an account of how the amiable middle-class Miller left his wife in the United States and rediscovered his soul amongst the prostitutes, drink and poverty that were to be found amidst the amoral underside of interwar Parisian intellectual life. Dylan Thomas called it 'the best modern fucking book'. Its appearance in early 1960s Britain helped to cement the atmosphere of sexual liberation. It arrived before female outrage at learning what was actually going through some men's minds had made itself publicly felt.

However, as the Whitehall files show, the publication of these books triggered a fierce struggle between the authorities over how liberal the new post-Chatterley regime should be. Customs and Excise was the first to raise the question of what to do about Henry Miller in February 1963 after widespread press reports that John Calder intended to publish *Tropic of Cancer* at the end of March. C.T. Cross of Customs wrote to Maurice Crump at the Director of Public Prosecutions' department asking for advice. During the previous decades courts in Willesden, Blackpool, Sheffield and Clerkenwell had all ordered *Tropic of Cancer* to be sent to the Scotland Yard guillotine. It had been confiscated 27 times from individuals coming through Customs and one bookseller had been prosecuted and fined for selling it in 1951. C.T. Cross told Crump:

I do not think that we at Customs will be able to consider this particular book in isolation from Miller's other works (e.g. *Tropic of Capricorn*, *Sexus*, *Quiet Days in Clinchy*). Provisionally my own view is that none of them differs essentially in kind from *Tropic of Cancer*, even though some of them may have more rude words to the page, but I should make it clear that this is a matter on which I have not yet had the benefit from my Board's solicitor.

The DPP also received complaints from the public. Miss Ruby Williamson of Dunraven, Church Road, Sefton Park, Liverpool, asked after reading in the *Sunday Times* of the impending publication, if 'it is necessary to add to the flood of such literature which is already here'. She blamed such novels for the increase in sex crimes and venereal disease. 'As a teacher I ought to be pleased that so many millions of people have developed the art of literary appreciation as shown by sales of *Lady Chatterley's Lover* but having taught for a long time I have my doubts,' she said, going on to claim that Britain was becoming as decadent as the empires of Constantinople and Rome.

Crump's reply to Miss Williamson demonstrates his lack of confidence in the 1959 legislation. He told her that the Obscene Publications Act was, as the Lord Chief Justice has pointed out, a very difficult piece of legislation, and no one could be certain that proceedings taken under it even if successful would have the desired effect. However, he pointed out to this Liverpool schoolteacher that it was open to anybody to take out a case under the Act.

Michael Evelyn, who had taken over the role of literary reader within the DPP's office, was asked for his 'appreciation' of *Tropic of Cancer*. He reported in a confidential note on 11 February 1963:

It is set in Paris of the 1920s, 1930s. It has no plot or story and is autobiographical in style. It describes in a

series of changing scenes, long and short, the left-bank
world in which Miller lived at the time. The people in
the book are for the most part writers, artists and
whores: everyone is broke. They talk, philosophise, eat,
drink and copulate, all in abundance. There are passages
which are coarse, bawdy, ribald, and disgusting,
depending on how you feel (e.g. pages 5, 6, 16, 41,
95, 109, 122, 126, 130, 195, 211 to 215) though some of these
I also found very funny. Words such as cunt, fuck and shit
appear on almost every page but after the eye has been
initially caught they seem quite natural in their context.
The book reveals an unusual command of language on
the part of its author and there are some fine prose
passages.

When I began reading the book I found it hard going,
rather like standing in front of an abstract picture waiting
for a glimmer of understanding. By the time I was a third
of the way through however I found myself absorbed in
the world Miller was describing, a world, above all of
individuals who shunned the conventions (religious, ethical
et al) of the society into which they had been born.

To me the book is never sensual or erotic as is *Lady
Chatterley's Lover*. Some of its passages may be more
disgusting but they are not, I would think, as titillating to
those who read such books simply for 'thrills'. It is a
book that has to be read as a whole for individual
passages as those quoted above to be seen in proper
perspective. I have no doubt that *Tropic of Cancer* if
prosecuted would have many defenders on the grounds
of literary merit. Literary merit is so subjective a reaction
and I can therefore say only that I think it qualifies.
Public opinion has become much more liberal in the
thirty years since the book was written, so the greater is
the pity that, as with *Lady Chatterley's Lover*, it is
bedevilled by its own history where the law of obscenity
is concerned.

Maurice Crump added in his own handwriting: 'Pages 5, 6, 16 are representative of the worst.' Page 16 was condemned on the basis of a single sentence in which Henry Miller describes 'walking through the Jardin des Tuileries and getting an erection looking at the dumb statues'. But the passage on pages 5 and 6 provide the full flavour of what upset Crump.

> O Tania, where now is that warm cunt of yours, those fat heavy garters, those soft bulging thighs? There is a bone in my prick six inches long. I will ream out every wrinkle in your cunt, Tania, big with seed. I will send you home to your Sylvester with an ache in your belly and your womb turned inside out. Your Sylvester! Yes he knows how to build a fire, but I know how to inflame a cunt. I shoot hot bolts into you, I make your ovaries incandescent. Your Sylvester is a little jealous now? He feels something does he? He feels the remnants of my big prick. I have set the shores a little wider. I have ironed out the wrinkles. After me you can take on stallions, bulls, rams, drakes, St Bernards. You can stuff toads, bats, lizards up your rectum. You can shit arpeggios if you like, or string a zither across your navel. I am fucking you, Tania, so that you'll stay fucked. And if you are afraid of being fucked publicly I will fuck you privately. I will tear off a few hairs of your cunt and paste them on Boris' chin. I will bite into your clitoris and spit out two franc pieces.[3]

On 22 February, John Calder's solicitors, Lawford and Co, wrote to the DPP announcing Calder's intention of publishing *Tropic of Cancer* at 25 shillings (£1.25) – twice the normal cost of a hardback. They said that they did not believe it was obscene and added that they had the support of 'many eminent writers and other authorities' that publication was justified as being for the public good on the grounds of its literary and other merits.

> Our clients would wish to make a formal publication of
> a copy of the book to a police officer, or other
> specifically appointed representative, before distributing
> the book to the general public. If it is the DPP's
> intention to institute proceedings we should be grateful
> if you would communicate with us to suggest a time and
> a place when publication can be effected.

The solicitors were obviously hoping for the kind of cosy and
financially painless gentleman's agreement that Penguin had
enjoyed over *Lady Chatterley*. The DPP, Sir Toby Mathew, consulted his deputy, Maurice Crump, and told him on 5 March:

> I don't think we need pass to counsel at this stage. As I
> find it almost unreadable the book almost certainly has
> literary merit. It is to be published at 25/- and I would
> have thought that at that price it would have few readers
> who were seeking pornography. For the present I do not
> think we need take any action.

But this time the DPP bridled at the publisher's request for a bit
of money-saving pre-publication voluntary censorship. The
next day on 6 March 1963 Crump wrote back to Lawford's,
saying the DPP would not act as a 'de facto censor' and argued
that such decisions must be for the courts. He pointed out that
the ruse used in the *Lady Chatterley* case of 'publishing' the book
by giving it to a police officer would no longer work: the courts
had in the meantime ruled that a constable, or at any rate not a
member of the dirty books squad, could not be depraved or corrupted by pornography. Crump asked for the list of eminent
writers prepared to support Henry Miller.

On 7 March Crump reported that the DPP had had second
thoughts and decided he would like the book to be sent to
Mervyn Griffith-Jones, the senior Treasury counsel, for his legal
opinion. Crump wrote:

The Director is motivated to send this to counsel now
because, if as seems probable, we do not take action the
Attorney-General will have parliamentary questions to
answer and it is easier for him to do so if senior Treasury
Counsel has advised. We are also particularly interested to
know if Mervyn [Griffith-Jones] thinks that a test case, if
wanted, is in law possible having regard to the fact that
publication to a police officer is not an offence.

John Calder had been busy building up a campaign to back
publication. Lawford's wrote back to the DPP on 11 March
saying that copies of the book had been sent to a wide range of
writers. Twenty-three experts had provided expressions of
support. The list included Brian W. Aldiss (then literary editor of
the *Oxford Mail* and later an important sci-fi author), Kenneth
Allsop (then literary editor of the *Daily Mail*), Professor A.J.
Ayer (Oxford University Professor of Logic), Samuel Beckett
(playwright and critic), E.M. Forster, Graham Greene,
Rosamund Lehmann, Colin MacInnes, Mary McCarthy,
Malcolm Muggeridge, Iris Murdoch, Anthony Powell, J.B.
Priestley, Kenneth Tynan and Angus Wilson.

The solicitors also sent to the DPP cuttings from the *Justice
of the Peace* magazine, the *Observer*, the *Sunday Citizen* and the
Sunday Pictorial, all welcoming publication of the book. The *Observer* described John Calder's decision to publish *Tropic of Cancer*
at the same time as Allen and Unwin's publication of a translation of the Indian erotic classic, the *Kama Sutra*, as the two
biggest tests of Roy Jenkins's Act since *Lady Chatterley*. The publication date for the *Kama Sutra* was set for 28 March 1963; it
was priced at 42 shillings (£2.10) to 'keep it away' from the dirty
book trade.

Cross of Customs wrote to Crump on 3 April:

The situation is now extremely pressing, as it would be
very embarrassing for us to find ourselves seizing imports
if a similar edition could be bought on the home market

without hindrance. As I said in my previous letter, we
would also have to reconsider the status of Miller's other
works in the light of your decision on this issue.

The day before, 2 April 1963, Mervyn Griffith-Jones had delivered his opinion on *Tropic of Cancer* from his desk in the Temple:

> In my opinion the book, *Tropic of Cancer*, is not obscene
> within the meaning of section one of the Obscene
> Publications Act 1959. It is an unpleasant and disgusting
> book but the manner in which it is written is quite
> unlike any other book which has been the subject of
> proceedings over the last few years in as much as, in my
> view, there is no tendency in this book to encourage in
> the reader conduct of a kind similar to that of the
> characters described nor to give rise in the reader to any
> prurient thoughts.
>
> Moreover, even if the book should be considered by
> some to be 'obscene', I think it is extremely doubtful
> whether a conviction would ever be obtained. In its
> curious style I find it well written – better written than
> *Lady Chatterley's Lover* – and with considerable humour
> so that the question of its literary merit would present
> difficulties. The author is apparently well recognised as a
> writer of distinction. It would appear that in the event of
> a prosecution there would be no shortage of
> distinguished 'experts' ready to speak on behalf of the
> book. For these reasons I advise that no criminal
> proceedings be instituted.

The DPP did not hesitate. Later the same day Maurice Crump
told Lawford's of the DPP's decision: 'I now write to say that it
is not proposed so far as this Department is concerned to take
any action in this matter at this stage.'

But the pressure for prosecution did not go away. The next
day the Revd Halley Viney of Hove, Sussex, wrote to the DPP:

'As a priest of the Church of England', he said that arguments that such books are 'art' left him cold. 'The ordinary man knows they stimulate the wrong desires. Must we have such stuff foistered on the public so that [the publishers] can make money?'

Tropic of Cancer was published the next day, 4 April 1963. The publicity had generated more than 40,000 advance orders. Henry Miller wrote in his diary that British publication had been a great success. The day after, on 5 April, Crump replied to the Church of England priest from Hove explaining the decision. Crump wrote that the courts had found obscenity a difficult definition to interpret:

> Parliament has set itself against there being any kind of
> literary censor. The only form of censorship is that which
> is obtainable under the Act through the courts.

On the same day a further letter arrived from an anxious Customs and Excise solicitor, D.J. Willson, to Crump at the DPP:

> My commissioners are extremely worried about the
> situation that has arisen due to the difference in the
> wording between section four of the Obscene
> Publications Act 1959 and section 42 of the Customs
> Consolidated Act 1876. At their request I have written to
> the Attorney-General asking for his advice.

Willson's letter to the Attorney-General, Sir John Hobson, said an 'embarrassing situation has arisen' because of the lack of any public good or literary or artistic defence under the Victorian Customs legislation. Willson said that he had read the book and was in no doubt that it was indecent and obscene and would be condemned by any court of law under the unreformed Customs legislation.

> This is undoubtedly a serious matter because if my

Commissioners are to allow the importation of the *Tropic of Cancer*, which is as bad an example of any indecent or obscene work as I have read it is very difficult for them to know to what type of book, if any, they should regard the prohibition as being applicable.

Meanwhile Scotland Yard's Obscene Publications Squad had only just woken up to what was happening with Henry Miller's book. On 5 April, Detective Inspector Webb was sent down the road by the Chief Superintendent to buy a copy of *Tropic of Cancer* at the Book House, 7 Whitehall, London SW1, where, to the surprise of Scotland Yard, it had been on sale for the previous 24 hours. Webb in his report said: 'This book contains numerous passages that can only be described as "utter obscenity".' The policeman quoted Miller himself to give a flavour of the book, saying 'the strong odour of sex it purveys is really the aroma of birth; it is disagreeable or repulsive only to those who fail to recognise its significance.' So eager was this porn squad officer to get this book into the dock, he did not even wait to get a public complaint; instead he insisted to his superiors that

we will undoubtedly be receiving a large number of complaints from members of the public concerning this publication. I ask for authority to hand this report together with the book to the DPP for consideration under the 1959 Obscene Publications Act.

Ignorant of the fact that Griffith-Jones had already ensured that *Tropic of Cancer* was not to be banned, Detective Inspector Webb's immediate superior, Chief Superintendent J. Kennedy, endorsed the police officer's plea to the Assistant Commissioner that the book should be suppressed:

This book outrages the mind of any normal individual. It is worse than *Lady Chatterley's Lover* but I don't doubt that there are those who, as in the case of that publication, will describe it as having literary merit. If it has I prefer to remain ignorant.

But not only did that well-known literary expert, Chief Superintendent Kennedy, prefer to remain ignorant, but also he saw it as a major chance to regain the ground that had been lost. He wrote:

> The publication of this book affords an opportunity to mount a counter-attack to avenge the repulse we have suffered in the *Lady Chatterley* case. In my opinion, and I do not speak without experience, in the light of modern trends, and certainly from our own aspect, no effort or expense should be spared to mount such a counter-attack, and thus vindicate the attitude of the vast majority of our populace.
>
> I earnestly hope that the DPP will decide to prosecute or, if he does not, that the law of obscenity will suffer a rapid and radical change.

That same day, 8 April 1963, the DPP received more letters of complaint, including one from Sir Cyril Black, the puritanical Tory MP for Wimbledon and a leading light of the Social Morality Council. He also regarded *Tropic of Cancer* as

> the most obscene book that it has been my misfortune to have to read. I hope you may decide that legal proceedings should be taken against those responsible. You are no doubt aware that most of the more reputable bookshops are refusing to stock and to sell this book and that quite a number of newspapers have refused to review it. Such reviews as there have been, have been largely of a condemnatory character.

But Black was wrong in his assessment of the reviews. The *Sunday Telegraph* described the book as a 'period piece published after thirty years'. The *Times Literary Supplement* said that it was always going to be a question of time before *Tropic of Cancer* was published and argued for a broadminded interpretation of the 1959 Act in this case. The *Sunday Express*, that historic scourge of the dirty book, the *Daily Mail* and the *Evening Standard* argued for its publication even if they did give it unfavourable reviews. Interestingly the *Police Review* said that prosecution would be a blunder that would only boost its sales and lead to millions rather than hundreds buying the book. *Justice of the Peace*, the magistrates' magazine, did favour prosecution but on the perverse grounds that it would be acquitted, which would prove that Miller's book was better literature than *Lady Chatterley* and was without the strings that the Bishop of Woolwich found attached to Lawrence's work. This could not amount to the rejection at the hands of the reviewers that Sir Cyril Black had claimed. Crump told Sir Cyril that it was open to anyone to take out a prosecution under the Obscene Publications Act but warned him that unsuccessful proceedings tended only to increase the sales of the offending book.

Four days later the Attorney-General formally announced in the Commons that, after consulting counsel in the shape of Griffith-Jones, it had been decided that legal proceedings would not be taken against *Tropic of Cancer*. Similar arguments were used to explain to the Scotland Yard Obscene Publications Squad why its plea had fallen on stony ground despite the opportunity for revenge. Crump wrote to the Metropolitan Police Commissioner:

> A prosecution that failed could only increase the sale of this book. The strength of the defence's literary merit witnesses is so great – it includes such distinguished people as T.S. Eliot – that one has to accept the possibility that the chances of prosecution being successful are too slight. I quite understand that this will be a bitter pill for those like Chief Superintendent Kennedy who feel outraged by the book but there is nothing I can do about it.

However, Chief Superintendent Kennedy was not ready to swallow this particular pill. His opportunity for revenge came a week later when Scotland Yard received a telegram from a Mr Edwards of 27 Woronzow Road, St John's Wood, London NW8.

> I think you should look into the programme being broadcast by the BBC on the Third Programme tonight, which is a reading from the book, *Tropic of Cancer*. Some of the foulest language I have ever heard has been read over the air and it should not be allowed in front of families. The broadcast was at 8 o'clock this evening.

The telegram was passed immediately to Detective Inspector Webb. He went round and had a word with Edwards but could tell him only that the Attorney-General had already decided not to ban the book. However, Webb decided that the complaint itself was sufficient to warrant a major police inquiry. He approached the BBC and asked to interview those in authority.

The programme was broadcast on what is now Radio Three, and took the form of a discussion between the distinguished literary expert Frank Kermode, and Peter Duval Smith, a BBC broadcaster, about *Tropic of Cancer*. Duval Smith claimed that *Tropic of Cancer* was 'a great novel that created a kind of earthquake in the novel and was one of the six masterpieces of the century'. The transcript of the broadcast in the police files shows that Frank Kermode did not share this flattering assessment of Miller.

The Scotland Yard inspector went to see Richard Jones-Marshall, an assistant solicitor at the BBC, who supplied him with the transcript of the programme. 'The complained of passage is on page five of the Calder edition and starts: "Tania, big with seed … After me you can take on stallions, bulls, rams, drakes, St Bernards".' One comment by Duval Smith was deleted because it was thought it would give offence. This was his observation: 'it would be hard to work out how many fucks he had in the course of the book'. Jones-Marshall explained that the BBC's Charter meant that the Director-General was responsible for the content of all broadcasts and it was left 'to good taste' to ensure that programmes contained nothing that was offensive.

> In confidence he told me other complaints had been received and that the Director-General [Sir Hugh Greene] who is answerable to the Postmaster-General [Reginald Bevins] is somewhat perturbed that such an extract from the book was utilised. Steps are being taken to see that there will be no such repetition in the future.

So Webb managed to get an assurance from the BBC that it would not broadcast extracts from a book which the Attorney-General had just told the House of Commons could be published in Britain. For good measure the policeman ended his report with the sentiment: 'It is indeed fortunate that the broadcast occurred on the Third Programme which caters for a minority of the listening public.'

Customs, which was still operating under its unreformed 1876 Victorian statute, was also unhappy and continued to insist it should seize all indecent or obscene works by Henry Miller regardless of literary merit. The Attorney-General told Willson that it would be 'ridiculous for the Commissioners to seize from the traveller a book which was openly on sale in bookshops here'. He agreed that the case highlighted what was now a defect in the law, which applied equally to the Post Office. This messy state of the law was to prove a continual source of difficulty for the authorities. The absence of the 1959 test of literary merit not only was absent in the Customs and Post Office legislation but also did not apply to books sold in Scotland and Northern Ireland, because the Obscene Publications Act covered only England and Wales.

Throughout the summer of 1963, Customs kept pressing the Home Office for clarification of this legal quagmire. In July, Cross of Customs told the Home Office that the *Tropic of Cancer* decision had 'not ended our troubles'. Copies of other works by Henry Miller had been seized by officers, including *Black Spring* and *Nexus*, which were being imported by Blackwell's. A consignment of 5,000 copies of *Tropic of Capricorn* had been seized and was being held at Shoreham Docks, Sussex. The solicitors acting for Customs did not agree with Griffith-Jones that the courts would not rule the books obscene. Cross also asked for a policy statement on William Burroughs's *Naked Lunch* and the Marquis de Sade's *Justine*, which were also being brought in by travellers in single copies from Paris.

The Home Office replied that Miller's other books, *Tropic of Capricorn*, *Nexus* and *Black Spring*, could no longer be regarded as obscene by Customs or the Post Office on the grounds that it was impossible in practice to go on drawing a distinction between them and *Tropic of Cancer*. The Home Office told Customs to continue to seize *Naked Lunch* and *Justine* since they were prima facie obscene. The civil servant urged Customs and the Post Office to adopt the literary test without worrying about the need to go back to Parliament, adding 'providing the difficulty can be resolved by administrative means perhaps it would be best to leave the law unchanged in such a controversial area'.

The debate went on across Whitehall throughout the autumn of 1963. The Economic Secretary to the Treasury, the minister in charge of Customs, who at this time was Maurice Macmillan, ordered the release of the 5,000 copies of *Capricorn* in September saying there was little difference between the two *Tropics* and the government did not want to be accused of 'unreasonable Grundyism'.

However, the Tory Treasury minister drew the line at *Sexus*, the fifth book by Henry Miller, saying on Customs advice he believed that 'it seems to go further than the usual run of his works and I feel we ought to consider it as a separate problem if the occasion should arise'. The Head of Customs assured him: 'We are fully alive to the need to take whatever steps we can to limit the degree of filth excusable by bogus literary merit.' This

does not sound like the attitude of a man fully in sympathy with
Roy Jenkins's literary test as set out in the 1959 Obscene Publications Act.

In this case the DPP agreed with Customs: *Sexus* was beyond
the pale. The mysterious, but literate, Evelyn was asked to read
Sexus for his considered opinion. His verdict was that it should
be regarded as obscene.

> It is obsessed with sex which is dealt with in the crudest
> and ugliest manner. On the other hand I have no doubt
> it would have its supporters on the grounds of literary
> merit and in view of Henry Miller's reputation, I am not
> suggesting criminal proceedings without a good deal
> more thought being given to the matter. In any event, it
> has not yet, I gather, been published in this country.
> However I sympathise with Customs' view of the book
> and wish them good luck in trying to keep copies out of
> the country!

This extract gives a flavour of what Evelyn was on about:

> I would ask her to prepare the bath for me. She would
> pretend to demur but she would do it all the same. One
> day, while I was seated in the tub soaping myself, I
> noticed that she had forgotten the towels. 'Ida', I called,
> 'bring me some towels!' She walked into the bathroom
> and handed them to me. She had on a silk bathrobe and
> a pair of silk hose. As she stooped over the tub to put the
> towels on the rack her bathrobe slid open. I slid to my
> knees and buried my head in her muff. It happened so
> quickly that she didn't have time to rebel or even to
> pretend to rebel. In a moment I had her in the tub,
> stockings and all. I slipped the bathrobe off and threw it
> on the floor. I left the stockings on – it made her more
> lascivious looking, more the Cranach type. I lay back and
> pulled her on top of me. She was just like a bitch in heat,

biting me all over, panting, gasping, wriggling like a worm on the hook. As we were drying ourselves, she bent over and began nibbling my prick. I sat on the edge of the tub and she kneeled at my feet gobbling it. After a while I made her stand up, bend over; then I let her have it from the rear. She had a small juicy cunt, which fitted me like a glove. I bit the nape of her neck, the lobes of her ears, the sensitive spot on her shoulder, and as I pulled away I left the mark of my teeth on her beautiful white ass. Not a word spoken.[4]

Maurice Crump decided to tread carefully. He agreed that *Sexus* should be regarded as obscene but suggested that no action should be taken unless there was a specific complaint and argued it should be seized only if it was found amongst a much larger consignment of other pornography. Nevertheless the ban on *Sexus* was to last a further three years. When Crump was pressed by John Calder's solicitors in January 1964 for the official attitude to *Tropic of Capricorn*, Crump replied: 'We have together fully explored the working or rather non-working of the Obscene Publications Act. There is nothing left for me to say.' The 30-year ban on the British publication of *Tropic of Capricorn* had finally been lifted. The official files show that chief constables around Britain continued to file complaints about the public sale of Henry Miller's books throughout 1964 and 1965. The police were not happy with the workings of the 1959 Act.

The case of Henry Miller demonstrated that the failure of the *Lady Chatterley* case had left the Director of Public Prosecutions dispirited and tired. Even Mervyn Griffith-Jones was determined not to repeat the mistakes that had led to defeat at the Old Bailey. No test case was allowed which would have reinvented the role of the DPP as an effective censor. No act of 'publication' was allowed to a police officer as a piece of cheap voluntary censorship and a certain official respect of the literary establishment was at last to be seen. The British publication of *Tropic of Cancer* marked the end of the era when publishers had to resort to a row of dots in a novel to indicate a four-letter word or a sexual episode. The week after it was published on 28 March 1963, the advance orders ensured that it was top of the bestseller lists even though the chain bookshops of the time, including Wyman's and W.H. Smith, refused to stock it and despite its expensive price of 25 shillings (£1.25). It even outsold Ian Fleming's Bond novel, *On Her Majesty's Secret Service*, and Harold Robbins's *The Carpetbaggers*. In the same week the *Kama Sutra* topped the non-fiction sales lists. But the history of literary censorship is by no means a simple one. It would appear that Henry Miller's *Tropics* had consolidated the historic gains made in the *Lady Chatterley* trial. It was not to be. The enforcement of the obscenity laws appears to ebb and flow with the phases of the popular and political mood, often driven by some new technological change in the mass media.

In the early 1960s the censorship of literary books became such a matter of routine that the Director of Public Prosecutions developed a simple form which included instructions that he sent to the 'readers' who were asked to assess whether a particular volume was obscene. The instructions were fairly straightforward:

> The reader is asked to summarise a story as briefly as possible and to draw attention to any passages of an obscene nature, e.g. page 23 – lesbianism. Young girl seduced by older woman. If the book has a fairly convincing story, and the obscene passages form an integral part, then reference should be made to this. Similarly if the story is merely a vehicle for sexual episodes or perversion, then this should also be noted. A test might be: are the 'objectionable' passages woven unobtrusively into the story or do they stand out as being 'filth for filth's sake'.[5]

Readers were not asked merely to give a general opinion as to whether they thought the book was obscene but to deal with it specifically. Readers were particularly asked:

> Please Do Not Mark The Book. It May Be Ordered To
> Be Returned.

One such completed form in the files deals with Mary Mc-Carthy's *The Group*. The DPP's reader reported that it was a dull and boring novel which concerned a group of girls who had just left Vassar Ladies College. A major part of the book was concerned with the sexual and reproductive lives of the girls. The passages relating to sexual matters were repulsive rather than anything else and the overall effect tended to suggest that perversions, particularly lesbianism, were recommended rather than normal sexual relations, reported the reader (who is named only as Lawrence).

Part of the form asks the reader to list all the obscene passages and suggests different kinds of description. The following qualified: sexual intercourse or sexual activity and whether a third person was present, lesbianism, rape, homosexual behaviour, flagellation (violence for sexual gratification), sadism, blackmail to obtain intercourse, etc. The reader of Mary Mc-Carthy's book duly complied. As far as he was concerned, pages 43–4 qualified as obscene on the grounds that they contain 'detailed description of obtaining female contraceptive'. Pages 46–8 were also obscene as a 'girl reports to her friend her conversation with her husband concerning pessaries, their storage and disposal' followed by pages 56–8 in which a doctor fits a girl with a pessary. On page 189 a description of a mother breast-feeding her child and her difficulties also catches his attention. The DPP declined to prosecute on the basis of this report.

Such routine censorship could not continue indefinitely: a new case – hard on the heels of the controversy over Henry Miller – involved another 'old-timer' on the banned list, *Fanny Hill: Memoirs of a Woman of Pleasure.* Mayflower, a paperback publisher which wanted to cash in on what was then seen as a banned book boom, announced that it was to be published in Britain in November 1963 at 3s.6d. (17.5p). *Fanny Hill*, who had made her first clandestine appearance 214 years earlier, was

Memoirs of a
Woman of
Pleasure,
*commonly known
as* Fanny Hill *by
John Cleland 1749.
The title page of
the first edition.*

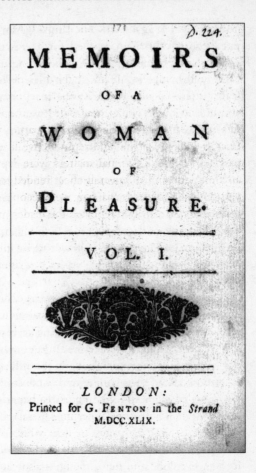

171 ꝑ. 224.

MEMOIRS

OF A

WOMAN

OF

PLEASURE.

VOL. I.

LONDON:
Printed for G. FENTON in the *Strand*
M.DCC.XLIX.

advertised as being available a few days before the official publication date in a Tottenham Court Road 'Magic Shop' run by G. Gold and Sons, a company which was to become a major publisher of soft-porn magazines.

The police raided the shop and seized 171 copies; a date was set at Bow Street magistrates' court in December 1963 for the hearing. Mayflower could have made a killing by distributing a further 82,000 pre-printed copies by the time of the case, but decided to wait for its outcome. The publishers, faced with the prospect of a long-drawn-out campaign through the magistrates' courts of Britain, pushed for a crown court jury trial whose verdict would apply throughout England and Wales.

The alternative would have been a guerrilla campaign waged in magistrates' courts wherever the local police decided to act against *Fanny Hill*. The contrite DPP was in no mood to rush back to the Old Bailey for another obscenity case; the book in this case advocated straight sex and its tone was bawdy rather than pornographic. Marghanita Laski called it a 'gay little book … a jolly book. It made me cheerful.' Mervyn Griffith-Jones ignored the lack of four-letter words and its roundabout approach to erotic episodes and instead concentrated on one untypical example of flagellation in which a client beat Fanny with sadistic ferocity. The episode follows a scene in which Fanny had given her 'gentleman' 30 lashes with a cane on his bare buttocks:

> All my back parts, naked halfway up, were now fully at his mercy: and first he stood at a convenient distance, delighting himself with a gloating survey of attitude I lay in, and of all the secret stores I thus exposed to him in fair display; then springing eagerly towards me, he covered all those naked parts with a fond confusion of kisses. And now taking hold of the rod, rather wantoned with me, in gentle inflictions on those tender trembling masses of my flesh behind, than any way hurt them, till, by degrees, he began to tingle them with smarter lashes, so as to provoke a red colour into them, which I knew, as well by the flagrant glow I felt there as by his telling me, they now emulated the native roses of my other cheeks. When he had then amused himself with admiring and toying with them, he went on to strike harder, and more hard, so that I needed all my patience not to cry out, or complain at least; at last he twigged me so smartly as to fetch blood in more than one lash, at sight of which he threw down the rod, flew to me, kissed away the starting drops, and, sucking the wounds, eased a good deal of my pain.[6]

The magistrate, Sir Robert Blundell, apparently untroubled by the recent history of the law, had no hesitation in finding *Fanny Hill* obscene after only two minutes' reflection. There was public uproar. Roy Jenkins said that it demonstrated that the legal authorities could be relied upon to mishandle any issue touching the censorship of books. He described Griffith-Jones as that 'indefatigable scourge of the impure'. The *Guardian* said that it was 'justice thwarted'. *The Times* noted that *Fanny Hill's* real offence was appearing in a cheap paperback edition and pointed a finger at the 'present immunity of an expensive (42/-) edition of the book'. Some commentators linked the prosecution to a panic reaction to the Profumo affair. But the *Express* newspapers and some Conservative politicians welcomed the ban as 'bringing universal relief'.

The ruling saw a crackdown on *Fanny Hill* around Britain with the magistrates in Manchester, Birmingham, Brighton and Sheffield all moving against bookshops which dared to stock it. Mayflower gave up for the time being and did not appeal. It brought out a bowdlerised edition of *Fanny Hill* and even that attracted the attention of the Edinburgh magistrates. Eventually in 1970 when the libertarian revolt was at its peak, Mayflower quietly put out an unexpurgated edition. Despite still being technically a banned book, it was allowed on the shelves without the threat of police molestation.

The backlash continued with the successful prosecution of Alexander Trocchi's *Cain's Book*, a decision that was seen more as an attempt to outlaw a lifestyle than to ban a text. *Cain's Book* was one of John Calder's new-wave American novels. It concentrated on a junkie's life in New York. The author was a leading light of the beat generation who stirred up huge rows at the Edinburgh Festival and orchestrated mass poetry readings, featuring Allen Ginsberg and Lawrence Ferlinghetti, at London's Albert Hall. The Sheffield police seized copies of *Cain's Book* in February 1964, on the grounds that it advocated the use of drugs in schools, so that children should have a clearer conception of art. It was enough to get the book banned in Sheffield. John

Calder pressed it to a higher court but the Lord Chief Justice, Lord Parker of Waddington, dismissed the appeal. In the process he extended the legal definition of obscenity. It now included highlighting the favourable effects of drug taking and tempting the reader to experiment with illegal drugs. 'There was no reason whatever to confine depravity and obscenity to sex,' said this important judgment.

A confidential report drawn up by the Home Secretary, Henry Brooke, for the Prime Minister, Alec Douglas-Home, on the formation of a London Committee against Obscenity was a further indication of the growing influence of the moral back-lash. This new body was pressing for a bill to close some loop-holes in the 1959 Act, not to reverse the *Lady Chatterley's Lover* ruling, but for tougher action against 'obscene' magazines for which nobody was making any claims of literary merit. The Home Secretary told the Prime Minister:

> The formation of the London Committee has been prompted mainly by a flood of obscene magazines and worthless paper-back novels coming from the United States. Our enforcement authorities have a good record.
>
> The Customs have seized over a million copies at the ports of entry, and, despite loopholes in the law which I want to close, the police have managed to bring before the courts a further large quantity of material which has escaped the Customs net.
>
> But these two measures have not by themselves been sufficient to prevent many publications of a disgusting depraving nature reaching the shops. I understand that the Director of Public Prosecutions hopes to be in a position to institute proceedings soon against the main importers in this country, and we shall see whether they are successful. The co-operation of the United States Government has also been sought; but since this is a matter of State law and in some states this material circulates freely, they may not be able to do much to

help. If we mean what we say about helping the young of
this country to grow up straight, I am sure we ought to
be seen to be doing everything we can to fight this evil
of pornographic magazines.

One new twist was that the 1 million magazines that had been
seized could no longer be burned. Legislation creating smoke-
less zones in London in an effort to combat the notorious smogs
of the late 1950s meant that they could no longer be sent to the
furnace because of the black smoke that was produced. Instead
the magazines had to be taken under guard to a shredding plant.
The summaries prepared for the destruction orders put before
the magistrates' courts give a flavour of the pulp fiction that was
now being condemned:

> *One Hell of a Dame* by E Seeley Jnr. A Chariot Book: The
> story is in three parts. Firstly of Sheila Watson's arrival in
> New York and her endeavours to establish herself as an
> actress and finding that all she can achieve are parts in
> strip shows and pornographic films. Secondly of her
> introduction to a famous film actress and becomes her
> dresser and understudy. Their acquaintance develops into
> a lesbian one and ends with the suicide of the famous
> actress. Thirdly Sheila's success in the stage role and her
> final submission to flagellation by blackmail from a
> journalist who has helped her in the past. Obscene
> passages: pp 44 sexual intercourse; pp 100 lesbianism; pp
> 103 sexual intercourse; pp 112 lesbianism; pp 157
> flagellation. Obscene.
>   *Harem Island*, Anthony Sterling, Monarch Books: A
> story of the Mormon Society in America. Jesse Strang
> became its leader. It recounts the trial and tribulations of
> the cult, and the reasons for its physical movement from
> one place to another. Strang instituted various reforms,
> one in particular being polygamy. He takes four 'spiritual'
> wives, and some of his bedroom scenes are described far

too vividly than appears necessary in an historical account of the Mormon cult (especially page 46 which has sexual intercourse vividly described). Obscene.

The Exotic Affair, Doreen Clarke, Magnet Books: The synopses on front and back are rather more lurid than the contents, but the people in the book spend most of their time deciding who to go to bed with eventually. Sex in nearly every chapter, with a hint of lesbianism here and there. The sexual passages are not described in detail, but taken as a whole this is obscene. Obscene.

These books and magazines were to become the bread and butter of the obscene publications squads in London, Birmingham and Manchester.

The advent of the Labour government in 1964, and particularly the appointment of Roy Jenkins as Home Secretary, saw a major shift in official attitudes towards obscenity and a serious rift open up between the Home Office, the police and the Customs. The first real battleground under Roy Jenkins came with the British publication of *Last Exit to Brooklyn*, which led to one of the more extraordinary obscenity trials of the twentieth century. The Labour Attorney-General initially refused to prosecute the book. A Conservative MP forced the eventual trial by taking out a private prosecution. The Old Bailey hearing itself was notable for the judge's extraordinary insistence on an all-male jury and the fact that it was the first case since Radclyffe Hall that the prosecution was actually able to find some literary experts ready to support the burning of a book.

Last Exit to Brooklyn by Hubert Selby had been published in the United States in 1964 to favourable if somewhat shocked reviews and the British firm of Calder and Boyars acquired the rights with a view to publishing it in January 1966. The book was a graphic view of the violent, lower depths of the drug-fuelled undergrowth of Brooklyn life in the early 1960s. It dealt in intense descriptions of violent and brutal gay and heterosexual sex. The publishers took the precaution of getting the opinion of the DPP and of Barbara Hardy, Professor of English Literature at the Royal Holloway College, University of London, and a literary adviser to the DPP. The DPP could offer no guidance: 'I get no help from the acts,' he told the publishers but Professor Hardy backed publication.

Calder and Boyars went ahead with a hardback edition at the then very expensive price of 30 shillings (£1.50) and by the autumn had sold more than 11,000 copies. The British reviews were mixed but agreed that it had literary merit. Anthony Burgess argued:

> no book could well be less obscene. We are spared
> nothing of the snarls and tribulations of pimps, queens
> and 'hip queers' but the tone is wholly compassionate,
> although sometimes whipped by the kinesis of anger.

Burgess thought it more likely to make you feel sick than to move you to lust.[7]

During the summer of 1966 a Conservative MP, Sir Charles Taylor, demanded in the Commons that the Labour Attorney-General, Sir Elwyn Jones, ban this 'filthy, disgusting and degrading' book which he refused to name on the grounds that it might boost its sales. But the Attorney-General and the DPP felt that the critics had testified to its literary merit and were far from sure that a prosecution would succeed. Both Professor Hardy and a psychiatrist had been consulted and agreed. The libertarian Labour MP, Tom Driberg, decided to tweak a few noses. He put down a Commons early day motion congratulating the law officers for not prosecuting this book, which he took care to name as *Last Exit to Brooklyn* specifically with the purpose of boosting its sales.

The move helped to provoke the Social Morality Council into a decision to try the expensive option of a private prosecution in the magistrates' court. As the DPP had reminded it many times, the 1959 Act left open the door to such a private action in cases where he felt unable to act. Sir Cyril Black once again took up the fight. The same Bow Street magistrate, Sir Robert Blundell, who had ordered *Fanny Hill's* death after only two minutes' deliberation, was again quick to agree to allow three symbolic copies of *Last Exit* to be seized pending a full hearing. In November 1966 a little army of literary experts gathered at Marlborough Street magistrates' court to debate the merits of Hubert Selby's dark work. On the prosecution side was H. Montgomery Hyde, who had appeared for the publishers in the *Fanny Hill* case, Robert Maxwell MP, who had described *Last Exit* as 'muck', and the deputy literary editor of the *Daily Telegraph*, David Holloway. The future Conservative Attorney-General, Michael Havers, acted as counsel for Sir Cyril Black. Ranged against them were Anthony Burgess and ten other leading literary figures.

The literary experts fought each other to a standstill. The magistrate banned *Last Exit* and singled out one particular passage that, he said, 'in its descriptions goes beyond any book of a merely pornographic kind that we have seen in this court. One passage I am thinking of is more likely to deprave and corrupt than any of those cyclostyled horrors,' he said in reference to the looseleaf pornographic novels sold in Soho at the time. The passage he had in mind, the death of Tralala, still appals. It is the most hideous of all the episodes in Hubert Selby's vision of his New York hell. It describes in a sub-Joycean stream of consciousness a brutal mass gang rape.

> Soon she passed out and they slapped her a few times
> and she mumbled and turned her head but they couldn't
> revive her so they continued to fuck her as she lay
> unconscious on the seat in the lot and soon they tired of
> the dead piece and the daisy chain broke up and they
> went back to Willies the Greeks and the base and the
> kids who were watching and waiting to take out a turn
> took out their disappointment on Tralala and tore her
> clothes to small scraps put out a few cigarettes on her
> nipples pissed on her jerked off on her jammed a

broomstick up her snatch then bored they left her lying amongst the broken bottles rusty cans and rubble of the lot.[8]

The publishers, though hopeful of getting a jury trial, indicated that they intended to continue publication, despite the ruling from the Marlborough Street magistrates. This time the DPP was left with no choice and *Last Exit* was committed for trial at the Old Bailey in November 1967.

Calder and Boyars had strong support. A joint letter from 18 publishers had gone out protesting against the ban. They had been particularly incensed by a proposal from Robert Maxwell during the magistrates' hearing that the book industry itself should set up a regulator to censor its output. Among the supporting cast were Professor Frank Kermode, Professor Barbara Hardy, A. Alvarez, Philip French, Kenneth Allsop and Professor Bernard Williams, alongside many more academics, critics, sociologists and psychologists.

This time the prosecution also had a cast list. It included the Revd David Sheppard, a former England cricketer who was to become Bishop of Liverpool, Professor George Catlin of Canada and Sir Basil Blackwell, the 70-year-old founder of the Oxford booksellers. But before this literary cast list could get into their stride, Judge Graham Rogers amazingly directed that the jury should be all male to 'spare the ladies possible embarrassment'. No doubt Judge Rogers had already decided in his mind that *Last Exit* was not fit reading for either his wife or his servants.

The glittering array of literary talent for the defence testified as to *Last Exit*'s qualities, with Frank Kermode arguing Selby had succeeded in his theme in biting terms.

The prosecution followed with the Revd David Sheppard claiming that even he had been corrupted by it:

It pandered to the worst in me and I would have to say that I'm not unscathed by reading a book like this.

Robert Maxwell, in a moment now filled with irony, claimed it would corrupt his children:

> If this prosecution fails the word obscenity in law is meaningless. We publishers have got to censor ourselves … There are passages which ooze with muck. One of my basic concerns is that this kind of literature is undermining the morale of the young. I speak as the father of young children … I am horrified that any one of my eight children may be exposed to this kind of filth.[9]

The Maxwell fears were reinforced by the Revd David Sheppard, who told the court that he was happy to have copies of *Catcher in the Rye* and *Sons and Lovers* on his shelves but this book 'weakens resistance to the idea of adultery or homosexual practices'. Sir Basil Blackwell also felt that reading *Last Exit* had defiled him, despite his experience of 70 years. The jury preferred their version to that offered by the literary world and after five and a half hours' deliberation returned a verdict of guilty.

The publishers arrogantly attacked the jury system, claiming that the 12 men had not read and understood the book properly and demanding that 'at least A levels' should be required of those who were to try obscenity cases. This elitist proposal was unsurprisingly scorned by the Conservative opposition. More constructively the publishers lodged an appeal, which was heard in July 1968. On a technicality they won. Judge Rogers had inadequately described the complexities of the 1959 Act to the jury. In particular he had not explained that it was possible for a book with 'corrupting and depraving tendencies' to be justified in its publication because it was 'for the public good'. The Court of Appeal said that the jury had been thrown in at the deep end of this particular problem and had been left to sink or swim in its dark waters. *Last Exit* had won the last round and the voices of Brooklyn drifters and deadbeats, prostitutes and drag queens, living in a morphine haze, were to be allowed to be heard in Britain after all.

At the Home Office plans were quietly drawn up to close the loophole in the 1959 Obscene Publications Act which had allowed Sir Cyril Black to take action when the DPP had refused. Roy Jenkins told the Cabinet in February 1967 that he did not want to close the door to private prosecutions but he did want to ensure that publishers were not deprived of the right to trial by jury.

The plan was to ban private individuals going to the magistrates' court to ask for a destruction order – a course of action that stopped the publishers having the case settled by a jury trial. The idea was that the destruction order route should be used only by the police or the DPP to deal with uncontentious pornography in bulk. The Metropolitan Police were now seizing about 50,000 such items a year. This represented only about one-third of the volume of material destroyed in the mid-1950s, despite the rapid growth in the porn trade. Private individuals would still be able to challenge individual books in the courts but they would have to do it at the Old Bailey before a jury – a far more expensive route. The state papers show that Roy Jenkins' deliberate intention was to prevent private prosecutions such as that initiated by Sir Cyril Black.

Mr Jenkins told the Cabinet that the Solicitor-General had in 1964 promised that a jury trial would settle any future case against a publisher where questions of literary merit were involved. He admitted that that promise had been broken in the *Last Exit* case when the destruction proceedings had been heard at Marlborough Street magistrates' court. 'The circumstances of the publication of this book were precisely those to which the Solicitor-General's undertaking was intended to apply,' the Home Secretary stated in a confidential Cabinet Office memorandum. So Sir Cyril Black should never have been allowed to proceed in the first place in the way that he did. The Home Secretary told the Cabinet that it had been an abuse for a private individual to use this method to test a particular work with claims to literary merit. The Cabinet had no hesitation in giving its backing to an amendment closing the loophole. It was quietly added in the final stages of the 1967 Criminal Justice Bill so that the supporters of the Social Morality Council would have little chance to create much of a parliamentary fuss.

The emergence of a more liberal attitude within the Home Office is also evident from the Whitehall records of an incident in January 1967, when Customs consulted the Home Office over the 129 copies of Henry Miller's *Sexus*, which had been imported by a Bradford book company from the United States and seized in October 1966. Miss Owen for the Home Office was unequivocal in her position. She said, no doubt confident in the knowledge that the Home Secretary himself had been involved in drafting the legislation nearly a decade before, that this was precisely the kind of book that the 1959 Act had been designed to protect. Summary proceedings in the magistrates' courts under the Victorian Customs legislation would be likely to 'stir up the same kind of public criticism as had proceedings in respect of *Last Exit to Brooklyn*'. Indeed there would be more criticism, she argued, as the 1876 Customs legislation did not allow for a jury trial or the question of literary merit to be raised at all. Britain was the only European country to ban publication of *Sexus*. 'We can at least point out to them the kind of hornet's nest they will undoubtedly stir up if they proceed with their intention to seize these books,' reported Miss Owen.

A note from a more senior Home Office civil servant, K.P. Whitney, an assistant secretary, agreed, saying that it would be very embarrassing if Customs went ahead with the seizure. Advice to Customs was delayed while Roy Jenkins himself considered the question. Meanwhile the Director of Public Prosecutions, Sir Norman Skelhorn, asked one of his now regular roster of literary experts to read *Sexus*. In this case Professor Barbara Hardy of London University undertook the task. On her advice the deputy director of Public Prosecutions decided not to prosecute under the Obscene Publications Act. 'Customs and Excise will find themselves in really deep trouble if they go ahead and institute proceedings under their own legislation,' Miss Owen noted on the file.

Customs said that the book was so obscene and possibly of such questionable literary merit that so far no British publisher had been prepared to publish it, unlike Henry Miller's other works. The books had been seized in October 1966 and Whitehall was still debating the matter some months later; the decision not to prosecute the Bradford book company was taken in the following March. In February 1967, the Home Office's Mr Whitney, using Miss Owen's words, wrote to G.C. English at Customs, telling him that Henry Miller's literary reputation was hardly insignificant. He pointed out that no other European country had banned the book, and that *Sexus* was precisely the kind of work that the 1959 Obscene Publications Act had been designed to protect.

'You will be inviting real trouble if this book is now to be made the subject of proceedings under Customs legislation,' he warned, before going on to stress that it would be

> seriously embarrassing to the Home Secretary whose personal views on this subject are well known from the part he played as a Private Member in introducing what is now the Obscene Publications Act 1959.

In the face of such a direct threat, resistance inside Customs collapsed: 'In light of the factors to which you draw attention we have decided to release the consignments currently under detention,' was the pathetic reply. Roy Jenkins congratulated his Home Office officials: 'A very good (and effective) letter to Customs and Excise.' It was a major victory for Miss Owen and Henry Miller.

Customs officials were not the only people that the Labour Home Secretary felt were getting out of control when it came to the enforcement of the Obscene Publications Act. Roy

Jenkins also began to question the activities of the 14 men who made up the Scotland Yard Obscene Publications Squad after they launched two raids on national art collections in London – at the Victoria and Albert Museum (V&A) and the Tate Gallery. Both cases led to personal protests to the Home Secretary from the Arts Minister, Jennie Lee, and from the chairman of the Arts Council and general fixer to Harold Wilson, Lord Goodman, who were alarmed that the police were now going around London seizing works of art from Britain's national collections.

A major exhibition of Aubrey Beardsley's Art Nouveau books, prints and original drawings was held in May 1966 at the Victoria and Albert Museum. The show was attended by more than 100,000 people and launched a Beardsley boom that led to his famous black-and-white line drawings appearing everywhere on record sleeves, in magazines, and even on mugs. Beardsley was to become an icon of British psychedelic culture and no more so than on the posters that were stuck on the bedroom walls of every 'swinging sixties' student.

The museum authorities had been happy enough to revive the works of one of the more controversial young artists of the 'naughty nineties'. But the intervening 70 years were not enough to allay their anxieties. The first problem the V&A faced was getting the catalogue printed. Sir Percy Faulkner, the controller of Her Majesty's Stationery Office, took exception to a series of erotic Beardsley illustrations for *Aristophanes, Lysistrata*, including the now famous *Lysistrata Haranguing the Athenian Women*, complete with pubic hair. Sir Percy was probably most exercised by the line drawing of the erect penis that appeared in *Cinesias Entreating Myrrhina to Coition*. He sent the catalogue to the Home Office saying that he was uneasy about some of the illustrations and asking whether they were obscene. The Home Office did him a service that was no longer available to the ordinary publisher and on his behalf asked the DPP whether it was illegal. The Home Office civil servant reported to his superiors that it was all done very informally:

Aubrey Beardsley,
Lysistrata
shielding her
Coynte, *V&A,*
Harari Collection,
E.294 – 1972.

LYSISTRATA.

I have returned the illustrations to Sir Percy. I told him I
personally would be disposed to suggest the omission of
one or two of the proposed illustrations. Sir Percy said
however he was sure that this would be strongly resisted
by the Museum and with the DPP's assurance he was
prepared to take responsibility for publishing the
catalogue with all the illustrations the Museum wanted.

Actually the V&A did respond to this pressure and absurdly
decided that five of the eight *Lysistrata* illustrations could be seen
only by special application. The entire series could already be
found in most books on Beardsley.

So the Home Office was already fully aware of the Beardsley
exhibition when in August 1966 the Scotland Yard Obscene
Publications Squad raided a gift card shop on Regent Street in

London. After 'several complaints from the public' one officer was sent round to the shop; he bought several of the Beardsley posters and postcards on display and took them back to Scotland Yard. A magistrates' warrant to seize the rest of the stock was secured and the squad raided the Regent Street shop seizing all the 'offending prints'. When the police were told that the Beardsley prints they had seized were actually on display at the V&A, the Metropolitan Police Commissioner himself went to the museum to see if it was indeed true that these 'obscene prints' were hanging in the galleries. He did not bother consulting the museum's director and the resulting outcry about a police 'raid' on one of the national art collections meant that the Home Secretary had to spend time trying to deal with the Met's growing 'Knacker of the Yard' image.

When the seized Beardsley posters and cards were sent to the DPP he was so deeply unimpressed by them he promptly ordered the police to take them back to the shop without any further ado. The Metropolitan Police Commissioner told the Home Office that some of the cards were of drawings in the V&A exhibition that showed fig leaves 'in the appropriate places' but the Regent Street reproductions 'showed not the fig leaves but what the fig leaves were supposed to cover'. Some of the other prints were of those *Lysistrata* drawings that the museum had decided to make available only by special application. This episode might have passed by with no more than a dressing-down from the Home Office to the Police Commissioner if it had not been swiftly followed in September 1966 by the squad's raid on a London West End gallery during which they seized 20 paintings and drawings by the American artist, Jim Dine. The owner of the gallery in Duke Street, Mayfair, was Robert Fraser, a key 'underground' figure who had become a police target. When the police charged Mick Jagger and Keith Richards of the Rolling Stones with drug offences, Fraser was caught in the net as well. Dine already had an international reputation and four of the pictures had already been sold for 250 guineas each – rather more than the then current going rate for a 'piece of porn'. The

official Home Office briefing note for the Home Secretary gave
something of the flavour of Jim Dine's collages.

> The pictures and drawings were of male and female
> private parts, and in one case of the two together and
> apparently conjoined. In about half the pictures there was
> nothing else whatsoever in the picture but the organ in
> question, the style of the draughtsmanship being very
> much that of the simpler graffiti on the walls of public
> lavatories.
>
> In most of those of female private parts, the latter
> formed the centre piece (fairly realistically painted in
> some cases) of a collage of what looked like cut-outs
> from anything from Christmas cards to seed catalogues.

There were a couple of problems facing the police, though. The
first was that this was a private art gallery and not a public exhibition. For this reason the DPP and the Attorney-General
decided that they could not prosecute under the Obscene Publications Act. However, if the police officer could testify that the
pictures could be seen from the street, the Fraser Gallery could
be charged under the ancient 1824 and 1838 Vagrancy Acts,
which banned the wilful exposure to public view of an obscene
picture. 'This is not as dotty as it sounds,' said the Home Office.

> Inspector Bill Moody [of the Obscene Publications
> Squad] said that if the Director of the Fraser Gallery had
> been prepared to take the pictures down and put them
> out of sight in a private room instead of in full view of
> all the passers-by in the street, that would probably have
> been the end of the matter.

The second problem was that the gallery's owners had told
Inspector Moody not only that Jim Dine was an artist with an
international reputation but also that his work was actually
hanging in the Tate Gallery. Inspector Moody quickly dispatched

a plain-clothes detective to the Tate Gallery to find out if he ought to seize that picture as well. The art world was outraged. A constable from the 'dirty squad' duly pressed his nose up against the window of the gallery and testified in court that the pictures were visible from the street. Robert Fraser was found guilty and fined £20.

These raids on the art world began to look like a sustained attack when the Leeds police in December 1966 seized some paintings by a Greek Cypriot artist, Stassinos Paraskos. The city's magistrates declared them obscene despite evidence from Sir Herbert Read that they were of some artistic merit. They obviously were not 'artistic' enough for the Leeds bench. These pictures were not even on public display but were being exhibited in Leeds Art School and the 'complaint' was that two 14-year-old schoolgirls had been seen sniggering at them.

The Labour Arts Minister, the redoubtable Jennie Lee, and the chairman of the Arts Council, Lord Goodman, decided that it was time to put a stop to this nonsense. Jennie Lee wrote to Roy Jenkins:

> Dear Roy,
>
> I am sure you were as shocked as Arnold Goodman and myself by the Jim Dine's prosecution. I should be very grateful to know how best you think this kind of incident can be avoided in future.
>
> Can I be sure at least that no policeman, plain clothes or uniformed, will again set up as an expert on works of art? There should be no great difficulty in devising means whereby an artist's work can be judged, in circumstances like those of the Dine's incident, by a committee of responsible experts.

Lord Goodman was equally vehement and made clear that he had personally offered Jim Dine his unofficial help as he regarded him as a serious artist:

Can there be any argument at all for a police officer invading a national collection such as the Tate? Surely here simple instructions could be given to the police that with accredited national collections – they could be given a list of them – they simply do not visit them to inspect alleged pornographic portraits on the footing that if the Director of the gallery is exhibiting pornography and not art, his Trustees can be expected to deal with him and not the police.

This I think would be very reassuring to enlightened humanity throughout the country. It does not, as I have been told, seem to me to require any legislation or to impose any objectionable fetter on police action nor would I suggest that it be extended to any other crimes committed on the premises such as murder, rape or the smoking of marijuana [sic] but simply that the pictures on the walls and in the cellars should be inviolate so far as artistic judgments by policemen are concerned.

Lord Goodman told the Home Secretary that if he were a director of an art gallery visited by a police officer without his knowledge, he would resign at once and 'make off by coracle for some other country where this could not happen'.

Roy Jenkins saw Jennie Lee and Lord Goodman and told them that he shared their unhappiness about what had been going on. He agreed that the police should in future consult gallery staff before they visited public museums or galleries so that nobody would be alarmed by their presence. The Home Secretary also told them that he had made quite clear to the police that they should steer clear of 'border-line cases in the arts and should concern themselves wholly with enforcing the law on hard-core pornography and its equivalent in the graphic and plastic arts'. Jenkins also promised to look into the idea of a committee of art experts to be consulted in such cases and to review the use of the vagrancy laws but neither came to anything. In a private note to Jennie Lee, the Home Secretary added in his own handwriting: 'We shouldn't assume it is a bad thing for police officers to visit galleries, provided they do not seize the contents!'

This clash did not, however, prevent the Obscene Publications Squad raiding and prosecuting the Institute for Contemporary Arts (ICA) on the Mall, London, in February 1967 for staging an indecent exhibition contrary to common law. A visiting German artist, Hermann Nitsch, had dismembered a dead lamb before an invited audience as part of a month of 'autodestructive happenings'. Biblical precedence was to prove no defence before the Guildhall magistrates.

This growing conflict between Roy Jenkins and Scotland Yard's Obscene Publications Squad was to reach its climax when the police raided one of the flagships of the London 'underground' hippie press, *International Times*, or *IT* as it was called after Times Newspapers threatened legal action. The magazine and an associated bookshop were strongly supported by John Lennon and Paul McCartney. It was the closest that the London police were to get to raiding the Beatles and it was to lead to a major split between the Jenkins-run Home Office on one side and the Metropolitan Police on the other.

The launch party for *IT* in October 1966 at the Roundhouse in Chalk Farm, north London, had seen Paul McCartney wandering around dressed as an Arab. While Richard Neville's, *Oz*, waved the banner of *Playpower*, *IT* was the more serious of the two samizdat magazines, carrying lengthy pieces on Vietnam, Latin America and European student protests within its mix of drugs, music, sex and nudity. It also carried columns of personal contact ads and it was these rather than any revolutionary or anarchist polemic that were later to prove its downfall. But this spaced-out newssheet of the London acid underground was to prove to have friends in surprisingly high places. The police first raided the offices of *IT* in March 1967 when they seized copies of the magazine together with a number of books. The raid immediately led to a complaint from the Labour MP,

Tom Driberg, to Roy Jenkins. Driberg asked the Home Secretary for the whole matter to be dropped.

Dear Roy,

I am a bit worried about the recent police raid on the offices of *International Times* [starts the original in the Home Office file]. As is usual when the police of any country take any sort of action against works of art or literature, their selection of books to remove seems to have been a fairly silly and random one. They took, for instance, a book called *Memoirs of a Shy Pornographer*. I do not happen to know this book, but I am told that it is not pornographic at all! They also took a copy, or copies of the *Naked Lunch*. I hope that this does not mean there is any question of action against this book or its publishers?

Since the raid was, I am told, carried out by the Drugs Squad, I suppose some of the articles in this paper about drugs were the pretext for the raid. I have not seen every issue of the paper, but I recall at least one editorial in it strongly condemning the use of heroin. The police apparently indicated that proceedings might be under the Obscene Publications Act. It is surely an improper broadening of this Act to relate it to writings about drugs.

The Home Secretary asked for a full report from the Metropolitan Police. Detective Inspector Leslie Alton explained that the raid had been carried out with the approval of the DPP. Detective Sergeant Terence Beale of the Obscene Publications Office, New Scotland Yard, had led the raid on the shop and basement of 102 Southampton Row, London WC2, using a search warrant from Bow Street magistrates which had been granted after the police produced issues 4 and 6 of *IT*. The Obscene Publications Squad had led the raid on 9 March 1967. Officers from the

Drugs Squad had also been present because more constables were needed than were available and there was information that drugs were in fact used on the premises.

> This was primarily a search by the Obscene Publications
> Squad, not as suggested by Mr Driberg a raid by the
> Drugs Squad, the reason for the search being the obscene
> nature of a number of articles published in the editions
> of *International Times*.

During the search the police seized 8,000 copies of various editions of *IT*, 25 copies of 'an obscene poem' allegedly imported to Britain from the United States and 35 books of 'an obscene nature', including two copies of a book entitled *The Naked Lunch*, five copies of *Memoirs of a Shy Pornographer* and two copies of a book, *I, Jan Cremer*. Detective Sergeant Terence Beale reported: 'All these books are, in my opinion, grossly obscene.'

The ground floor of 102 Southampton Row was occupied by Indica Books, an enterprise that had been set up with strong support from John Lennon, who paid its legal bills. Four people were interviewed. They included Michael Henshaw, who was 'undoubtedly the person in authority'; Thomas McGrath, aged 26, who was the editor of *IT*; and Peter Stansill, aged 23, the business manager. Also seen was Christine Uren, a secretary, and George Redpath, a printer. All were cautioned and told the matter would be reported to the DPP. Indica Books was searched in the presence of Barry Miles, then a director of Indica, and now Paul McCartney's biographer.

The initial Home Office advice to Roy Jenkins was to give a non-committal reply to Driberg, saying the whole affair was for the DPP to sort out. The only question from the Labour MP they could answer was to justify the presence of the Drugs Squad officers by pointing out that drug taking had become an obscene publications matter since the prosecution of Alexander Trocchi's *Cain's Book*. Mathers of the Home Office advised the

Home Secretary to say that the whole matter was *sub judice* and it would be improper for him to comment further.

His colleague, Miss Owen, did a little digging about the seized books. The legal position of William Burroughs's *The Naked Lunch* had been considered by the DPP following an interception by Customs in 1963. Miss Owen wrote:

> It was reckoned to be obscene but to have literary merit. No action was taken. But apparently there has been at least one occasion when it has been made the subject of a forfeiture order by a magistrates' court. Our files also show that there was a correspondence between Miss Jennie Lee [the Arts Minister] and the Attorney-General about it in 1965 when the latter stated that he did not consider that the 'public interest would be served by proceedings against the publisher' but that decision was not necessarily final.

In her view Tom Driberg need not have any fear that the literary merits of the books involved would be overlooked, she said.

The Home Office drafted a reply for Roy Jenkins to send to Driberg saying that it would be wrong for him to interfere in the enforcement of the law in individual cases.

> I do not say this in any spirit of indifference, but because the principle that there should be no censorship of publications by the executive has its negative as well as its positive obligations which I am bound to respect.

This drafted reply remains in the file. It was never sent. In fact what happened was that there was a furious row between the Home Secretary and some of the most senior civil servants inside the Home Office. One of them, Mr Guppy, who drafted this original reply for the Home Secretary, exploded at the idea that Roy Jenkins should even consider criticising the police for their raid on *IT*. He said that the idea that the Home Secretary was some kind of unofficial Court of Appeal was 'highly dangerous'. Guppy told his colleagues:

> action by the police on the instructions of the DPP is in no way the responsibility of the Home Secretary. He should not be expected to accept any implied responsibility.

But a note on the file from his colleague D.E.J. Dowdler makes plain that the Home Secretary did take a very serious view of the action of the police in this case, and had rejected the letter as drafted.

> It seems to him a matter for deep concern that officers of the Obscene Publications Office should think fit to seize copies of *The Naked Lunch* without apparently being aware that this book is by a serious author; that it has been on sale in reputable bookshops in this country for a number of years; and that it has been respectfully reviewed in serious journals and newspapers; and that a decision was taken some time ago by the Director not to proceed against it.
>
> This incident re-inforces the Home Secretary's view that the officers in the Metropolitan Police, as unfortunately in some other forces also, concerned with this sort of work are not sufficiently well chosen; and he is particularly disturbed that this incident should have occurred after the assurances he was given by the Commissioner following the Beardsley seizure.
>
> In due course the Home Secretary will want to see the Commissioner himself about this case. But before he does he would be grateful if the Department would ask Scotland Yard, in writing, why the police seized the *The Naked Lunch* in spite of the considerations I have referred to above.

In practice this amounted to an official declaration of war by the Home Secretary on Scotland Yard's 'dirty squad' and it had all been prompted by their decision to target a small-circulation hippie magazine.

Roy Jenkins sent Driberg a short holding note saying:

> Dear Tom,
>
> I am sorry not to have been able to reply earlier to your letter of March 15 about the action taken by the police at the offices of the *International Times* and even now I am afraid that I am not in a position to let you have a final answer.
>
> As you know my responsibility in matters of this kind is confined to the form of the law; I am not, in my official capacity, concerned with its enforcement in individual cases. Nevertheless there are aspects of this matter which cause me concern, and I am therefore making further inquiries and will write to you again as soon as I can.

This note was sent on 17 April 1967. In the face of all this pressure the DPP dropped all the charges against *IT* and all the seized books and magazines, after much foot-dragging by the police, were eventually returned to them.

Two days after Roy Jenkins had made clear to Driberg that he was not happy with the police, the Home Office's most senior civil servant, the permanent secretary, Sir Philip Allen, wrote to the Metropolitan Police Commissioner, Sir Joseph Simpson. He told him that Jenkins was deeply unhappy about the performance of the Obscene Publications Squad and the Home Secretary wanted to see him about it. But first the Home Secretary wanted a written explanation as to why the police had seen fit to seize a book by a serious author, which had been on sale in reputable bookshops for a number of years and which the Attorney-General had decided not to prosecute.

As regards the last of these considerations, it is possible, I imagine, that the police are not aware of the views of the Attorney-General (and of the DPP) and if this is so, I think this raises the question whether the existing arrangements for ensuring that the officers are familiar with the views of the prosecuting authorities are satisfactory.

The Metropolitan Police Commissioner's confidential reply could not hide his obvious embarrassment:

As a result of assurances which I gave the Home Secretary some months ago in the Aubrey Beardsley case, I had the procedure in C1 [the Obscene Publications Office] overhauled to minimise any chance of what might be regarded as stupid or precipitate action being taken.

He said that there was a record of 30,000 different publications that had been held to be obscene at that time. They were aware that there had been five successful prosecutions of the Paris-printed Olympia Press edition of *The Naked Lunch* but did not know that the Attorney-General had decided not to take action against the British John Calder edition.

Once again, as they had in the early 1950s, the Home Office tried to spare the Home Secretary's blushes from police blunders by proposing that a 'white list' be drawn up. Miss Owen wrote to the DPP's office to ask if this was possible:

We have recently been considering whether some means can be devised to prevent the kind of embarrassment to the Home Secretary that has occurred in one or two recent instances of police action under the OPA where copies of quite well known books by established authors have been taken away under search warrant, despite the fact that the book may already have been considered and rated not obscene by our Department.

There is no problem over the hard core pornography but would it be possible for you to let the police have a quite short white list covering only the kind of books that cause trouble? By this I mean books by serious authors. *The Naked Lunch* is an example of what I mean or Henry Miller's *Sexus* or Cleland's *Memoirs of a Coxcomb*.

A fortnight later the DPP himself, Sir Norman Skelhorn, sent a three-page reply explaining his opposition to such an idea.

It is impractical because it is not my province to act as a censor of books ... this is a position I always maintain and try to make clear to publishers when they submit a book in advance of publication with a request for a ruling.

Interestingly he added that no action had been taken against *The Naked Lunch* because the publishers had stressed the special safeguards they intended to take in marketing the book. He claimed, somewhat incredibly, that if it could be shown that the Burroughs book was being sold indiscriminately to young teenagers then the question of taking proceedings would be revived. This surely must have been an unlikely prospect – banning a book that was already widely available. But Sir Norman argued that was why he could not give it a 'clearance certificate'. He said that such a white list could be circulated confidentially but it was bound to leak and 'would clearly stamp me as a censor in the eyes of the public'.

Miss Owen said that they had little choice but to accept the DPP's arguments against having a list of cleared books. She confessed:

With the best will in the world junior officers cannot be expected to make themselves masters of all the byways of avant garde literature (for the record I had not heard of

> 'I, Jan Cremer' or 'Memoirs of a Shy Pornographer',
> although I do read the weeklies – and even avant garde
> literature for that matter).

On 7 July 1967, the Home Secretary finally confronted the Metropolitan Police Commissioner over the incompetence of the 'dirty books squad'. He told the police to stop seizing books and instead to make a note of those titles about which they had doubts and buy them in a bookshop in the ordinary way. He insisted that new instructions were issued to the police officers concerned so that they would stop seizing books by obviously reputable publishers. The confidential memorandum was also designed to ensure that there was no repeat of the embarrassing 'raids' on the V&A or the Tate Gallery: 'It should be pretty clear from the way a book is produced, regardless of whether it is hard or soft cover, whether or not it is hard core pornography,' Roy Jenkins told Sir Joseph Simpson bluntly. The Commissioner agreed to do as he was told.

The confidential memorandum that Sir Joseph Simpson sent to his officers in 1967 said that the recent more tolerant attitude to obscenity meant that there were times when police action led to criticism by responsible people in the worlds of literature and art.

> Such instances can be reduced to a minimum by the
> application of certain elementary tests which do not
> demand a detailed examination of the material
> concerned.

The Commissioner said that in a recent House of Lords debate, the Lord Chancellor, Lord Hailsham, had noted that anybody familiar with pornography had not the slightest difficulty in dividing the works involved into 'dirt for dirt's sake' and perfectly legitimate books. The Commissioner offered an even simpler test for officers on the dirty squad.

The material and quality of printing used in the
production of 'dirt for dirt's sake' is usually as dirty as its
contents. Where, however, the material has, in the eyes of
at any rate some experts, literary merit, the publication
will usually be of a reasonably high quality. Paper,
printing and binding will be of a fair standard, which
shows that the publisher has made a deliberate, and
thereby responsible, decision that his business is not likely
to be placed in jeopardy by publication. The same
principles apply in the case of prints and drawings by
well known artists.

The procedure laid down said that the police could carry on
raiding the purveyors of 'dirt for dirt's sake' with impunity but if
there was any doubt, they were to make an 'incognito visit' to
the premises and consult the DPP even before a test purchase
was made. No material which was 'classed as a responsibly produced production' was to be seized. So in four pages the Metropolitan Police had wiped out a century of argument over the
definition of obscenity. The new test appeared to be: if the ink
came off on your hands it was porn; if it did not it was literature.

By 1970 these guidelines had been refined somewhat further.
The updated confidential Met rules stated:

> Seizures of unquestionably hard-core pornography from
> the 'dirty bookshops' do not attract very much publicity
> or any real protest. Clearly, in this field it is relatively
> simple to assert that the seized articles are 'filth for filth's
> sake'. However, it is clear there is a level of pornography
> which is exceptionally delicate, where any police action
> will obviously attract much publicity, subsequent analysis
> and criticism … Obvious examples are: displays in
> recognised galleries and books expensively published;
> works of alleged or real masters; exhibitions of famous,
> infamous or notorious individuals; or films at private
> clubs and associations, etc.

If only Roy Jenkins had realised at the time that these new guidelines actually gave a corrupt Obscene Publications Squad an even freer hand to consolidate the secret monopoly they already had over the Soho bribery and corruption rackets. In an effort to protect legitimate literature and art, the new instructions actually provided them with an even greater opportunity to exploit their power to their own massive profit. At their peak in the late 1960s, the dirty squad was able to 'recycle' the easily seized hard-core porn back on to the market, with each officer said to be clearing a profit of up to £2,000 a month.

Perhaps if Roy Jenkins had read this description of life in the Obscene Publications Squad in 1972 he might have demanded more fundamental action:

> The dirty squad were a great bunch to work with and I
> had more laughs with them than at any other time. It was
> probably the right attitude. If we'd taken a serious
> interest in everything that we saw we'd have ended up
> like the dirty old men whose fun we were out to spoil.
> Basically we were the DPP's runners, as far as obscene
> publications were concerned ... I saw some very odd
> sights. I wasn't shocked and I stopped being amazed.
> After all there's a physical limit to what can be done in
> the sex act, and basically, when you've seen one dirty
> book you've seen them all. Even the action with animals
> – pigs, donkeys, horses and dogs – was so remote from
> the real thing as to be idiotic. If that is what people
> wanted ... it didn't bother me as long as they didn't do it
> in the road. What I didn't like were the scenes showing
> beatings, cuttings and burnings, really vicious stuff that
> made me feel quite ill. Most of the time the material we
> saw was just a source of rude comments, comparisons
> and cues for jokes. This particularly applied to the films
> ... Occasionally on a Friday evening we might have a
> special showing for selected friends and acquaintances in

C1 – a sort of stag party … Whichever way you looked
at the dirty squad – dull it wasn't.[10]

In this atmosphere the police did not forget the trouble that *IT*
had caused them. On the 'they'll keep' principle they targeted
the underground magazine again in November 1970 once the
Labour government had left office. This time they had more
success and the pillar of the underground press was closed
down, using charges of conspiracy to corrupt public morals by
prosecuting it for the gay contact ads it carried in the personal
columns buried away at the back of the magazine. It would be
another six and half years before the biggest ever police corruption trials would see 18 Scotland Yard officers sent to prison. Detective Inspector Bill Moody and Detective Inspector Leslie
Alton, who had persecuted Jim Dine and *IT*, were sent to prison
for 12 years and 10 years respectively in March 1977 for their
part in the corruption ring. But it was to be their raid on
another hippie magazine that was to help them along the road
to the Old Bailey.

The Lord Chamberlain regrets ... the end of Aunt Edna

The first Baron Cobbold and owner of Knebworth House in Hertfordshire, or Aunt Edna as his fellow peers in the House of Lords preferred to call him, was the last ever Lord Chamberlain to wield the power to censor what appeared on the British stage. The theatre had been under the vice-like grip of the Lord Chamberlain since 1737 and with hindsight it now appears inevitable that once *Lady Chatterley* was on sale in every high street Woolworth's and ITV and BBC had established a mass audience for television, his days would be numbered.

Perhaps because he was more easily identifiable as a one-man, authoritarian censor and operated out of Buckingham Palace, the Lord Chamberlain was the target of much easy abuse. It was widely believed that Baron Cobbold, aided by his military comptrollers, used his notorious blue pencil, not so much to protect the public from what might deprave or corrupt them, but to maintain the blue-blooded values of the royal aristocracy. When his office was finally abolished in 1968, Baron Cobbold had the grace to realise that the game was up but as the confidential Cabinet and Home Office papers show, he fought an important rearguard action, the effects of which are still felt today. Lord Cobbold was so concerned that the reputation of the royal family and of foreign heads of state would be maligned on the stage that he wanted it made a criminal offence to make 'crude or vicious mockery of them' in a play.

Under the Lord Chamberlain no offensive representation of a living member of the royal family was permitted, nor of any other heads of state, except for those of Communist countries, of whom it was positively encouraged. Religious leaders, including the Pope, were also well protected by the law. Baron Cobbold was so keen to see this protection remain after the abolition of theatre censorship in 1968 that he waged a campaign within government and even nobbled Harold Wilson to overrule an attempt by the then Home Secretary, James Callaghan, to gag him. The Lord Chamberlain did not succeed but his campaign did have an impact. Even up until the mid-1980s references to the royals on stage, or for that matter on television, were mostly neutered and cosy, as the effects of his campaign lingered on in the 'good taste' of television directors and theatrical directors. For example, it was still regarded as something of a shock to see Prunella Scales's intimate portrayal of the Queen in *A Question of Attribution*, Alan Bennett's drama about Anthony Blunt on BBC television in 1991. It is only in more recent years that full-frontal attacks on the reputation of the royals in satirical programmes such as *Spitting Image* have finally demolished this taboo.

The Lord Chamberlain's delicate approach to the stage was notorious. For example, he once put his blue pencil through an anodyne limerick that began 'There was once a young man from Newcastle'. When the author complained that the limerick used was inoffensive, the Lord Chamberlain explained that it was being banned because he personally knew a much dirtier version that the audience was bound to think of when they heard it.

The explosion of talent in the English theatre probably sounded the death knell of the Lord Chamberlain. The likes of

John Osborne, Joe Orton, Arnold Wesker, Harold Pinter and Edward Bond were never likely to suffer quietly the kind of censorship that novelists and poets had just shaken off. John Osborne had a particularly torrid time with the Lord Chamberlain. His play, *The Entertainer*, suffered badly from cuts and he was forced to remove words such as 'pouf', 'rogered' and 'had Sylvia'. A lengthy correspondence ensued when Osborne's agent objected to cutting 'balls' from the script: 'No, a thousand times no. Who does Mr Osborne think he is?' The Lord Chamberlain's reader described the play as 'verbal dirt' with 'traces of blasphemy and disloyalty'. He said the whole play was impregnated with sex and general lavatory dirt.

Joe Orton fared little better. Lines in *Entertaining Mr Sloane* such as 'You wanted to see if my titties were all my own' were simply cut. Harold Pinter was prevented from putting his play, *Landscape*, on the English stage simply because the Lord Chamberlain refused to allow him to use the words 'fuck all' and 'bugger'.

By the early 1960s it was not only the plays of John Osborne and Joe Orton which were regularly provoking apoplexy in Buckingham Palace. The Lord Chamberlain even once ordered a raid on the musical *Fings Ain't Wot They Used T' Be* in which lines such as 'Don't drink that stuff, it will rot your drawers' were banned. Sometimes the Lord Chamberlain did show rare flashes of sanity, such as the occasion when he received a letter demanding a play be banned because it used the word 'maidenhead'. 'Dear Sir, Maidenhead is a town in Berkshire in which over 17,000 people contrive to live without embarrassment', began his reply. But the Cabinet papers show that it was two particular plays, John Osborne's *A Patriot for Me* and Edward Bond's *Saved*, which finally delivered the fatal blows to the Lord Chamberlain's power over the stage. The censor's notes in the archives show the Lord Chamberlain's depths of contempt for Osborne's play about homosexuality and especially a scene set at a transvestites' ball. It featured Lady Godiva wearing a gold lamé jockstrap.

This play looks like a pansies' charter of freedom ... Mr
Osborne's overweening conceit ...and blatant anti-
authoritarianism causes him to write in a deliberately
provocative way. He almost never misses a chance to be
provocative. By presenting homosexuals in their most
attractive guise – dressed as pretty women – it will to
some degree cause the congregation of homosexuals and
provide the means whereby the vice may be acquired ...
The piece might well corrupt since it reveals all the
details of homosexual life usually left blank even in the
newspaper reports.

A Patriot for Me was the joint winner of the *Evening Standard*'s
Play of the Year for 1964 and when the Attorney-General
refused to endorse a request from the Lord Chamberlain to
prosecute a 'club production' at the Royal Court theatre, his authority suffered a major blow.

Edward Bond's bleak play, *Saved*, was to finish him off. The
Lord Chamberlain's reader described the play, in which a baby is
stoned to death, as being about a group of moronic youths that
behaved as 'apelike yobs'. The Home Office note reads:

The 'heroine' is a brainless slut, who sleeps with anyone, a
daughter of sluttish parents. The language is 'stylised
cockney, but in an unreal way'. The writing is vile and
the language worse. The LC [Lord Chamberlain] requires
many changes in language – list runs into 4 pages.
   The main character is Fred – father of girl's child. The
main scene to which LC objects runs to 10 pages. Fred
has deserted girl, Pam. Pam meets gang in park, pushing
pram. After row leaves pram with gang. Baby is ill-treated
and finally stoned to death. Only Fred is charged, gets off
with light sentence and everyone is pleased when he gets
out. Then he sleeps with girl's mother and another of
gang watches.

The Lord Chamberlain sent the script back to the Royal Court in the summer of 1965 with the instructions that the scenes in which the baby is murdered and in which Fred has sex with the girl's mother were to be cut. Also twelve 'Christs', three 'sods', and two 'get stuffeds' were to go.

Edward Bond decided to try the same route as that trodden by John Osborne's *A Patriot for Me. Saved* opened in November 1965 as a 'club performance'. The Lord Chamberlain believed that the Royal Court's English Stage Society with its rather loose membership rules was really a public performance by another name. The Lord Chamberlain demanded that the Attorney-General prosecute. At a meeting on 22 November 1965 at the Home Office between the Home Secretary, Sir Frank Soskice, and Baron Cobbold, the Lord Chamberlain made clear that if the law officers failed to prosecute the Royal Court for *Saved* then 'he would feel it his duty somehow to represent to Parliament that it was impossible for him to carry out his duties under the Theatres Act, 1843'. The government took his threat to resign seriously and when the curtain went up on the performance of *Saved* on 1 January 1966 a number of police officers had taken their seats in the audience. Despite an appearance by Laurence Olivier, the Royal Court management was found guilty of presenting an unlicensed play and fined 50 guineas (£52.50).

The Lord Chamberlain had already conceded the bigger battle at his meeting with the Home Secretary, however. He agreed with the Labour government's proposal that there should be an official inquiry into the whole future of theatre censorship but he warned that it would be difficult for it not to stray into questions of television and film censorship. Home Office ministers, already under fire from Mary Whitehouse's National Viewers' and Listeners' Association, were anxious to keep television out of the picture. Tony Benn, as Postmaster-General, had managed to do this by arguing that as an unscripted medium it was impossible to impose censorship of any traditional kind on the output of the small screen.

The confidential minutes from the Cabinet's Home Affairs Committee setting up the inquiry into theatre censorship make clear that abolition was on the agenda from the very start. They point out the absurdity that a play to be performed before a few hundred spectators could be banned by the Lord Chamberlain while it could safely be broadcast to millions of viewers without hindrance and that no other country censored stage plays. In Parliament the Lord Chamberlain had few friends. Lord Annan, who opened the special debate in the House of Lords authorising the select committee inquiry, dubbed him the Aunt Edna of British theatre and in the Commons, Roy Jenkins as Home Secretary also made it clear that his time had gone. Lord Cobbold, anxious to leave the scene with dignity, proposed that he should abdicate in favour of a board of theatre censors along the lines of the film world's British Board of Film Classification. Cobbold feared that he would be seen as a lame duck once news of his impending demise got out and so he proposed that this board would take over until a final decision was made on what, if anything should replace his role. But the Labour Lord Chancellor, Lord Elwyn Jones, blocked this delaying tactic. The Cabinet papers note that the Lord Chancellor argued that from the point of view of those interested in the free exchange of ideas in the theatre, a Board of Theatre Censors would be as objectionable as the present censorship. His private secretary recorded his actual words as: 'Over my dead body'.

The fight was to go on for another two years and Edward Bond succeeded in provoking the Lord Chamberlain's wrath when he submitted a new Royal Court play, *Early Morning*, in November 1967. Designed to outrage, it portrayed Queen Victoria as a lesbian who slept with Florence Nightingale while a sadistic Gladstone and a Machiavellian Disraeli ran the government like a branch of the Mafia. Baron Cobbold rose to the bait when it was given two 'club' performances in April 1968.

This play appears to this reader to be the product of a diseased imagination [said the confidential report for the

Lord Chamberlain]. The author must have a very sick
mind. Cannibalism and lesbianism may be legitimate
themes for dramatisation but not in this context. Banned.

Scotland Yard's vice squad made sure that they obtained tickets
but they agreed that the prospects of any legal action 'depends
on what Marianne Faithfull gets up to'. The chanteuse and
Rolling Stones' girlfriend played Florence Nightingale. 'I mentioned last night to the Queen the present position of *Early
Morning*. HM agreed that this should be put firmly in the Attor-
ney's lap,' he reported. But despite the Queen's own endorsement, the Labour Attorney-General decided that it was better to
side-step this particular piece of provocation and wait until the
Theatres Bill became law in September 1968. He refused to
prosecute and spared Mr Bond's further martyrdom.

Throughout those final months in office, Baron Cobbold
fought a fierce campaign to provide some specific legal protection for the royal family and heads of friendly foreign states. The
recently released government papers show that this was not an
idle question. Indeed the political censorship exercised by even
Harold Wilson himself over the portrayal of friendly foreign
heads of state now, with hindsight, looks perhaps more sinister
than the hounding of playwrights such as Edward Bond and
John Osborne.

The files released under the 30-year rule have brought to
light some new examples alongside the better known ones, such
as the attempt by Lord Cobbold to ban Peter Brook's 1966
Royal Shakespeare Company (RSC) production, *US*, which
criticised American involvement in Vietnam. As Brook himself
put it:

The birth of *US* was allied to the reaction of a group of
us who quite suddenly felt that Vietnam was more
powerful, more acute, more insistent a situation than any
drama that already existed between covers … We were
interested in the theatre of confrontation. In current

events, what confronts what, who confronts who? In the
case of Vietnam it was reasonable to say that everyone is
concerned, yet none is concerned; if everyone could
hold in his mind through one single day the horror of
Vietnam and the normal life he is leading, the tension
between the two would be intolerable. We wanted actors
to explore every aspect of this contradiction.[1]

Brook said the group, many of whom were dedicated socialists,
was frustrated at the lack of any reflection in the British theatre
on the subject of Vietnam.

This inescapable fact shamed us into trying to make one
collectively as quickly as possible giving ourselves a
deadline believing that if one side of the ... coin is to
spend infinite time on a single gesture the other side of
the same coin is speed. In this case urgency outweighed
art.

The play, much of it improvised, portrayed American torture
techniques, and had no formal end. When it had run its course
an actor brought a lighter and burned a paper butterfly in
silence. The cast then stood silently on the stage. This provoked
the critic, Kenneth Tynan, at the opening night to shout: 'Are
you waiting for us or are we waiting for you?'

The Lord Chamberlain's reader was in no doubt what he
thought of the original script submitted in 1966:

Hysterically subjective anti-Vietnam war propaganda.
Turgid text. A history of Vietnam with snide references
to the evil influence of the French. Text gets progressively
more obscene. Anti-States and all the other antis are
discussed. Dangerous and insulting attitude to an ally. The
war in Vietnam is, so to speak, *sub judice*. Would we have
permitted a play about Suez during the Suez crisis. Not
recommended for a licence.

The Lord Chamberlain regarded *US* as 'beastly' and 'offensive to responsible foreign opinion'. He considered whether the authors could be charged with incitement to riot when they proposed getting around the censorship by suggesting that the audience read out the offending passages. Lord Cobbold also consulted the Foreign Office and tried to enlist its support for a ban. But in this case, the Foreign Secretary, George Brown, did not want to become involved. At the same time the RSC chairman, George Farmer, went to see Lord Cobbold to persuade him it was a responsible production. In these circumstances the Lord Chamberlain was forced to withdraw. He did, however, succeed in banning *MacBird,* an American satire that presented President Johnson as the murderer of John F. Kennedy, on the grounds that it was hostile to a foreign power.

Less well-known cases documented in the files demonstrate the lengths to which the Foreign Office was prepared to go to protect the reputation of friendly heads of state and in particular tried hard to ban outbreaks of anti-American sentiment. In March 1967, an educational Jackdaw dossier on the assassination of President Kennedy, published by Jonathan Cape and designed for use in school history lessons, led to an anxious exchange of confidential transatlantic telegrams between the British Embassy in Washington and the Foreign Office in London. The kit had been written by Len Deighton, who was already famous as the author of the *Ipcress File*, and two members of the staff of Jonathan Cape. Jackdaws were a series of educational folders, which contained source material about a historical event. This particular Jackdaw included a full-scale drawing of Lee Harvey Oswald's rifle, a cardboard model of Deeley Plaza, where the President's motorcade was when he was shot, a photograph of Kennedy's bloodstained shirt, copies of the Bethesda Naval Hospital's pathological reports, and brief essays on Kennedy, Dallas, the Warren Commission inquiry, Jack Ruby and 'unanswered questions'.

US Customs seized 500 copies of this Jackdaw at New York on the technical grounds that it contained unauthorised reproductions of the Presidential seal. The Foreign Office scrabbled around to find a copy. Bizarrely the British Embassy in Washington believed that it was produced by somebody called Jack Straw. This was based on a report from the British Consul in St Louis, who said he had seen a photograph of the kit on which the words 'Jack Straw' were identifiable. But Tony Blair's Home Secretary was not guilty.

The American ambassador in London put them in the picture when he officially lodged a protest to the Foreign Office. He said that the US government was upset not only about 'the questionable taste of some of the documents' but also more importantly about 'the fact that the whole thing is slanted to the Mark Lane thesis' (i.e. that the official Warren Commission inquiry had been a whitewash). The Foreign Office complained: 'The pale blue folder is in fact anti-US administration propaganda' and said it well understood the Americans' complaints. The Foreign Office panicked and considered a legal action in Britain to ban the export of Jackdaws to America. It was worried that 'criticism in the United States is likely to be widespread and will reflect not only on British publishers but possibly on British exports to the US in general'. The British ambassador in Washington said that the government should consider stopping its distribution 'either by legislation, or by private persuasion, or be ready to express official repugnance'.

It was even suggested that a Foreign Office civil servant should have a private word with Graham C. Greene, the chairman of Jonathan Cape, to suggest that it was bad publicity for the company and would affect future sales of its books in the United States. But the Foreign Office was prepared to go even further. One civil servant suggested:

The news department should drop a discreet word to a reliable British journalist. The issue of the kits is a news story and there should be no difficulty in inducing a newspaper to denounce the publication as being in deplorably bad taste.

In the event wiser counsels prevailed and the Foreign Office in London settled on issuing a couple of official statements saying that it regretted that the boundaries of good taste had been overstepped by Jonathan Cape. It was decided that a legal action would not succeed, as it would be difficult to prove that the Jackdaw was insulting to a foreign head of state.

This undue sensitivity about American feelings was again in evidence in November 1967 when the Foreign Office took exception to the inclusion of some cartoons by Gerald Scarfe in an official exhibition in New York to be opened by Lord Snowdon, who was then married to the Queen's sister, Princess Margaret. After Foreign Office censure, Gerald Scarfe had to withdraw, before the exhibition opened, a cartoon that depicted the Statute of Liberty as 'a negro woman, with obvious implied criticism of the United States' racial situation'.

When the Design and Art Directors Association exhibition finally opened, the Foreign Office was dismayed to learn that it included many other Scarfe political cartoons, including two 'highly uncomplimentary' attacks on Harold Wilson and Edward Heath. The British Information Services in New York reported to London:

> There are also one or two cartoons dealing with
> Vietnam, at least one of which can be described as
> extremely insulting to President Johnson. This is all the
> more unfortunate since the Prime Minister issued a
> statement today welcoming the show and encouraging
> this effort to sell British graphics and design in the USA.

'Imagine the row here if a US exhibition insulted the Queen,' minuted a senior Foreign Office civil servant.

Lord Snowdon, who it might be said was somewhat closer to the royal family than this anonymous Foreign Office man, defended Scarfe and warned that there would be a violent reaction among the other exhibitors if his cartoons were banned. So the Foreign Office had to content itself with organising a defensive line and making clear to Lord Snowdon that he should have been more vigilant about Scarfe in the first place.

It was not only towards the United States that the Labour government was particularly sensitive. Harold Wilson also got himself into a terrible fuss over a play about African governments based on a novel written by Ronald Millar, a former Downing Street press officer to the previous Conservative government and a future speech writer for Margaret Thatcher. The play, *Number Ten*, was to be performed during British Week in Toronto in October 1967. The Queen's cousin, Princess Alexandra, was scheduled to attend. The cast included Alastair Sim, Michael Denison and Dulcie Gray. Harold Wilson's state papers describe the play as about the reactions in the British Cabinet to the fictional Zimbadian Federation nationalising British copper mines under Chinese pressure.

The Commonwealth Office in London said that it clearly referred to President Kuanda's Zambia and depicted one section of the British Cabinet advocating the armed overthrow of an African government and preparing to assassinate the president.

> The Cabinet 'hawks' make a series of disparaging references to African Nationalist regimes, savages, the unreliability of African Ministers compared with the South African Government and contemptuous remarks about the African President himself, all of which are liable to give offence to African opinion.

The Commonwealth Office advised that, given that the author might be credited with knowledge of British Cabinet procedures, it was unsuitable for official sponsorship. When the British government threatened to withdraw all support for the play, however, the organisers in Canada made clear that they would ensure that there was a barrage of bad publicity if the play was boycotted in any way. A huge fuss then ensued with telegrams flying back and forth between Harold Wilson's office, the Commonwealth Office and the British High Commissioner in

Toronto. It was finally decided not to give the play any financial support and that Princess Alexandra would attend not the opening night, but the second night. Everybody kept their fingers crossed that the fact that elections were being held in Ontario on the same day would mean that local press interest was too distracted to make much of a fuss. It was also decided to send the play to Baron Cobbold to see if the Lord Chamberlain's blue pencil would do the job on their behalf.

This was no idle threat. In May 1967 Lord Cobbold had had his censorious way with another anti-establishment satirical play based on *Private Eye*'s *Mrs Wilson's Diary*. The Prime Minister's papers show that the script for *Mrs Wilson's Diary* – the predecessor of Dear Bill during the Thatcher years – was vetted not only by Lord Cobbold but also by Mrs Mary Wilson herself, the Foreign Secretary (George Brown), the Chancellor of the Exchequer (James Callaghan), Mrs Callaghan and even Colonel George Wigg, Wilson's confidant. By the time it had been through all their hands no fewer than eight separate passages had been cut. One of the scenes to go depicted a social evening at Number Ten with Harold and Mary Wilson entertaining James and Audrey Callaghan and George Brown.

> Harold: 'Ah, Audrey, do come in. We were just playing a little game we picked up during our brief stay at Balmoral Castle. It's called Crawling Round Under The Table Pretending You're Drunk.'
> George: 'Yes. I've been playing it for years.'
> Audrey: 'I think a little drink is called for.'

The Lord Chamberlain said it was one thing to make fun of George Brown's addiction to drink 'which I suppose everyone knows about' but he was not going to have the royal family portrayed in this light. Nor would he allow a line in which Gladys (Mary Wilson) says she would never forget the time that Audrey Callaghan had got 'taken short by the tea place' during a Lake District hiking trip they had all been on in their youth. It was no wonder that the play lacked a certain satirical edge when it finally reached the stage.

In this atmosphere it is no surprise to learn that when a year later Lord Cobbold launched his behind-the-scenes campaign for a new crime to be created of making 'inexcusably coarse and indecent' references to members of the royal family and foreign heads of state, it was taken very seriously. But the Queen let it be known that she was anxious not to be accorded any special treatment by the law and so the proposed change in the law was drafted to provide protection for the reputation of 'living persons and the recently dead'. This was widely taken to mean banning offensive portrayals of politicians as well as the royal family. If the measure had succeeded it would have killed political satire in Britain for a generation.

By now James Callaghan was Home Secretary and the Home Office was firmly opposed to this proposal to end theatrical censorship only to replace it with a new crime which, in its words, could only be 'secured by massive inroads on the principle of free speech'. The Home Office advised Callaghan that

> we should all deplore cheap jibes at the Sovereign but the feeling of outrage that would result from any such performance would vindicate approved standards of taste more effectively than any criminal prohibition.

Cobbold continued to press his case in April and May 1968 with his supporters arguing that those offended, including religious leaders, should be able to take out a High Court injunction to ban grossly offensive, personally abusive, menacing or scurrilous references to them. Not only would this have dealt the 'satire boom' a savage blow, but also, as far as the Home Office was concerned, it would involve an unacceptable extension of the law of defamation.

Baron Cobbold told Callaghan in no uncertain terms that he was prepared to go public and take on the government in order to secure this protection for the royal family. 'I must in conscience

repeat reservations I have made on certain points, particularly
on the treatment of "living persons",' he told the Home Secretary before a key House of Lords debate. Callaghan made clear
to Cobbold that he strongly objected to him speaking out publicly. He feared that it would be portrayed as a Labour government in a head-on political clash with the Queen. The Home
Secretary said that he would be placed in great difficulty if the
Lord Chamberlain urged a different course of action from that
which the government had decided to adopt. There was a
further difficulty:

> Will it be possible in your position in the Queen's
> Household to avoid creating the impression that you are
> conveying Her Majesty's own views?

The Home Office knew that this was all Cobbold's campaign
and the Queen had said nothing more than that the royal family
should not be accorded any special protection.

Cobbold went behind the Home Secretary's back straight to
the Prime Minister. The Lord Chamberlain demanded and got
a meeting with Harold Wilson in Downing Street. Wilson
agreed and told Callaghan that Cobbold should be allowed to
speak out on the issue. 'A speech from Cobbold given his deep
knowledge of the subject would be welcomed,' the Prime Minister told the Home Secretary. The gag had been lifted and the
sky did not fall in. During the House of Lords debate, ministers
argued against his ideas of special protection for royals, religious
and political leaders, and instead made clear that the law of sedi-
tion – which includes acts that tend to vilify or disgrace the
Queen – was still on the statute book. As it remains to this day.

Mrs Whitehouse meets the Wizard of Oz

When Mary Whitehouse first launched her crusade to promote a Christian way of life and to end the stream of 'disbelief, doubt and dirt' she claimed that the BBC was broadcasting into millions of homes, Harold Wilson believed that she could be safely ignored. Her 'Clean-up TV' protests to Downing Street demanding the removal of Alf Garnett or the banning of the latest Play for Today were met with disdain and even contempt. 'Mrs Whitehouse is clearly a most tiresome woman out for all the publicity she can get,' one senior Downing Street official confidentially advised Harold Wilson in 1965. Number 10 was so fed up with her misconceptions about who actually ran broadcasting in Britain that it sometimes accidentally 'lost' her letters. On one occasion the Prime Minister's office even worried that she would produce the Post Office registered letter stub proving that one such binned protest had actually been delivered and so was in need of an official answer.

> The ground is not very firm under our feet. She has created a great stir about this missing letter. We are apprehensive that the Post Office will produce evidence that the letter was registered,

they anxiously reported after yet another fruitless search of the office files for the missing tirade had been ordered. As far as Mrs Whitehouse was concerned Hugh Carlton Greene, the Director-General of the BBC from 1960 to 1969, was the man most to blame for Britain's moral collapse.

By 1970 the social atmosphere was rapidly changing. As the Scotland Yard 'dirty books' squad and their colleagues in the Drugs Squad created mayhem amongst London's new rock and roll elite, so the 'underground' press grew stronger. There was a retreat from the 1959 Act, with the police falling back on increasingly obscure ancient laws to justify their activities. In 1970 the police raided an exhibition of John Lennon's lithographs at the London Gallery in Bond Street. The police seized the drawings and prints and prosecuted the gallery's owners under the 1839 Metropolitan Police Act, under which it was necessary to prove only indecency and not the tougher test of obscenity. The Lennon Lithograph Bag One exhibition showed John and Yoko Ono making love in various positions. The lithographs, which had a 500 guinea price tag, depicted the marriage and honeymoon of John and Yoko. But the gallery owner was acquitted on a technicality under the 130-year-old Act. The section he was charged under related only to the exhibition of indecent prints to 'public view to the obstruction or annoyance of residents or passengers': it had been designed to protect the public when they travelled on buses. Detective Inspector Frederick Luff, who also was to play a role in the raids on *Oz* magazine, had some difficulty in proving to the magistrates that there were any 'passengers' present in the gallery at the time. Indeed the gallery had remained stationary throughout the raid. Dismissing the case the magistrate, Mr St John Harmsworth, said:

> As I understand the word 'passenger' it means someone
> on the move, but people who enter the gallery are not
> passengers – they then finish, for the time being,
> passaging. If, of course, the action had been taken under
> another Act, it might have been a different kettle of fish.[1]

A new generation was testing the limits of its freedom. When Kenneth Tynan staged his naked revue *Oh! Calcutta!* at the Roundhouse theatre in Chalk Farm (subsidised by the Arts Council), north London, it appeared to the authorities to be a deliberate provocation. The contributions from Joe Orton and Samuel Beckett set alongside a John Lennon sketch about masturbation were calculated to unleash a spate of 'state handouts for filth' headlines. But it also led Sir Alan Herbert and Norman St John Stevas and others behind the 1959 obscenity reform movement to shake their heads in despair. In an article for *The Times*, Herbert was bitterly saddened 'that the worthy struggle for reasonable liberty for honest writers' should have ended in establishing 'a right to represent copulation, veraciously, on the public stage'.[2] But those seeking to live out the drug-induced dreams of the *Playpower* society were not without friends in high places. An Arts Council working party, convened while under the influence of changes in the Danish obscenity laws, recommended a complete end to censorship and the repeal of the 1959 and 1964 Obscene Publication Acts for a trial five years. The utter lack of any consensus on a practical definition of obscenity was compounded by the Arts Council working party report. Its chairman, John Montgomerie, argued that the better written the obscene material, the more likely it was to debase the reader. Obscenity was truly now held in the eye of the beholder.

The police, still operating under the shadow of corruption, stepped up their activities with the advent of the 1970 Conservative government. They went back for *IT* in November 1970, and got a conviction on an obscure charge of conspiring to corrupt public morals. This law had been used only once before to close down a prostitutes' contact magazine, *The Ladies' Directory*. This time it was not the editorial content that the Obscene Publications Squad was worried about but the personal ads tucked away at the back of the magazine which offered now legal gay contacts. One example cited at the trial was:

> Passive masculine good looking graduate 36 seeks
> sexually demanding active male with own pad in
> London. Daytime preferred.[3]

The guilty verdicts closed down one of the pillars of the 'underground press'. A fresh purge was under way.

The trial of Paul Ableman's *The Mouth and Oral Sex*, in
March 1971, was notable for Margaret Drabble's polite willing-
ness to testify to the literary merit of a book that suggested that
many couples spontaneously invent games involving eating
strawberries out of their vaginas and sucking liqueurs off their
penises. During Margaret Drabble's testimony, the judge was
moved to ask: 'Why is it important to read about it now ... we
have managed to get by for a couple of thousand years without
it.'[4] The jury refused to share his sense of self-denial and duly acquitted the publishers and in the process the public discussion of
oral sex in Britain.

Those involved in the moral backlash in the early 1970s,
which included Mrs Whitehouse, the Festival of Light, which
had started life as a Christian protest outside *Oh! Calcutta!*, Lord
Longford's private commission into pornography and the anti-
abortion Society for the Protection of the Unborn Child, were
not just interested in banning filth. For Mrs Whitehouse the real
target was the extreme left which, to her mind, was behind this
rising tide of pornography. She believed that revolutionary
Marxists were using it for the same purposes that Hitler had
flooded Poland with pornography before the Nazi invasion. She
saw the dissent of the 'hippie underground' as a conspiracy to
attack the moral fibre of the youth of Britain. But while Mrs
Whitehouse found little sympathy amongst the coming generation for her views, she found some unlikely allies amongst those
who were developing the first radical feminist critiques of
sexual politics. Feminists, such as Kate Millett and Germaine
Greer (who was a major force on *Oz* magazine), soon noticed
that the permissiveness to be found in books like *The Joy of Sex*
or magazines such as *Forum*, was still all about male dominance

and female submission even if the positions had got more varied.

As Caroline Coon, the founder of Release, the drugs advice service, put it in a 1999 *Guardian* article:

> It is no coincidence that the big trials in the 60s, like *Lady Chatterley's Lover*, were all about male access to a more liberated sexuality. The paradox was that they did not want the same freedom for women. By the end of the 60s, sexual liberation was turning into a kind of ghastly celebration of sexual violence against women. Those optimistic, loving images of naked young men and women dancing with flowers in their hair at Woodstock were eliding into pictures of women being tied up and beaten. Album covers and magazines showed images of women handcuffed or with black eyes – images that were desirable to men.
>
> At the same time our boyfriends were asking us what our fantasies were and when we didn't present sado-masochism as an exciting experiment to broaden our sexual menu, we were accused of being straight. The upsurge of degrading pornography and S&M was like the first backlash against women who had tried to be sexually liberated in the 60s. It was a shock for us, frightening and heartbreaking.[5]

This was not only hindsight speaking. By 1971 *Oz* magazine was carrying letters from women angry that the magazine was no more than 'an underground version of *Playboy*' and attacking it as an example of 'penis power and not sexual liberation'.

Such criticisms first about the treatment of rape and then of domestic violence and later about child abuse and pornography were all highly influential in driving the Yippie 'why don't we do it in the road?' sentiment out of popular youth culture. By the end of the 1970s, and with the advent of AIDS and HIV in the 1980s, the politics of sex had taken on a very different tone.

Kate Millett's landmark feminist book, *Sexual Politics*, identified the works of D. H. Lawrence, Henry Miller and Norman Mailer as representing a mood of reaction against the literary sexual revolution pioneered by Thomas Hardy, the Brontës and Virginia Woolf, and provided a rigorous analytical framework to this response. At the same time Mrs Whitehouse was persuading Scotland Yard to move against the British 'underground press'. It was a concoction that was to prove fatal for the London 'hippie' publishing scene.

The first target in 1971 was the English translation of a Danish work, *The Little Red Schoolbook* (*LRSB*), which was modelled on Mao's manual for the Red Guards of the Cultural Revolution. *Time Out* told children:

> You should read the *Little Red Schoolbook* which is
> written by people on your side and gives masses of really
> useful information on how to cope with school.
> However old you are you have a right to be told the
> truth about sex, contraception and homosexuality.[6]

The attitude of the *LRSB* to pornography was widely quoted: 'It is quite possible that you can get some interesting ideas from it and may find something interesting that you have not tried before.' So was its advice on premarital sex:

> People go to bed with one another for many reasons ...
> People who warn you against strong feelings and sex are
> generally afraid of both.[7]

Less quoted was its straightforward views about relationships:

> The only way to avoid unforeseen consequences in
> sexual relationships is for both people to be honest with
> one another about what they are looking for. Someone
> seeking security rarely finds it with someone who only
> wants sexual satisfaction. Someone who feels under

pressure to have a sexual relationship may not find sexual satisfaction.

What some people really objected to was its descriptions of sex:

> When a boy puts his stiff prick into a girl's vagina and moves it around it is called intercourse, or making love, or sleeping together (even if they don't sleep at all). The usual word for intercourse is fucking.[8]

Its critics were less interested in its views on smoking:

> If you haven't started smoking [tobacco] don't. Some of your friends or other people at school may smoke themselves and encourage you or dare you to try it. Saying no is sensible, not cowardly.[9]

Or on homework:

> Homework shouldn't just be a routine duty, set because it says so in the timetable. It should give you a chance to work on things on your own, and develop the ideas discussed in class. It's important for you to learn to think things out for yourself and express yourself clearly.[10]

Lord Longford was predictably incensed:

> It recommends that children should read pornography if lessons were boring to find ideas; and that children should press for contraceptives to be on sale in schools.[11]

He said that its opening sentence, 'All adults are paper tigers', showed that it was as much concerned with politics as education. Lord Longford conceded that there was much reasonable advice in the section dealing with sex but said what was objectionable was its bland assumption that every boy and girl had a right to indulge in any form of sexual activity that he or she liked. It was this explicit recognition of adolescent sexuality more than anything else which was the real target of the police raids on the *LRSB* and later that year more famously on *Oz* magazine.

The *LRSB* actually ran to 208 pages and only about 50 of them concerned advice on sex, particularly contraception, and drugs. Its wider concentration on how to handle homework failed to attract the same level of press interest. Despite this it was continually labelled as a sex and drugs manual for schoolchildren rather than a handbook of children's rights. It should be noted that in the previous year, 1970, the BBC had started broadcasting a sex education programme for schools aimed at children aged eight and over, but then this was at a time when even the production staff of *Jackanory* included members of the Workers' Revolutionary Party.

The police ransacked the offices of Richard Handyside's Stage One publishing house, which also brought out works by Fidel Castro and Che Guevara, when they carried out their raid on the *LRSB*. John Mortimer led the defence of *LRSB* at Clerkenwell magistrates' court but despite what Mary Whitehouse sneeringly called 'Mortimer's travelling circus' of experts, Handyside was found guilty and given a token £50 fine. The publishers were to spend further years fighting a fruitless battle through the European Court of Human Rights in an attempt to quash the verdict. Mary Whitehouse declared herself 'greatly relieved – for the sake of the children' at the news of the conviction. But in the same month she was to enjoy a greater victory barely two miles away at the Old Bailey, where the three editors of *Oz*, the second pillar of the 'underground establishment', were facing the full might of the law.

The invitation to its younger readers to edit a *Schoolkids Oz* was issued by the magazine's editors, Richard Neville, Felix Dennis and Jim Anderson, at a time when they were becoming increasingly fractious, bored and exhausted by the regular rhythm of magazine production. It coincided with the news of Charles Manson's Californian acid murders and the publication of Baroness Wootton's official report that took a tough line on psychedelic drugs and linked LSD to sociopathic violence. The *Schoolkids Oz* followed an *Acid Oz*, a *Flying Saucer Oz*, a *Gay Oz* and even a Germaine Greer-driven, *Cunt-power Oz*, or *Women's Liberation Oz*, as Neville more coyly referred to it in court. The invitation simply appealed for 'injections of youthful vigour in our ageing veins'. In his autobiography, Richard Neville says the dozen or so kids who turned up to do the job seemed confident, sceptical and cheerful:

> One was a true-blue hippie, with a satin cloak and a job
> at the Roundhouse; another was a skinhead look-alike
> who contemplated a career in advertising.[12]

Amongst them was the 18-year-old Charles Shaar Murray, who claimed he had the sex appeal of a mouldy sock. But he was to write such a perceptive piece on the then state of rock music that it later moved the presenter of Radio One's 'Top Gear', John Peel, to tell the Old Bailey: 'I wished I'd written that.'

Neville reported that most wanted to write about the horrors of school exams, bullying and corporal punishment. But the trouble really lay in the last two contributors, whom he describes in his book, *Hippie Hippie Shake*:

> On my left knelt Berti, a fifteen-year-old from Aldershot
> who was sweet and pretty and wanted to live in a
> commune. Beside her was Vivian Berger, 16, the wildest
> of the bunch, a self-proclaimed anarchist who claimed to
> have smoked pot at nine and tripped at eleven.[13]

It was Viv Berger's contribution to the 48-page issue of *Oz* 28 that was to cause the most outrage. The magazine was mostly made up of cartoons, readers' letters and articles concerning school, sex, drugs and discipline. Mrs Mary Whitehouse's verdict was based on a misconception shared by nearly everybody involved in the subsequent prosecution:

The cover of Oz
28, the school kids
issue.

> I do not have anything personal against the three men
> but I think it is an unmitigated disaster for the children
> of this country. If they cannot be protected by the law
> from this kind of material then the law should be
> tightened up.[14]

The point was that this was not an adult magazine produced to
corrupt or abuse children. Its contents were conceived and produced by children. What Mrs Whitehouse failed to appreciate
was that this was what children were already like. If they were a
bit wild for her taste, well this was what was already going on in
their heads. Unsurprisingly a major preoccupation of sassy
London teenagers growing up in the middle of psychedelic
London was experimenting with sex and drugs.

The personalised pieces attacking exams, school uniforms
and discipline, including beatings, were all ignored. The call for

legalising soft drugs would not have looked out of place in *The Times*. It was the tales of guilt-free adolescent sex that got the juices of the establishment going. In particular the attack crystallised around a collage of the *Daily Express* comic strip, Rupert the Bear, and a Robert Crumb American 'Gypsy Granny' comic. In this bit of fun the head of Rupert the Bear was stuck on a naked figure which proceeded to have sex with 'Gypsy Granny'. It had been put together by Viv Berger, who was a pupil at an Islington Inner London Education Authority grammar school. The strip had captions in the style of the old Rupert the Bear cartoons: in the first frame when 'Rupert finds Gypsy Granny', the young bear is seen staring at her vagina. The second frame is headed 'Rupert's way barred' and the caption reads: 'Then Rupert starts to push and peep. But finds the hole is much too deep.[15]

At the Old Bailey, the artist Feliks Topolski went so over the top in his description of the strip that his evidence probably seriously damaged the defence:

> This is a tremendously clever and witty putting together of opposite elements from the 'comics' culture, thus creating a profound clash. I think it is a great invention, if one accepts the satirical basis of the whole magazine.[16]

As the prosecution counsel, Brian Leary, put it to one of the three *Oz* editors, Jim Anderson, who had made the mistake of describing the collage as the work of a youthful genius:

> 'The youthful genius set to work by snipping out of the *Rupert Annual* the head of the bear. That's right?' asked Mr Leary.
> 'Yes, I suppose that is what he did,' replied Anderson.
> 'And then if we were keen to watch a genius at work, we would see him sticking it on the cartoon?' asked Leary.
> 'Yes,' said Anderson. 'Where lies the genius?' 'I think it is in the juxtaposition of two ideas, the childhood symbol

of innocence ...' Anderson began to reply. 'Making Rupert Bear fuck?' interrupted Leary. 'Yes,' said Anderson.[17]

This was matched only by Leary's cross-examination of Edward de Bono, the Cambridge philosopher:

'Mr de Bono. Why is Rupert the Bear equipped with a large organ?' asked Leary. 'I don't know. What size do you think would be natural?' replied the inventor of lateral thinking.[18]

Viv Berger himself seemed under no illusion that it was anything but a good piece of agitprop. As he told the defence counsel, John Mortimer, during the Old Bailey trial:

'I subconsciously wanted to shock your generation: to portray us as a group of people who were different from you in moralistic attitudes. Also, it seemed to me just very funny, and like anything else that makes fun of sex.' Mortimer asked: 'You say you did it to shock an older generation? What relevance did Rupert have as a figure or as a symbol?' Berger replied: 'Well, Rupert would probably be known to many generations as the innocent young character who figures in magic fairy tales. Whereas here, he's just doing what every normal human being does.'[19]

Mortimer suggested:

'Was it part of your intention to show that there was a more down-to-earth side to childhood than some grown-up people are prepared to think?' Berger answered: 'Yes. This is the kind of drawing that goes around every classroom, every day, in every school,' he said to the Judge's obvious horror. 'Maybe I was

portraying obscenity, but I don't think I was being
obscene myself.' He was later to explain that this meant:
'If the news covers a war or shows a picture of war, then,
for me they are portraying obscenity – the obscenity of
war. But they are not themselves creating that obscenity,
because it is the people who are fighting the war that are
creating that obscenity … For example, I consider that
the act of corporal punishment is an obscenity. I do not
consider the act of reporting or the writing about
corporal punishment is obscene.'[20]

Indeed it was hard to see how two cartoon characters could be
accused of an obscene act. The distinction between sex as obscenity and violence as obscenity as articulated in the witness
box by Viv Berger was to prove far more enduring than the
harsh sentences passed at the end of the longest ever British obscenity trial by Judge Michael Argyle.

Richard Neville has said the worst moment during the case
for him was when the prosecution read out a small ad for a sex
magazine on page 28.

It was what I most dreaded – the ad for *Suck. I can open
my throat pretty well if a guy has a really long cock. Actually, I
prefer ones that are not too long – six inches is plenty – but I
love fat ones that fill up my mouth. If the guy is really groovy,
he's stroking my neck and shoulders and breasts …* 'Why was
that put in the magazine?' demanded the prosecution
counsel, Brian Leary.

'It is a miniscule advertisement for a European sex
paper.' 'But it has nothing to do with the children who
produced this magazine.' 'No.' 'And what it does, that
little extract you've chosen from the magazine, *Suck*, is to
glorify the act of fellatio. By printing that, you have the
effect of encouraging people to do that sort of way-out,
sexual thing. Now if you're dealing with children, and a
particular experiment is written up in an attractive and

passionate way, chances are it's going to encourage that
sort of behaviour, isn't it?' 'Yes that is possible. But there
is nothing harmful about that paragraph. It coincides
with *Oz*'s general approach to sex, which is one of
openness and honesty and not trying to sweep it under
the carpet.'[21]

By now the liberal literary establishment was becoming wary
of being recruited to Mortimer's 'travelling circus of experts'.
On this occasion the cartoonist, Ralph Steadman, and the
philosopher, A.J. Ayer, were among those who refused to take
part. Nevertheless there was a ready sprinkling of expert witnesses from the hot-panted Caroline Coon, to the jazz musi-
cian, George Melly, and Viv Berger's own mother, Grace, then
chairman of the National Council for Civil Liberties, and his
staunchest defender.

Some witnesses were less than helpful. The eccentric comedian, Marty Feldman, outraged the judge by insisting that the
Bible was more obscene than *Schoolkids Oz*. Some witnesses
trotted out the old faithful that the obscenity laws would have
banned Shakespeare for his description of the stewing of dead
children in *Titus Andronicus*.

Mortimer ran the defence on the basis that the charges were
an attack on dissent and on those who asked society to reconsider its complacent values and were anxious to build a better
world. In the past, religious dissenters had thundered their de-
nunciations from small chapel pulpits while dressed in dark
clothes:

Now the dissenters wear long hair and colourful clothes
and dream their dreams of another world in small bed
sitting rooms in Notting Hill.

Judge Michael Argyle was not impressed. After six weeks the
jury under the influence of his summing-up took only three
and three-quarter hours to reach their verdicts. On the princi-

pal charge of 'debauching and corrupting the morals of children and young persons and to arouse and implant in their minds lustful and perverted desires', the jury found them not guilty. But they did find the three *Oz* editors guilty under the 1959 Act of publishing an obscene magazine and of sending indecent articles through the post under the 1953 Postal Act. In his summing up, Argyle had echoed the words of Jix nearly 50 years earlier when he quoted from the Book of Matthew:

> But who shall so offend one of these little ones which believe in me, it were better for him that a millstone were hanged about his neck and that he were drowned in the depths of the sea.

Argyle also told the jury that if *Oz* were a window on the hippy world – then windows sometimes needed cleaning.[22]

Much to the amusement of some newspapers, Judge Argyle remanded the three editors for social, mental and medical reports. While they sat in Wandsworth Prison awaiting sentence, their shoulder-length hair was forcibly shorn to regulation prison length. The outcry in the press that greeted the prison haircuts overshadowed Argyle's savage sentencing. He sent Richard Neville down for 15 months and Jim Anderson for 12 months; Felix Dennis – now a major publishing magnate – was given nine months on the insulting grounds that he 'was much less intelligent' than the other two. Among the crowd of 400 who burned the judge in effigy outside the Old Bailey were John Lennon and Yoko Ono. One factor in the severity of sentences may have been a series of death threats that Argyle received. He believed that they had come from the hippies. In fact the wife of the clerk to the court had sent them. She was later to be found guilty of fabricating threatening notes and wasting police time. As Angry Brigade bombs were exploding around London at the time, the threats were taken seriously and Argyle had been heavily guarded against assassination.

The Court of Appeal quashed the obscenity verdict on a

technicality and suspended the original six-month prison sentences for sending indecent articles through the post. John Mortimer had successfully convinced the Appeal Court judges that the naughty bits in *Schoolkids Oz* were so disgusting that the effect was emetic rather than erotic. Geoffrey Robertson in his book *The Justice Game* says that one of the Appeal Court judges sent his clerk, a former merchant seaman, to Soho to buy £20 worth of the strongest pornography he could then find on open sale. He believes that when the Lord Chief Justice, Lord Widgery, saw the strength of what was available, he was persuaded that the contents of *Oz* paled in comparison.[23]

Mary Whitehouse was in no doubt about the importance of the *Oz* trial:

> Thousands of parents who had seen their children's lifestyle changed through the impact of the underground press were only too well aware of its significance. They knew Richard Neville not as some hard done by humorist, but as the editor of *Playpower* which became the handbook of the international dropouts and bemused pot-smoking youngsters, who persuaded them to believe that society was rotten, life was too hard, and the odds too heavily stacked against them and the best thing was to drop out and bum around. The purpose of the underground press is not so much to dissent as to disrupt, and its editorial policies seek to overthrow society as we know it, and of this it makes no secret.[24]

Thirteen Labour MPs, including Tony Benn, put down a Commons early day motion condemning the sentences as 'an act of revenge by the Establishment against dissenting voices'. Neville had claimed that pornography was as important a weapon in the battle for social and cultural revolution as getting British troops out of Northern Ireland or the United States out of Vietnam. As Richard Neville put it in *Hippie Hippie Shake*:

Orgies in Amsterdam were never the key to the New Jerusalem but it was an age of hedonism and, steeped in the sexism of the time, I took to it like a duck to water.[25]

Lord Longford's counter-blast was equally media-wise. The decision to include Cliff Richard and Jimmy Saville alongside Malcolm Muggeridge and Peregrine Worsthorne on his 16-month inquiry into pornography ensured massive publicity. No tabloid newspaper could resist the idea of Lord Longford visiting Copenhagen to see a live sex show in a strip club. They were not to be disappointed as they witnessed a half-naked girl invite the peer to whip her. It was an invitation that he turned down only when her whip was entwined around his neck.

The Longford Report (1972) was a bestseller with its simple 'things have gone too far' message and its claim that 'the public at large' would no longer stand for it. Longford's programme of reform centred on a plan to scrap the public good test in the 1959 obscenity law and replace it with a new *Alice's Adventures in Wonderland* crime of 'outraging contemporary standards of decency'. Longford tried to establish a firm link between pornography and crime and took refuge in Richard Nixon's denunciation of the US Presidential Commission on Pornography. This commission, which had reported in 1970, said the available research evidence demonstrated no significant link between exposure to or use of explicit sexual materials and harmful human behaviour, such as crime, delinquency, sexual deviancy or severe emotional disturbances. The commission recommended that censorship be abolished and adults given the full freedom to read what they wanted. Much of the 'problem' stemmed from the inability of adults to be open and direct in their dealings with sexual matters, it argued. More sex education was what was needed. Longford praised Nixon for rejecting this dangerous permissiveness after the President condemned it as a 'morally bankrupt' report. The debate about the evidence for the existence of a link between porn and crime has not moved much further forward in the intervening years.

The Longford Report was easily ridiculed. *Private Eye* dubbed Longford 'Lord Porn', and even some of its more distinguished authors, such as Kingsley Amis, found the need to put in a dissenting note from its conclusions. But it took evidence from a wide range of sources and gave a valuable account of the then booming nature of the British porn industry, which was expanding exponentially largely under the enterprise of David Sullivan, now the owner of the *Sport* newspapers and Birmingham City Football Club. Longford's report alongside the growth of the born-again Festival of Light set a tone which future politicians, particularly Conservative ones, felt that they could ignore only at risk of the wrath of their constituency associations.

Confidential Home Office papers released to me for the purposes of this book show that the *Oz* trial had ramifications for the Metropolitan Police that the editors of the magazine were totally unaware of at the time. The *Oz* trial, far from being the middle-class 'Yippie' teenage tantrum that it appeared, actually rebounded on the Met to such an extent that it helped create the atmosphere in which a Conservative Home Secretary finally ordered the mid-1970s anti-corruption drive in the police. This purge of Scotland Yard was to lead to the imprisonment of senior officers, up to and including the rank of commander, and hundreds of detectives leaving the force under a cloud of suspicion. The papers, which under the 30-year rule were to be kept secret until 2003, show that the then Home Secretary, Reginald Maudling, was so stung by the criticism that the police were prosecuting *Oz* and the *LRSB* while far worse was being sold unmolested in Soho, that he ordered an internal inquiry.

As the 'personal' letter from Sir Philip Allen, the permanent secretary at the Home Office, to Sir John Waldron, the then Metropolitan Police Commissioner, put it:

> The Home Secretary is a little concerned at the volume of opinion which is asking why certain publications, such as *Oz* and *Red School Book*, are singled out for

prosecution while at the same time not all that much is done about hard core pornography openly on sale on a large scale in Soho. I expect you have heard a good deal to the same effect on the wireless and elsewhere.

Sir John Waldron's reply on 17 August 1971 was a prime example of what James Callaghan was later to describe as his fault of being 'too loyal to some serving under him who were undeserving of his confidence'. Sir John, a rather stiff man with a high standard of personal integrity, said he understood Maudling's difficulties because the view was very much a reflection of what was being said in the national press. First he blamed the journalists: 'The contrariness of the press is illustrated in the tremendous publicity given to the *Oz* and *Little Red Schoolbook* cases but none to the Old Bailey trial' of three men, the Sicka brothers, an Indian family running a network of bookshops and massage parlours, who had been fined £7,500 after pleading guilty to obscenity charges.

Then Sir John blamed the Director of Public Prosecutions:

> My officers are of the opinion that there could be more prosecutions if the Director was so minded but it is appreciated that like everyone else he has a staff problem. About 12 months ago I did contemplate mounting a special exercise to try and clear up the whole of the Soho area, particularly in regard to pornography but because of manpower problems and the liberal view taken in regard to *Love Camp 7* and *Oh! Calcutta!* I decided against it. Officers of C1 act impartially and all papers are submitted to the DPP, it is he who makes the decisions. At the present time I do not consider it justified to add to the present squad of 14 officers all of whom are working diligently and consistently.

Even more interestingly the Metropolitan Commissioner included a report from Detective Chief Inspector George

Fenwick, the officer then in charge of the Obscene Publications Squad, who was later to be sentenced to ten years' imprisonment for receiving bribes from the porn barons. Fenwick explained why the police had targeted *Oz*:

> In this country at the minute there are somewhere in the region of 80 publications which advocate what in the current idiom is called the alternative society. These are published at varying intervals according to circulation figures and money available.
>
> Of these about 25 can be termed 'Underground' press and a number of them contain articles which can be described as indecent. However by far the worst of these are '*Oz*', '*Frendz*' and '*IT*' in that order. These in fact are the only ones against whom action has been taken or indeed contemplated in the last 12 months.

Detective Chief Inspector Fenwick noted that alongside the rise of these underground magazines, 'sex instructional' literature had also emerged, into which category he placed the *LRSB* and magazines such as *Curious*, *In Depth*, *New Directions* and *Forum*. The last had amongst its later distinguished contributors Tony Blair's press secretary, Alastair Campbell. 'All have been subject of enquiry or prosecution by this department during the past year,' said Fenwick. 'Apart from the *Little Red Schoolbook* which advocates a change in the structure of society, they deal solely with sex.'

Fenwick then made an astonishing admission:

> It is an unfortunate fact of life that pornography has existed for centuries and it is unlikely that it can ever be stamped out. It is in this situation that the current legislation was passed making an offence to publish or possess for gain an obscene publication but accepting the right of an individual to possess pornography for his own gratification. I would rather question the assertion that pornography was on 'open sale' in Soho or indeed

anywhere else in London on a large scale. I would
however agree that it can be found in various bookshops
when it is particularly asked for.

Had this explanation been made public at the time, no doubt it
would have been a distinction lost on Mary Whitehouse or
indeed the supporters of *Oz*. It did not impress the Old Bailey
judge, Mr Justice Mars-Jones, when later he sent Detective
Chief Inspector George Fenwick down for ten years along with
four of his colleagues.

In his report to the Home Secretary, Fenwick went on to
give his own explanation as to why *Oz* and the *LRSB* were
prosecuted:

> Both publications deal in some way with children and
> the statute book has always contained laws which
> specifically protect the young. The Obscene Publications
> Act does not draw this distinction, but it may
> nevertheless be felt they are still entitled to all the
> protection the law can provide.
>
> Complaints from members of the public regarding *Oz*
> started to arrive in this office on 27 June 1967 and
> continued through the various issues until No 28 which
> the DPP considered obscene. At his request the premises
> of *Oz* were raided on June 8 1970 which resulted in the
> recent prosecutions.

The rest of Fenwick's report to Maudling details the Met's claim
that it had submitted more than 350 obscenity cases for action to
the DPP but prosecutions followed in only 43 of them. The
Home Office was highly sceptical of these figures.

The real reason why the police prosecuted only the hippies
while letting the Soho pornographers off free is contained in
the replies from the DPP, Sir Norman Skelhorn, to Maudling's
inquiry. He pointed out that this was because as far as most Soho
bookshops were concerned it was true.

'The traders in hard-core pornography appeared to escape with nothing more than the destruction of the material in question,' said a Home Office minute of a meeting with the DPP. Within months the Home Office was to be questioning whether this disclaimer system, which was the cause of much police bribery, was itself the right side of the law. The DPP said that he had always had reservations about whether it was legal but said it had proved 'a convenient method of saving the time of all those concerned and of achieving the result contemplated by the statute'.

As for the harassment of the underground press, Sir Norman explained that when the 1959 Act was going through Parliament, undertakings had been given that a publisher who was determined to carry on publishing the material would be given the opportunity to be tried before a jury. In the case of the Soho bookshop owners, they simply regarded the seizure of their magazines as a hazard of their trade and let it go. The net result was that there were few prosecutions of Soho porn merchants and a series of high-profile court cases that put the middle-class hippie establishment on trial.

In this atmosphere it was no wonder that, as the Home Office put it, the apparent inviolability of Soho continued to excite comment, which was reinforced by allegations that the position in Soho might be attributable to police corruption. The alarm inside the Home Office was reinforced by an article in the *London Evening News* on 19 August 1971, which quoted 'senior Yardmen' saying they did not believe the *Oz* trial would herald a new crackdown on porn. The 'permissive society' had arrived and there could be no turning back. Such cases consumed too many personnel and 'one can go into Soho today and see far worse pornography than was in the *Oz* magazines. Any child can buy it,' one unenthusiastic officer was quoted as saying. It was no surprise that when specific allegations of police corruption were made in the winter of 1971 by a consultant employed as a by-product of Lord Longford's pornography inquiry, Reginald Maudling took them very seriously.

Longford's investigator, a private detective called Matthew Oliver, named seven men running the pornography trade, alleged that they had bribed police officers and that one of them had given parties attended by members of the Obscene Publications Squad. Oliver also identified a number of Soho bookshops that he alleged were immune from police attentions on the grounds of corruption. The Home Secretary demanded a full report after the allegations had been aired in the *Sunday People* newspaper. But the firm at the Yard was more than up to parrying the blow. The police interviewed five of the seven men named by Oliver. The Home Office file says that these rigorous in-depth interrogations included speaking to one of the men on the telephone in Dublin. No allegations of corruption were substantiated. All denied making payments to the police, or owning any Soho bookshops: 'The police report seems disposed to take these denials at their face value,' said the Home Office.

The result of the other Scotland Yard inquiries was equally fruitless:

> The investigating officer questioned every existing
> member of the obscene publications section, and
> employees at 33 of the shops listed by Oliver as selling
> pornography in Soho. These enquiries proved negative.
> Every officer denied any suggestion of a bribe, and those
> interviewed in the shops denied that they had ever been
> asked for, or offered a bribe. The report shows that,
> contrary to Oliver's allegations, all the shops in question
> had in fact been raided a number of times in recent years
> and material seized on most of these occasions.

The counterattack was not to succeed for long. In February 1972 the *Sunday People* carried details of a holiday enjoyed by James Humphreys, one of the seven pornography barons named by Oliver. He had just returned from two weeks in Cyprus with Commander Kenneth Drury, the head of the Met's Flying Squad. Both men had taken their wives and Humphreys had paid the hotel bill in Famagusta and the cost of a two-day jaunt to Beirut. Drury claimed they were looking for Ronnie Biggs, the escaped Great Train robber. Initially the newly released Home Office files show that the official view was that the relationship between Drury and Humphreys was 'almost certainly not corrupt though it plainly was a colossal misjudgment'. But as a more detailed investigation got under way ordered by the new Metropolitan Commissioner, Robert Mark, it was in the end to prove enough to reveal the operations of a 'firm within a firm' and the existence of systemic corruption at the heart of the police. By 1976, when Roy Jenkins was once again Home Secretary, nearly 400 officers had been dismissed or left the force voluntarily during the course of criminal or disciplinary inquiries. At least ten faced criminal trials, including Detective Chief Inspector George Fenwick.

When the Old Bailey judge, Mr Justice Mars-Jones, sent Fenwick down for ten years along with four of his colleagues for having been in the pay of the porn barons for years, he described him as 'the arch villain' in the whole affair. 'Thank goodness the Obscene Publications Squad has gone. I fear the damage you have done may be with us for a long time,' said the judge at the end of the first of three separate porn squad trials.

It was an outcome which the radical left in Britain has long speculated about but even the staunchest hippie supporter of *Oz* magazine could not have possibly had an inkling that there was a direct link between their court battle over Rupert the Bear and the jailing of the very officers charged with enforcing the obscenity laws against them.

From *Deep Throat* to 'Reclaim the Night'

Growing concern about the retreat of the law from the field of pornography and obscenity reached a peak in January 1976 with the acquittal at the Old Bailey of the publisher of *Inside Linda Lovelace*. The high quality of the publisher's legal team of John Mortimer and Geoffrey Robertson was not matched by the book that they had to defend. Its style was that of a confessional diary on the theme of oral sex, buggery and the use of vibrators, with Linda Lovelace claiming that as the star of the film, *Deep Throat*, she was as famous in the United States as Henry Kissinger. The British publisher of *Last Exit to Brooklyn*, Marion Boyars, claimed at the trial that *Lovelace*'s oral philosophy allowed women the active participation in sexual pleasure previously monopolised by men.

Among the other defence experts called by Mortimer and Robertson was the journalist Anna Coote, who testified that it was an honest book which put forward a positive attitude to sex. Others in the witness box included Johnny Speight, the creator of Alf Garnett, and Dr Lionel Howard, a consultant forensic psychologist. The hearing attracted the biggest press coverage for an obscenity case since the *Oz* trial and the jury's decision to acquit led to some hyperbole. The Metropolitan Police declared that if they could not get a conviction from a jury for *Linda Lovelace* then it was unlikely the law would be invoked again against the printed word. Both the judge and the police took the view that it would be difficult to imagine what written material a jury would regard as obscene.

If there were any lingering doubts amongst liberals about the deeply cynical nature of the ghosted memoirs, *Inside Linda Lovelace*, they were dispelled by the publication of a second volume. This was also ghost-written, but now Linda Lovelace or rather Linda Boreman was portrayed as a born-again Christian who described her previous life as one of being regularly beaten and raped and forced to perform regularly for private parties and the film cameras. In Parliament, the Conservative opposition used the resulting furore from the collapse of the prosecution to mount an attack on the state of the obscenity laws. It was the same complaint that was heard after the *Lady Chatterley* trial. Why had the Crown not matched the defence expert for expert, they demanded to know, and they drew a link between the failure of the prosecution and the activities of the Cambridge Rapist. This was a notorious serial rapist who had taken to wearing a hood inscribed with the word 'Rapist'; he told the police it saved time on the introductions.

The architect of the 1959 Obscene Publications Act, Roy Jenkins, was once again Home Secretary and the Conservatives saw it as a useful stick to beat the prime creator of the permissive society. A number of private members' bills were introduced by Tory backbenchers trying to reform the law to ensure that it was literature and not pornography that it protected. Meanwhile the Law Commission was pressing for action in exactly the opposite direction and recommending the abolition of the offence of 'conspiracy to corrupt public morals'. Jenkins turned to a Royal Commission under the philosopher and Provost of King's College, Cambridge, Professor Bernard Williams, to try to inject some sense into this increasingly confused debate.

The sense that the obscenity laws were in full-scale retreat was reinforced in the autumn of 1976 and spring of 1977 with the start of three major corruption trials involving the Met's Obscene Publications Squad. The evidence that came out was truly shocking to the general public. Pornographers were being 'licensed to trade' in exchange for large bribes, which were systematically shared out amongst the officers. The 'licensed' porn merchants were given early warning of impending raids – W.H. Smith or Rymans were common codewords indicating the clean standard that the stock had to meet – or were invited to buy back the publications that had been seized. It seemed that as with prohibition in 1920s America, the corruption unleashed by the law was actually worse than the crime it was designed to prevent.

In this atmosphere Mary Whitehouse, Raymond Blackburn and other members of an organisation called the Responsible Society continued to look for ways of stemming the moral decline of Britain. Despite years of onslaught, the BBC's charter had left it immune from their attempts to initiate private prosecutions under the Obscenity or Theatre Acts. Mrs Whitehouse had considered using the archaic blasphemy laws against a 1972 episode of *Till Death Us Do Part* in which Alf Garnett asked: 'Wot abaht yer virgin berf, then?' The BBC's charter prevented such actions. But by the mid-1970s Downing Street was no longer losing Mrs Whitehouse's letters. Her share price had risen considerably. Her opportunity came when a Danish porno filmmaker proposed to make *The Many Faces of Christ* in London after the Vatican had complained about the project when it was to be filmed in Copenhagen. Mrs Whitehouse prevented its arrival on British shores after securing assurances from the Prime Minister, James Callaghan, and the Archbishops of Canterbury and Westminster that this Danish blasphemer would be repulsed.

So when in June 1976, *Gay News* published a poem by James Kirkup called 'The Love That Dares to Speak its Name', it seemed she could do no wrong. The title and its theme were taken from Lord Alfred Douglas's sonnet about guilt and homosexuality that was quoted in evidence against Oscar Wilde at his

The Love That Dares To Speak Its Name *by James Kirkup. Still banned in Britain as blasphemous.*

trial. Printed alongside the poem was a large illustration of the corpse of Christ being lowered by a Roman centurion from the Cross. It depicted Christ with a large penis. The poem suggested that the Roman left alone with the 'well-hung' body before burial had revived the corpse one final time and engaged in an act of buggery. The poem's metaphysical conceit reflecting

Christ's love for all mankind was, for the prosecution, its worst stanzas. They were simply too odious for words. They ran:

> For the last time
> I laid my lips around the tip
> Of that great cock, the instrument
> Of our salvation, our eternal joy.
> The shaft still throbbed, anointed
> With death's final ejaculation.
>
> I knew he'd had it off with other men –
> with Herod's guards, with Pontius Pilate,
> with John the Baptist, with Paul of Tarsus,
> with foxy Judas, a great kisser, with
> the rest of all the twelve, together and apart.
> He loved all men, body, soul and spirit – even me.

The centurion then went on to embrace the body of Christ in a section which the judge said was so profane not even the defence counsel, Geoffrey Robertson, dared to read it out in court:

> And then the miracle possessed us.
> I felt him enter into me, and fiercely spend
> his spirit's final seed within my hole, my soul,
> pulse upon pulse, unto the ends of the earth –
> he crucified me with him into kingdom come.[1]

Mrs Whitehouse felt that the *Gay News* poem was the 'climax of anti-religious attacks. I had to do something.' She took out a private prosecution for blasphemous libel against Denis Lemon, the editor of *Gay News*, in November 1976. The author, James Kirkup, was left alone once the Viewers' and Listeners' Association had discovered he was a university professor and Fellow of the Royal Society of Literature. It was a development that shocked liberal Britain. Nobody had been convicted for blasphemy since

1921 when John William Gott published a secularist pamphlet which claimed that Christ had entered Jerusalem like a circus clown astride the backs of two donkeys. Mr Justice Argyle, sentencing Gott to nine months' hard labour, told him that any person of strong religious feelings who read his pamphlet would instinctively want to give him a thrashing. He died soon after completing his sentence.

Again John Mortimer and Geoffrey Robertson were leading the defence team. John Smyth appeared for Mrs Whitehouse. As this was a blasphemy case, the judge ruled that no expert witnesses were to be allowed. Instead Geoffrey Robertson tried to get round the ban by calling Margaret Drabble and Bernard Levin to testify to the good moral character of Mr Lemon and of *Gay News*. The prosecution argued that its blasphemy was self-evident, while the defence wondered whether the whole courtroom had not been transported by some time machine back to the Middle Ages. The jury was out for five hours before they returned a split ten to two majority verdict of guilty.

Judge King-Hamilton in sentencing Denis Lemon to a suspended nine months' prison sentence and a £500 fine said that he had no doubt that the poem was quite appalling and was the most scurrilous profanity. The judge acknowledged that it had been touch-and-go whether Denis Lemon was sent to prison. He told the court:

> It is past my comprehension that a man like James
> Kirkup can express himself in this way and that the paper
> should publish it with reckless disregard for the feelings
> of Christians and non-Christian sympathisers.[2]

The defence took the judge's failure to take into account the intention of the defendant in publishing the poem all the way to the House of Lords. But the final appeal was rejected by the Law Lords by three votes to two with Lord Scarman arguing that the blasphemy law should be updated to cover all religions, not just the Anglican Church.

It was perhaps the zenith of Mrs Whitehouse's powers, although the censorship debate has continued under her shadow. *Gay News* flourished after the trial. The hearing had revived the idea of a private prosecution for blasphemy. It was a precedent that was to fuel the Salman Rushdie affair a decade later when a section of the Muslim community tried to persuade the Bow Street magistrate to issue a summons against the author of *The Satanic Verses* for blasphemous libel. The magistrate refused on the grounds that the blasphemy law applies only to the Christian religion. There was an appeal to the High Court which started with the judge and counsel all receiving a badly-written death threat. But it did not stop Lord Justice Watkins confirming that the blasphemy law did not cover Islam. The Home Office announced in 1989 there would be no future blasphemy prosecutions by the state, but the law still remains on the statute book.

The full aftermath of the *Gay News* ruling was seen outside London. In Greater Manchester, the evangelical Chief Constable, James Anderton, who made no secret of his belief that pornography was sinful, conducted some 355 raids under the obscenity laws in 16 months. Not even W.H. Smith was safe. Amongst the magazines seized were *Men Only*, *Mayfair* and *Penthouse*. In Leicester, the magistrates tried to ban the Sex Pistols' album, *Never Mind the Bollocks, Here's the Sex Pistols*, on the grounds that putting it in a record shop window amounted to an indecent display. After the etymology of the English word 'bollocks' had passed the equivalent of Norman Tebbit's cricket test, the magistrates reluctantly threw out the charge.

The main significance of the post-*Gay News* ruling was Mary Whitehouse's successful campaign to put the evils of what she called 'kiddie porn' on the agenda of the new Conservative Leader of the Opposition, Mrs Margaret Thatcher. Mrs Whitehouse claimed that Britain was in danger of being swamped from the United States with pornography involving children as young as three. The campaign was taken up by the Festival of Light and found widespread support in the press and with head

teachers. When Cyril Townsend, the Conservative MP for Bex-
leyheath, brought forward his Protection of Children Bill, few
MPs could resist joining the moral stampede and the bill quickly
made it on to the statute book. It was to be some time before
the police took a serious interest in the activities of the Paedophile Information Exchange and the wider subject of
endemic child abuse.

On the eve of the election of the first Thatcher government
it was obvious to all that the political atmosphere had under-
gone something of a radical change since Roy Jenkins had appointed his Royal Commission. He had asked the Cambridge
philosopher, Professor Bernard Williams, to review the law on
obscenity, indecency and violence and to look at the way film
censorship operated in Britain. When the inquiry completed its
two-year investigation and reported in October 1979, there was
no longer a Labour government. Mrs Thatcher and her Conservative Home Secretary, Willie Whitelaw, were never going to
give it a warm welcome. Yet it remains perhaps the best analysis
of the problem in Britain and deserves to be taken off the top
shelf of the Home Office cabinet, where it has languished for
too long, and once again given serious consideration.

Williams agreed with Lord Longford's unofficial inquiry that
for many years the law on obscenity had been in retreat and
recognised that the *Inside Linda Lovelace* judgment had left large
parts of the 1959 Obscene Publications Act unworkable.[3] It was
unlikely that ever again the written word would find itself the
subject of an obscenity conviction in Britain. From there the
two inquiries parted company. Professor Williams and his 12
committee colleagues, including the *Guardian* columnist, Polly
Toynbee, a retired chief constable and a bishop, reached their
conclusions after a cool, elegant and incisive analysis of the
problem.

They decided that what was needed was to limit the availability and public display of pornographic publications, but to
make all but a small class of hard-core pornography, involving
child exploitation and physical injury, available in restricted

circumstances. This would mean that designated adult-only cinemas and Swedish-style licensed sex shops in restricted circumstances could show material that was more hard-core than that legally available in the UK at that time. The shops could 'announce their nature but not allow their contents to be seen'. The aim was not to ban what could not be suppressed but to remove it from public view and control access behind closed doors or plain paper wrappers. It recognised that the public had a legitimate interest in not being offended by the display and availability of material. In other words, 'not in our face, thank you'.

The Williams committee also suggested a new definition of obscenity. Material which would be illegal was that which was 'offensive to reasonable people by reason of the way it portrays or deals with violence, cruelty or horror, or sexual, faecal, or urinary functions or genital organs'.[4] It was proposed that there should be safeguards to protect children and animals. Films or videos showing real acts of torture or the mythic 'snuff movies' would also remain illegal. This definition was much wider than traditional official notions of obscenity and recognised that society no longer saw it simply as a matter of sex alone. Nevertheless for some critics it did not go far enough. They complained that it did not embrace incitement to racial hatred, which actually was already on the statute book as a crime and had been incorporated into the 1968 Theatres Act.

The Williams committee acknowledged that the state of law on obscenity was in complete chaos. It was necessary to start all over again. The existing jungle of contradictory laws needed to be scrapped and replaced by one comprehensive new statute. Its object should be to prevent certain kinds of material causing offence to reasonable people or being made available to young people. The confused and vague terms of 'obscene', 'indecent' and 'deprave and corrupt' had outlived their usefulness. Williams argued that what was important was not to ask whether the material caused depravity or was evil but to question what harm it did and whether more harm would be done if it was banned.

The report concluded:

> Only a small class of material should be forbidden to
> those who want it, because an objective assessment of
> likely harm does not support a wider prohibition.[5]

Williams would allow no censorship of books and the printed
word. He believed that the

> written word should be neither restricted nor prohibited
> since its nature makes it neither immediately offensive
> nor capable of involving the harms we identify, and
> because of its importance in conveying ideas.[6]

The theme that runs through these proposals is that what is offensive to reasonable people should not be thrust in front of
them – but that people who are not offended by the material
concerned should not be denied access to them. Their study of
the market for pornography led them to believe that it was not
just a few perverts who used pornography but that around 4
million people had read some kind of porn magazine in the last
month. This market for porn was changing and with it ideas of
what was offensive to the reasonable person. Williams argued
that this 'community standard', as the courts in the United States
dubbed it, was far more useful and objective in coping with
those changes in taste than the confused and subjective 'deprave
and corrupt' language of the 1959 Act.

Williams considered that most pornography was trash, ugly,
shallow and obvious. He added that its 'tastelessness and depress-
ing awfulness' made it easy for its critics to attack it as responsible for all sorts of other evils as well. He reasoned that such
attacks on pornography might really be assaults on other cultural changes that were 'new, unfamiliar, and perhaps threatening', but which were not caused by pornography. This view rests
principally upon the question of whether or not there is a strong
link between the use of pornography and crime. The Williams

committee, as had the US Presidential Commission before it, concluded that this link was not proven. The Williams report said:

> Clinical opinion and our impression of the anecdotal evidence cohere: the cases in which a link between pornography and crime has even been suggested are remarkably few.
>
> Given the amount of explicit sexual material in circulation and the allegations often made about its effects, it is striking that one can study case after case of sex crimes and murder without finding any hint at all that pornography was present in the background.[7]

The committee said that its 'expert witnesses had more reservation about violent material, though again we heard no direct evidence of cases in which it was considered that crime had resulted from a particular stimulus'. The report was particularly dismissive of press speculation that in cases such as the Cambridge Rapist, sex crimes had been the result of reading pornographic material.

This debate has raged for as long as the argument over censorship itself. In the mid-1960s the works of the Marquis de Sade were cited as an influence on the Moors murderers, Myra Hindley and Ian Brady. In the early 1990s, a senior police officer investigating the murder of two-year-old James Bulger suggested that a video, *Child's Play 3*, in which a small boy was killed, might have been a factor in the case; this prompted renewed debate and research into the existence of such a link. The latest Home Office research looking at the viewing habits of convicted teenage offenders and the effect of their watching violent videos was published in 1998. It concluded that violent teenagers did indeed have a taste for violent videos. But it said that the most important factor was whether they came from violent homes. In the absence of any background of family violence, there was no significant relationship between offending and

preference for violent films and character. The debate will no
doubt continue, with the next serious research to be published
looking at the 'drip-drip effect' of computer games on teenagers.

The Williams committee said that the broadest arguments
put to it as to social harm caused by pornography were 'in terms
of cultural pollution, moral deterioration and the undermining
of human compassion, social values and basic institutions'. It
said, though, that there was often real difficulty in identifying
what the harmful effect of the material was supposed to be.

> And whether indeed it is really an effect of the materials
> circulating that is in question rather than the circulation
> itself which is regarded as intrinsically an objectionable
> thing ... it may be an expression rather than a cause of
> an undesirable state of society.[8]

The reception that the Williams report got left its authors
feeling bitter. It was out of sympathy with the times. Some
critics complained that its deep analysis had little to say about
the impact of the latest 'menace' – the growing ownership of
video recorders at home.

To a future chairman of the Conservative Party, Dr Brian
Mawhinney, it was nothing less than a 'pornographer's charter',
while Mary Whitehouse claimed that Williams had been 'unbe-
lievably naïve'. Willie Whitelaw was more modest in his language than Richard Nixon had been in rejecting the US
Presidential Commission on Pornography. He nevertheless
made his attitude clear. In a Commons debate on 16 January
1980, he said that there would be 'no early action' on Williams.
Instead a private members' bill banning 'indecent displays' first
proposed by the Conservative Home Secretary, Robert Carr, in
1974 was revived and pushed through Parliament by Tim Sains-
bury, the Conservative MP for Hove. All the difficulties in defin-
ing such words as 'indecent' raised by Williams immediately
became apparent. The Soho sex shops seized on the new
measure when it became law at the end of 1981. Instead of per-

secuting them they loved it. Every shop window, regardless of the 'strength' of the stock, carried a notice: 'Warning, sexually explicit material inside. Do not enter if you are easily offended.' Business boomed again.

Nevertheless Mary Whitehouse was in buoyant form and when the last Conservative leader of the Greater London Council, Sir Horace Cutler, walked out of the first night of Howard Brenton's play, *The Romans in Britain*, at the National Theatre, she felt once again the call to carry out God's work. On 17 October 1980 she wrote in her diary:

> Three Roman soldiers are apparently tearing off all their clothes and raping three young, male Britons in full view of the audience. It has been known for two thousand years how the Romans – some of them – behaved in Britain. We haven't needed to wait all those years for the National Theatre to come and show us.[9]

The abolition of theatre censorship in 1968 had specifically barred prosecutions by private individuals and when the Attorney-General, Sir Michael Havers, refused to take action himself or give his permission for a private prosecution in the case of Howard Brenton's play, Mrs Whitehouse had to turn elsewhere. And so yet another piece of legislation was invoked against an artistic enterprise, albeit one that was regarded as execrable by the critics. Some objected to its agitprop analogy with the British army's role in Northern Ireland. By the time the attack came, it was as much a political assault by the new Thatcherite ascendancy flexing its moral muscles as it was a defence of a drive to defend a 'decent Christian society'. The moral crusaders found the loophole they were looking for in an obscure clause of the 1956 Sexual Offences Act. This was more often used against the practice of 'cottaging' in public lavatories than against a play at Britain's major theatre. Mrs Whitehouse secured a summons against the director, Michael Bogdanov, for 'procuring an act of gross indecency between two actors'.

In the scene in question the three Roman soldiers come upon three naked Druids. They kill two and the third soldier grabs the wounded third, MARBAN, and holding his thighs 'attempts to bugger him'. But after complaining that he won't 'keep his fucking arse still' it seems his penis has slipped out. As the script puts it:

THIRD SOLDIER. This in't no – in't no – at all –
SECOND SOLDIER. In trouble, comrade?
THIRD SOLDIER. In't no arse at all.
The THIRD SOLDIER *rolls away.* MARBAN *begins to struggle.*
MARBAN. Hunh hunh hunh –
THIRD SOLDIER. Not even got it up anymore!
MARBAN. Hunh hunh –
The SECOND SOLDIER *hits* MARBAN *on the top of the head with the butt of his sword.*
MARBAN *is knocked unconscious. His left leg twitches twice then is still.*
A silence.
THIRD SOLDIER. Oh. (*He sits up.*) Oh oh.
SECOND SOLDIER. I said, are you in trouble comrade?
THIRD SOLDIER. Arseful of piles. Like fucking a fistful of marbles. I mean, what do they do in this island, sit with their bums in puddles of mud all year long?
He stands.
And I'm covered in shit.
…
THIRD SOLDIER. I don't want you talking about this.
SECOND SOLDIER. Did I say a word?
THIRD SOLDIER. I don't want to hear a word.
SECOND SOLDIER. If that's your attitude.
THIRD SOLDIER. Marcus Clavius. I do not want to hear, one night out drinking, back home, years from now on a lovely evening, surrounded by admirers, sons. I do not want to hear – of me not getting it up a British arseful

of piles. Right?
SECOND SOLDIER. Right.
THIRD SOLDIER. I know how rumours start.[10]

Mary Whitehouse versus the National Theatre at the Old Bailey was the kind of trial few in the media could resist. Yet it never got off the ground. Graham Ross-Cornes, Mrs Whitehouse's solicitor, had claimed that he had seen the actor playing the Roman soldier hold his penis in an apparently erect position, put it between the wounded Druid's legs and make a number of thrusting movements. All this was done under bright lighting. But at the trial, under cross-examination by Lord Hutchinson, Mr Ross-Cornes revealed he had sat in the back row some 90 yards from the stage and had to admit that what he saw might not have been an apparently erect penis at all but the actor's thumb. Sir Peter Hall, the director of the National Theatre, gave evidence that the attempted rape was as horrifying as the gouging out of Gloucester's eyes in *King Lear* and was a precise metaphor about the brutality of colonialism. As the Attorney-General announced the withdrawal of the prosecution, Mrs Whitehouse insisted that she had made her point. She had won a judicial ruling that such a private prosecution of a play was possible, but it was to be her last outing to the Old Bailey, even if there was to prove plenty of life in the old moral crusader yet.

The utter chaos of the obscenity laws in Britain that continues to this day was highlighted yet again in the mid-1980s with one of the more bizarre Customs operations. Once again the powers used were under the 1876 Customs Consolidated Act, which gives the authorities the power to seize 'indecent and obscene' articles without any of the public good or literary and artistic safeguards available in the 1959 Act. This new Whitehall farce in 1985 went under the Customs codename of Operation 'Tiger'. It involved charging the directors of Gay's The Word bookshop in Bloomsbury, London, with conspiracy to import 142 indecent books. The operation involved 35 Customs officers over an 18-month period. Works by Tennessee Williams and

Gore Vidal ended up in the net 'because they had the name of a homosexual author on the cover' alongside some old, previously cleared, war-horses by Henry Miller, Jean Genet, William Burroughs and J.P. Donleavy. It was as though the battles of the previous 30 years had never taken place and had been expunged from history by Customs and Excise.

The case eventually collapsed after a European Court judgment involving German inflatable sex dolls had ruled that imports from the European Union to Britain could not be banned by Customs if they were not already illegal in Britain. Amongst the other books seized were works by Allen Ginsberg, Truman Capote, Armistead Maupin and even Kate Millett. It was a stern warning that the claim that the obscenity laws were no longer used to suppress literature was mistaken. This was reinforced again in 1996 when Customs once more used its arcane powers under the 1876 Act to try to ban the work of the American cartoonist, Robert Crumb, from being imported into Britain. Crumb, whose work had featured in the *Oz* trial and who had created *Fritz the Cat* and *Mr Natural,* was cleared of obscenity charges only after a year-long battle which ended when the Uxbridge magistrates in West London ruled his book, *My Trouble with Women,* was not obscene.

In the late 1980s the argument took on a fresh lease of life as new, wider definitions of obscenity clamoured to be acted upon. This impetus came from the feminist movement, which by the late 1970s had achieved a new coherence and sophistication. Women saw pornography as a typically unpleasant male pastime, which unquestionably exploited women. As in the wider debate, there was little consensus about what to do about it. In the early 1980s some radical feminists had tried to 'Reclaim the Night' by photographing men entering and leaving sex shops, daubing their windows and supergluing their locks, and sticking 'Sexist Crap' stickers on advertisements for Bond films.

The British publication in 1981 of Andrea Dworkin's *Pornography: Men Possessing Women* and Susan Griffin's *Pornography and*

Silence were both hugely influential in stimulating this debate. Dworkin starkly argued that 'the Left cannot have its whores and its politics too'. She consciously went one step beyond the traditional maxim that pornography is to rape as theory is to practice to go on to claim that pornography is tantamount to rape itself.[11] In the United States in 1983, Andrea Dworkin and Catherine McKinnon drafted an amendment to the Minneapolis Civil Rights Ordinance, which said that pornography was a form of discrimination based on sex and so was a fundamental infringement of civil rights. The idea was that once Minneapolis had adopted the ordinance, women and children could pursue civil actions against pornographers and their distributors on the grounds that they had suffered direct harm. It was justified on the grounds that women had been coerced into pornographic performances to produce it; that women had been forced to see pornography in their daily lives, and that women had been assaulted and attacked as a result of pornography. The Minneapolis City Council passed the ordinance but after a four-year battle the Supreme Court ruled it unconstitutional in 1988. This ruling also prevented any similar law being passed anywhere else in the United States.

11

The film censor: the last of the old-time regulators?

When James Ferman, Britain's last chief film censor, or classifier as he preferred to be known, stepped down in 1999 after spending 23 years in his Soho Square screening room, he reflected that the British public had grown to accept increasingly frank depictions of sex on the screen. His verdict reflected the steady liberalisation of erotic content in both film and video throughout the 1990s. Ferman wrote in his final report to Parliament as the director of British Board of Film Classification (BBFC):

> No sexual image has been cut from any mainstream
> cinema film since 1989, and explicit sex education
> videos, gay and straight, have become commonplace on
> the shelves of W.H. Smith's. But sex education is not
> pornography, which has a different function. The role of
> censorship in this area seems to me to be one of limiting
> the kinds of fantasy that porn inspires. That is why we
> have stressed the importance of non-violent sex between
> consenting adults. The problem that remains is where to
> draw the line on explicitness. It is a problem I have failed
> to resolve, and I wish my successors well in dealing with
> it.[1]

Burn your video nasties. *Front page,* The Sun, *November 26 1993.*

That thorny issue of where to draw the line on explicitness was to lead to a behind-the-scenes clash between the BBFC and the Home Secretary, Jack Straw. That scrap saw the Labour Home Secretary try to roll back the liberal tide, if only by a few feet, and was to prove an important marker for the kind of regulatory framework that would shape the multimedia future. We shall look at this episode in more detail later.

If sex still had the power to provoke fierce political battles, Ferman was surely on firmer ground when he argued that it was

the screen depiction of violence that now worried most people
and represented the thorniest problem for the censor. He asked:

> To what extent should the goal of free speech vindicate
> scenes of brutality and blood-letting? Even in America,
> judges have begun to wonder if the legal test of 'clear and
> present danger' is any longer adequate to stem the drip-
> drip effect of 'designer violence' on inner-city teenagers
> with access to guns.[2]

This is a debate that intensified after the 1999 Columbine High
School mass shooting in Colorado which, to the disgust of
some, sparked a more intense debate over the violent face of the
modern Hollywood movie than any actual reassessment of the
absurd gun control laws in the United States.

Ferman, whose BBFC is paid for by the film industry, always
liked to portray himself as the industry's conscience rather than
its protector. Yet he explicitly distanced himself from the more
liberal view of his predecessor, John Trevelyan, that the board
could not assume responsibility for the guardianship of public
morality. Ferman said he had once agreed with Trevelyan on that
point but had changed his mind:

> I realised that public morality is actually at the centre of
> our concerns and must remain there. If we don't want
> entertainment to influence human behaviour in a
> harmful or anti-social direction, then we can only
> intervene on grounds of public morality.[3]

Ferman had been responsible for film to be brought within the
terms of the Obscene Publications Act in 1977. This meant that
directors could at last mount a public good defence on the
grounds of artistic merit and that the courts, as well as the board,
had to consider the film as a whole and not just face condemnation on the strength of a particular clip.

The influence of the Williams committee has had an enduring effect in this area as well. As a result of the 1999 Human Rights Act, which incorporates the European Convention of Human Rights into British law, 'harm' has replaced 'offensiveness' as the prescribed legal test to be used when censors place limits on freedom of speech by insisting on cuts or refusing a film a certificate. The Convention has explicitly written the right to freedom of expression into British law for the first time. But it also includes a separate article that makes clear that that freedom can be curtailed by the state on the grounds of the 'prevention of crime or disorder' or the 'protection of health or morals'. In the case of film and video, this covers a large amount of ground, especially the protection of health and morals. This means that it is not just sex, violence and horror that are considered potentially harmful but also the depiction of criminal behaviour and the use of illegal drugs. Sexual violence is regarded as the most disturbing and potentially harmful by the law. It is to be hoped that these legal phrases will have a happier life than the confused history of the 'deprave and corrupt' test in the 1959 legislation that the BBFC has long told its classifiers and the film industry that it interprets as meaning 'making morally bad'.

At first sight it is surprising how much power the BBFC wields within the film industry when it is realised that the board has no statutory authority from Parliament to decide what should not be shown on British cinema screens. In fact that statutory power belongs to the 350 local authorities whose duty it is to license cinemas in their areas. When the board was set up in 1912 by the film industry, it was to get round the problem of the censorship lottery created by the local licensing committees and which made national distribution impossible. Local authorities were mostly only too willing to pass this controversial task over to the board, although they still retain the power to override its decisions in their particular area. For example, some local authorities classified Mrs Doubtfire (1993) as a PG rather than the BBFC's recommended 12-certificate after pressure from local parents' groups. Westminster and Camden councils in London have often demonstrated their independence from the BBFC. Camden, for example, licensed the showing of *The Story of O* and *Texas Chainsaw Massacre* as 18-certificate films in its cinemas long before the board got round to similar decisions.

As he left his job, Ferman made clear that his main concern had been to curb the excessive violence in modern American screen entertainment. He was particularly disturbed that the European and Asian film industries were beginning to ape this US trend and were doing so merely for commercial gain.

> In Britain, we held the line on violence, particularly on video, but a new generation may have different views. My instinct is still to reduce the level of violence in action adventure films, simply to have less of it. Too often in my view it functions like a drug, like the pounding beat of rock music which keeps the serotonin levels up. I worry that violence has so little meaning, that younger cinemagoers take the view that 'violence is cool', a view which seems to me to be simply an excuse for not empathising with the victims.[4]

This is plainly a censor with a social conscience speaking and a generation and a million miles away from the attitude of Lord Cobbold, the last Lord Chamberlain, with his anxiety to protect the reputations of the royal family and of the heads of state of friendly foreign powers.

The chief film censor has no statutory powers of his own. His authority to classify films is delegated to him and his expert examiners by the hundreds of local authorities around Britain, which alone have the right to decide what it shown within their municipal boundaries. His power to censor videos, and for that matter computer games and digital CD-ROMs, is delegated to him by the Home Secretary. The film and the porn industries are prepared to submit their output for classification only because it is cheaper, easier and the outcome more certain, than the alternative of risking prosecution in the courts under the

Obscene Publications Act. All this makes the chief film censor a more powerful figure than even the Lord Chamberlain was in his heyday. A softly spoken Cambridge-educated American, Ferman was a former television director who had suffered his own share of heavy-handed censorship in his day. He believed that during his quarter-century he turned the BBFC from a board of censors to a board of classification. Others disagreed, including some of his own examiners, who attacked his autocratic style.

Nevertheless, he was able to boast at the end of his career that far fewer cinema films were cut before release than when he started. The proportion declined from some 40 per cent in 1974 of films cut before release to just 3.6 per cent in 1998. Marginally more videos faced cuts, reflecting the stricter standards laid down by law for films viewed in the home, where there is so much less control over the age of the audience. Others argued that the film industry simply got wise to the ways of Ferman and exercised such a stringent self-censorship that they considered it a matter of professional shame if the BBFC examiners insisted on further cuts. Most film companies are only too keen to cut their own movies if they believe it will lead to a lower category and guaranteed entry to the more lucrative younger teenage market. As if to underline the stringency of the British film classification system, in 1998 the BBFC even insisted on cuts in a Disney feature cartoon, *Mulan*, before it could get a U-certificate.

As in literature, the use of four-letter words has become tolerated even if the process has taken somewhat longer. The comedian Billy Connolly's 'How does he bloody do that?' in the U-rated *Muppet Treasure Island* movie provoked so many complaints that it was cut from the video. But the censors have become much more tolerant even in children's films. *ET* was given a U-certificate despite the boy saying 'penis' and 'prat'. 'Shit' is now acceptable at PG level. Ferman has indicated that the F-word has gradually become acceptable at 15. *The Commitments* had a lot to do with this, and the 11 F-words allowed in the opening moments of *Four Weddings and a Funeral* were something of a record.

At his farewell speech to the British film industry in February 1999, Ferman summed up the current state of the British public's attitude to film censorship:

> Nudity doesn't seem to bother many people nowadays.
> Bare backsides are at the bottom of the list of the public's
> anxieties. Naked breasts no longer attract outrage either.
> The portrayal of violence and drug abuse remains the
> great worry on the minds of the British public.[5]

Film in the UK faces the strictest censorship in Europe and part of the reason for this lies in the early 1970s when the system of film censorship was almost tested to destruction. 'There was a lot of rape about in the 1970s,' said Ferman, who put it down to a 'backlash by male film-makers against the Women's Libbers'. The worst example, in his view, came from Michael Winner's *Death Wish 2*. The offending scene showed two women putting up next to no resistance to the gibbering rapists who gangbanged them. 'I cut 3 minutes 42 seconds of that stuff. A record I think. Winner was furious.'[6]

The advent of the mass home video market in the early 1980s could have proved the downfall of the BBFC. Like all massively popular new inventions, the politicians were deeply suspicious of the home video machine. The newly born video industry was keen to follow the practices of its older brother and was quick to submit its output for BBFC approval within a newly devised voluntary code of practice.

The film censors were keenly aware that there were fewer controls over what children might watch at home on the video compared with the cinema. Nevertheless the examiners were determined that they would not restrict video certificates to those which could safely be watched by a five-year-old. They successfully argued with the government that since only one-third of homes have children under 16 living in them, the whole audience for video should not be censored down to the level of a PG certificate.

This proposition was to be sorely tried when Mary Whitehouse started her 'video nasties' campaign with a compilation screening for Tory MPs at the 1983 Conservative Party Conference. At that time the biggest selling video was a comic-chiller, *The Evil Dead*, which was branded the 'number one nasty' by Mrs Whitehouse. It was distributed by Stephen Woolley's Palace Pictures. Others such as *The Driller Killer*, with its deliberately provocative advertising – the video's cover line ran: 'The Blood Runs in Rivers ... and the Drill Keeps Tearing Through Flesh and Bone' – suffered from their own publicity. Serious film critics argued to little avail that *The Driller Killer* was the only gore movie genuinely to approach art. The juvenile taste that these videos catered for not surprisingly upset the indignant housewife tendency found in profusion amongst the ranks of Conservative Party activists. The *Daily Mail* quickly joined the bandwagon, denouncing the 'video-pushers' for pedalling their sadistic wares as though they were major drug importers.

The pressure became so intense that the Director of Public Prosecutions drew up a list of 60 'potentially obscene' titles to help guide the Metropolitan Police. The 'big 60', as it became known, even included films such as Francis Ford Coppola's Vietnam war film, *Apocalypse Now*. More importantly it also led to the 1984 Video Recordings Act, which was introduced by the backbench Conservative MP, Graham Bright, an undistinguished businessman who had made his money in artificial sweeteners.

As far as the government was concerned, new legislation became urgent only after a jury at Snaresbrook Crown Court refused to find *The Evil Dead* obscene. As David Mellor, the responsible Home Office Minister at the time, put it: 'The classic simplicity of the bill is its proposal that the only matter of concern to the courts will be whether a video has a certificate.' So the verdict of the public – in the shape of a crown court jury – had to be replaced by the expert opinion of Ferman and his colleagues. The courts could no longer be trusted to enforce the Obscene Publications Act and so somebody else had to be given the task. The BBFC was in business and it already had a backlog of 10,000 titles that it could get to work on. Few mourned the passing of the 'cheap video nasties' which were swept away by this action. More worryingly, their place was taken by ever more violent big budget Hollywood movies.

Mary Whitehouse had successfully insisted that Graham Bright include a clause in his bill requiring the censors to have 'special regard to the likelihood of video works ... being viewed in the family home'. The BBFC examiners had already made clear that they had little intention of censoring all videos down to the level of what was acceptable to a PG audience. They had proudly declared that they had no intention of being put into the position of policing homes where the parents were unwilling or unable to regulate their children's viewing habits.

However, a few test cases soon demonstrated that the will of Parliament was not being thwarted in Soho Square, the offices of the BBFC, when it came down to making the actual decisions. The classic example was *The Exorcist*, which had been passed by the censors in every country to which it had been submitted but was to be banned on video in Britain. Ferman was concerned in the late 1980s about reports of child abuse, particularly claims of satanic abuse, and he had regular contacts with Warner Brothers, its distributors, about its possible release on video. Ferman told the film company that there was one scene that would have to be cut before it was given a video release for home consumption. This was the scene in which the 'possessed child' masturbates with a crucifix while she shouts, 'Fuck me, fuck me.' But the executives of Warner Brothers refused to make the cut. They knew that a film buff of Ferman's standing could not bring himself to insist on cutting a film as famous as *The Exorcist* and so no formal request for a video certificate was made while he was in charge.

The other film that gave Ferman the greatest difficulties was Sam Peckinpah's *Straw Dogs*, which he regarded as the worst example of sexual violence in British film because its four-minute rape scene suggested that women secretly enjoy being raped. Although there is little evidence to show that a jury would be any more censorious about a video than a book, more than half the 60 videos on the DPP's original list still remained banned in Britain when Ferman stepped down.

But if Ferman and his fractious band of examiners did a better job as far as the Home Office was concerned of 'holding the line' than juries could be trusted to, they too found themselves the target of concerted campaigns by pressure groups. Perhaps the most famous example in the 1980s was the controversy over Martin Scorsese's *The Last Temptation of Christ*. The BBFC received more than 1,870 letters complaining about its depiction of sexual fantasies involving Mary Magdalene and demanding a ban on its distribution. Mrs Whitehouse threatened a rerun of the *Gay News* blasphemy case at the Old Bailey unless Ferman acted. He knew perfectly well that a ban on a film made by America's most prestigious living director would have fatally damaged his credibility in the eyes of the film industry and the critics.

Ferman decided to adopt what Jack Straw calls an evidence-based policy. He invited 28 bishops, priests and deacons to the Soho Square viewing room to see the film. It was a smart move. They did not like the film but they did not think it was blasphemous either and, more importantly, were prepared to say so in public. It defused the entire argument and the *Last Temptation* was released to little public fuss, despite advice from Cardinal Hume to the Roman Catholic community not to see it.

Ferman constantly worried in particular about the portrayal of weapons that could be abused by juveniles. He completely confounded Bruce Lee fans and some of his fellow examiners by having a particularly strong line on any film that contained an actor using 'nanchukas' or chainsticks. At the time there were serious concerns in criminal justice circles about the availability of various knives and weapons and specific legislation banning the sale of certain knives was passed following the murder of a

London headmaster. But the policy on nanchukas reached its nadir with the children's film, *Teenage Mutant Ninja Turtles*, in which one cartoon turtle, Michaelangelo, was believed to be swinging the dreaded chainsticks. The scene was cut. It was not even reinstated when another examiner pointed out that the turtle was not using the nanchukas but a string of sausages.

In the 1990s Ferman also showed that it took more than what the sociologists call a moral panic to move him. Perhaps his sternest test came in the wake of the murder of the two-year-old toddler James Bulger in Liverpool by two ten-year-old boys in February 1992. One police officer involved in the case drew a link between the murder and a video, *Child's Play 3*, which the murderers were alleged to have seen. It prompted a huge national debate about the influence of violent videos on juvenile crime, with MPs pressing for new legislation. In this atmosphere Ferman felt that he had to ban the release of Quentin Tarantino's *Reservoir Dogs* on video even though he had declared there was actually very little violence in the film and what was there was justified by the context. A similar film, *Bad Lieutenant*, directed by Abel Ferrara of *The Driller Killer* fame, starring Harvey Keitel as a corrupt police officer, was also banned on video at the same time. As Ferman said at the time, both films just 'simply happened to be around'. It was to be another three years before the BBFC allowed the two films to be released on video. When *Bad Lieutenant* finally made it in 1995 it was cut by 1 minute 47 seconds and when *Reservoir Dogs* was released on video in the same year it came with a warning that it contained bloody and shocking violence.

Perhaps the biggest influence of the Bulger murder on the film censorship debate was to spark a series of major Home Office research projects on the influence of violent videos. Dr Kevin Browne of Birmingham University compared the viewing habits of 82 convicted young offenders with 40 other boys in their age group. He found that both groups were watching the same films and videos and both had a strong preference for macho heroics. The research came to the conclusion that most young people were not influenced by video violence, however, although some could be and they included the most violent and potentially dangerous young people in Britain. Although violent youngsters sought out violent videos, the researchers concluded that a violent family background was a far more important factor in the development of their antisocial behaviour than watching films had been.

More recently Ferman's independence was tested by the controversy that blew up over *Crash*, the film adapted from the J.G. Ballard book. It dealt with the disturbing idea of a group of people who tried to find sexual satisfaction amongst the carnage of car crashes. The obsessive leader of the group believes that car crashes resulted in a 'liberation of sexual energy' and so spends his time reconstructing the fatal car crashes of film stars who had became sex symbols by dying young. He dies pursuing his obsession. The film's director said that it was a study in eroticism and technology. The *Daily Mail* and the London *Evening Standard* started a campaign to have it banned after it was screened at the London Film Festival in June 1996. The *Mail* said that it contained 'some of the most perverted acts of sexual deviance ever witnessed in the mainstream cinema'. This view led to a decision to ban it from London's West End cinemas by the Conservative-controlled Westminster City Council. The papers could not resist mentioning the fact that one of the councillors involved in the decision was named John Bull.

Ferman and the BBFC spent five months worrying about *Crash*, as the Conservative Culture Secretary, Virginia Bottomley, voiced her own anxieties about the film in November 1996 and pressed for him to act. But Ferman felt that the sight of Holly Hunter taking her clothes off in a car that was damaged did not warrant a ban and *Crash* was passed uncut. The *Daily Mail* called for the sacking of 'this feeble censor'. Lord Birkett, one of the two BBFC vice-presidents, summed up the syndrome:

The circumstances have become depressingly familiar.

Somebody sees the film in question in its country of origin, or at a film festival prior to its international release, and writes an article attacking it as the most dangerous film ever to be offered to the public. The press then canvasses the opinions of dozens of prominent figures, almost none of whom has seen the film, and then, long before the BBFC has had a chance to view it and make its own painstakingly objective analysis, it is deluged with warnings and injunctions not to permit the showing of the film.[7]

In this atmosphere, Lord Birkett said that it was difficult for the public to believe that the film was not exceptional and there were film-makers who were not above hoping that scandal would be good for the box office. But sometimes the results were not as predicted. In the case of *Crash*, there was actually little violence in a film that had been condemned for its violence. It was also accused of glorifying depravity. It was depraved, argued Lord Birkett, but it certainly did not glorify it. Instead he stood back in icy astonishment at the desperation of a tiny minority who regarded car crashes as sexual stimuli. The BBFC vice-president used this example to emphasise why the test of whether a film was acceptable or not had to be whether it would produce lasting harm and not simply shock, outrage or offence: 'Harm in the sense of injury, something it is hard to recover from,' said Lord Birkett. Such a liberal approach from such a senior figure in the world of film censorship was to shock the new Labour Home Secretary, Jack Straw, in November 1998, to such an extent that it ensured that Lord Birkett did not go on to become president of the BBFC. The episode also underlines how the film censors' lack of any democratic accountability leaves them open to direct political pressure from the government.

The fight was sparked by a decision by the BBFC to allow hard-core videos to be sold in licensed sex shops under the limited R-18 category. Those licensed included explicit scenes with penetration, including buggery, and oral sex, as long as they were non-violent and appeared to be consensual. One of the videos that was given an interim R-18 certificate by the BBFC was called *Makin' Whoopee!* Birkett and Ferman argued that the thriving black market operating through unlicensed sex shops traded in very degrading material including torture, bestiality and sexual violence. The 80 or so licensed sex shops, set up under the influence of the Williams committee, were failing because as one Conservative Home Office minister, Tom Sackville, had informally suggested, they were not allowed to sell anything the punters who went to the black-market shops wanted to see. Without any parliamentary approval or political debate, Birkett and Ferman went ahead with the experiment and the licensed sex shops quickly stocked up with videos that included erect penises engaged in non-violent, consensual sex.

But when Jack Straw became Home Secretary and discovered that this shift in policy had taken place he summoned Lord Birkett. Lord Birkett later told John Ware on BBC TV's *Panorama*:

> It was quite obvious that the Home Secretary himself was in a genuine state of outrage about the whole thing. He said: 'Do you really mean that you are going to allow oral sex and buggery and I don't know what else? That you're actually passing this? You are giving a certificate to it?' And I pointed out of course it is a very limited certificate. The R-18 certificate is for films that can only be sold to people over 18 and in licensed sex shop premises and as it happens buggery is no longer illegal as it was until quite recently.[8]

Jack Straw, for his part, said that the BBFC had failed to consult the Home Office, the police, Customs and Excise or the Crown Prosecution Service about its action. He said that Customs had advised him that some of the new R-18 videos would fall within their criteria for seizure and in changing its policy the

BBFC was out of step with the other enforcement authorities. 'It subsequently became clear to me at a meeting with Lord Birkett that he had failed properly to exercise his responsibilities,' said Straw. The Home Secretary also took the opportunity to restate his belief that the 1959 Obscene Publications Act remained a useful piece of legislation, describing it as a 'flexible regulatory tool' which allowed for 'changes in society's moral standards'. It was notable that when the government later announced a major review of the law relating to sex crimes, changes to the obscenity laws were specifically excluded. One suspects that if Mr Straw were to open the Pandora's box that is the current state of the obscenity laws, what he claims is a 'flexible regulatory tool' would quickly be unmasked as an implement that long ago stopped being of much use to either conservatives or libertarians.

The BBFC was of course powerless in the face of this intervention from the Home Office. Its authority to act as a censor came only from the power delegated by either the Home Secretary in the case of video or the local authorities in the case of film. If the elected Home Secretary objected to its actions, it had no other recourse. The BBFC withdrew the interim R–18 certificate for *Makin' Whoopee!* and the other videos. The episode demonstrated the weakness of the board's legal and political position and as a result Lord Birkett, who was acting president during 1997 and 1998, was not confirmed in the job.

In his place Straw appointed Andreas Whittam Smith, the former editor of the *Independent* newspaper, as president of the BBFC. The Home Secretary insisted on a complete clear-out at the top. Two new vice-presidents and a new director, Robin Duval, who was an experienced television regulator, were also appointed. The new team has consciously been more open and accessible in an attempt to improve the accountability of the board. A number of controversial matters were left over from Ferman's reign for his successors to deal with in their first few months.

The first involved a new decision about whether to release

Sam Peckinpah's 1971 *Straw Dogs* on video. Andreas Whittam Smith and Robin Duval decided that they would maintain the ban. Whittam Smith said he shared Ferman's view that the main difficulty with the film was the brutal rape scene in which Susan George playing Amy is raped by her ex-lover, Charlie, and then at gunpoint by his friend. The film conveys a clear indication that Amy comes to enjoy being raped. The BBFC when it confirmed the original decision not to release *Straw Dogs* on video said that the film condoned the male rape myth that 'women really like it'. The censors justified their decision on the grounds that, if anything, concern about sexual violence had grown and not diminished over the previous 30 years.

The censors did finally decide to allow a video release of *The Exorcist*, saying that there was little, if any, hard evidence that it had caused actual harm. The previous refusal of its release on video had rested on reports of incidents on its original cinema release in the 1970s, of hysteria involving young women and concern that it might cause severe emotional problems in those who believed in demonic possession. Whittam Smith and Duval said 20 years later that it had to be acknowledged that there was little, if any, hard evidence that *The Exorcist* had harmed its viewers.

Similarly the new board felt that it was time to allow the video release of the *Texas Chainsaw Massacre* and of the notorious *The Driller Killer*. The 1970s slasher movie was given a video certificate without cuts on the argument that the modern young adult audience used to the macabre shocks of the horror films of the 1980s and 1990s would not find it particularly challenging. *The Driller Killer* was given a video release only after the scenes showing the drill actually boring through bone and flesh had been deleted. On this basis the new board looks set to carry out a similar policy to that pursued by Ferman for the previous quarter-century. The exception is the continuing row over Jack Straw's interference in the R-18 category, which rumbles on towards the first High Court case for many years, which will discuss just how far a film-maker may go in *Makin' Whoopee!*

When the new regime at the BBFC reversed the Ferman verdict on these films, their decision was rejected by the Video Appeals Committee (VAC), which continued to apply the 'harm' test in the 1984 video nasties legislation. This requires the classifiers to have special regard to 'any harm that may be caused to potential viewers, or through their behaviour to society' by the subject matter in the video. When the VAC applied this test, it allowed *Makin' Whoopee!* through to the shops. Whittam Smith and Duval contended that the VAC's interpretation was incorrect and would have fundamental implications for all the board's decisions, including those turning on questions of unacceptable levels of violence. Straw had lent on the board to ensure that in the face of this conflicting legal situation, the line continued to be held on the stricter 1959 'deprave and corrupt' test. Shepton-hurst, the distributors of *Makin' Whoopee!*, argued that since it had been allowed through, seven other of their similar videos should also be given certificates. The BBFC said no. The VAC said yes. It was left to the High Court to sort out this shambles and in a ruling that left Jack Straw fuming, Mr Justice Hooper said that the Video Appeals Committee had acted within its powers when in May 2000 he overruled the BBFC and said the seven explicit videos, including *Horny Catbabe*, *Nympho Nurse Nancy* and *Office Tarts*, should be give R-18 certificates. He said, on the present evidence, the risk of the videos sold in adult-only sex shops being viewed by, and causing devastating harm to, more than a minority of children or young people was insignificant.

The *Daily Mail* went apoplectic at this new 'flood of filth' and demanded to know why nobody in politics had the moral conviction or the courage to halt it. Mr Straw quickly made clear he was up to the task. He announced that he was not happy with the high court ruling, made clear that he had appointed Andreas Whittam Smith to avoid precisely this situation and said he was prepared to change the law if necessary to keep such hardcore videos out of Britain.

But as Ferman himself has speculated, the game may well be

over. The advent of digital television will eventually mean the merger of the Internet and the home television screen. Already the technology is shaping up to deliver video over the Net. Ferman predicted in his final report:

> It may well be in the 21st century that it simply becomes impossible to impose the kind of regulation which the Board exists to provide. After all what is the point of cutting a gang-rape scene in a British version of a film if that film is accessible down a telephone line from outside British territorial waters? I am probably the last of the old-time regulators.[9]

12

Patrolling the Internet

The argument about censorship and obscenity in Britain in the first half of the twentieth century concentrated almost entirely on the printed word with little or no discussion about the merits of the books to be burned. A single episode was sufficient to send a book to the furnace. It did not even have to be considered in the wider context of the book as a whole. In post-war Britain the obscenity debate centred increasingly on whether or not the courts had the right to declare a literary or a scientific book obscene. The 1959 Obscene Publications Act finally gave some protection to serious works although (as we have seen) police attempts to ban the written word – although nearly all unsuccessful – continued right up into the 1990s.

But as a fairly libertarian consensus developed about the written word so the argument shifted on to cinema and then to video. In some ways both lend themselves much more readily to a system of classification than published books – if only because a more limited number are produced each year. But the media are once again going through a period of rapid technological change and with it new ways of presenting and marketing material. The introduction of the personal computer in the home has been followed by satellite and cable television and then by the rapid growth of the Internet. These new technologies, particularly with the promise of a merger between the Internet and the home television, look like much more difficult media for the authorities to patrol. The very technology itself completely changes the nature of the debate. It is no longer a moral question about what should or should not be published but whether or not there is any practical way such a decision can even be enforced. The law is already trying to catch up. Having looked back at some of the failures, however well intentioned, of the authorities over the past century to control the flow of 'obscene' material in Britain, it is now time to look forward. In this final chapter I want to examine whether or not the future will be libertarian.

When it comes to the World Wide Web the conventional wisdom is already well established: 'Oh, you can't censor the Net' is the constant cry of those who claim to have a little learning. Yet the same pundits will go on to agree that one of the biggest problems facing parents now is that their teenage children can view hard-core sexual pictures on their computer with just a couple of knowing clicks of the mouse in the privacy of their own bedroom. It is anxiety that afflicts all parents who are faced with a technology they do not feel they understand. Even Tony Blair is not immune and has said he worries about the kind of information his three 'very computer-literate' children, Euan, Nicky and Kathryn, can find on the Net. In an interview with Bun.Com (the *Sun* newspaper's website), Mr Blair said:

> I'm very concerned. We try to keep a careful watch on what our children are getting access to on the Internet. There are organisations that give advice to people, but it's very difficult if the parents aren't around watching what is going on. There are tremendous opportunities, but there are dangers. In the end I think it is more a matter for parents than for governments. We can do what we can, but it's down to the parents.[1]

For a politician this represents a very liberal stance compared with the kind of law and order 'let's get tough' actions that have developed among those competing to crackdown on the Net in the United States and Australia. In Britain the government appears more concerned at the beginning of the twenty-first century to encourage the spread of the Net and to avoid the creation of a society divided into a wired-up superclass and an information underclass. Corporate tax breaks are being made available to encourage companies to allow their staff to borrow computers for home use and plans have been drawn up for cheap computer leasing schemes so poorer families can get online. By 2002 Tony Blair has said he wants to see all 32,000 schools in Britain connected to the Internet and hopes that around 400,000 teachers will be trained so that they are fully computer-literate. Already some 75 per cent of secondary schools and about 35 per cent of primary schools have their own websites.

With this kind of government backing the spread of the information superhighway looks as though it will be as rapid as its most fervent enthusiasts hoped. By 2001 one in two adults told a *Guardian*/ICM opinion poll that they had access to the Internet either at home or at work and the number getting wired up is likely to accelerate.

The arrival of digital technology, with its promised merger between the domestic television and the Internet, is already leading to a new revolution in home information and entertainment. At the same time it threatens to render the current systems of media regulation, as practised by the BBC, the Independent Television Commission and the British Board of Film Classification, redundant within a decade. Eventually the digital set-top box will not only bring dozens of extra television channels into the home but also provide a choice of hundreds of thousand of new stations, each broadcast through a separate website available throughout the world.

Opinion poll surveys have revealed that some of the old familiar anxieties that have greeted the arrival of every powerful new technology from the printing press onwards are already making themselves felt among a significant section of the public.

For example in a poll for *Which? Online*, some 58 per cent of the sample said they believed that the Internet undermined the morality of the nation by making pornography and other illegal materials freely available. The challenge is recognised to be an international one. As Janet Reno, the former US Attorney-General, told a meeting of the G8 countries, in December 1997: 'The fight against lawlessness on the Internet will be one of the greatest law enforcement challenges of the century.'

Certainly Britain's Home Secretary, Jack Straw, has no intention of scrapping the present obscenity laws in Britain. Indeed despite their history, he believes they still represent a 'flexible prosecutory tool' which has managed to adapt to changing times and tastes. The Home Office told me:

> Under UK legislation what is illegal offline is illegal online. The Obscene Publications Act 1959 therefore applies to material published via the Internet, as does specific legislation relating to child pornography – including the Protection of Children Act 1978.[2]

The idea of going further and bringing specific new government laws to control the content of Internet sites accessible in Britain has already been canvassed at the highest levels. Home Office sources tell me that there was a completely unpublicised effort by Michael Howard when he was Home Secretary, and his criminal justice minister, David Maclean, to use government regulation to ensure that the Net was a clean and safe place for British children to play. But wiser heads among the Home Office civil servants persuaded them that it was a dangerous and complicated path to get involved in and they dropped the whole idea. Instead the Home Office took the position that elementary forms of self-regulation by the Internet industry should be given the chance to develop the kind of protection that British parents, such as Tony Blair, are looking for. A Home Office civil servant told me:

Most commercial adult websites require a credit card to verify the user's age. The possession of a credit card generally excludes children and that and the additional information required, such as an address and telephone number, usually provide some safeguards against unauthorised access. Rating and filtering mechanisms are being developed which will assist parents in monitoring their children's use of the Net.[3]

But behind the scenes a whole new network of regulatory controls is being put in place and without any real public or parliamentary debate. It is a regime that will extend the definition of what is acceptable in a public medium far beyond the twentieth-century debates over the meaning of 'obscene' or 'indecent' and introduce a new concept of 'intolerance'. The new system of Internet controls is being pioneered with the backing of the British government for adoption across Europe. It is worth saying again that the UK already has the strictest form of censorship in the whole of Europe and now it is trying to set the standard for the rest of the EU in this highly controversial area. The Home Office says the new standard will be based on a system that will control access to sites on the grounds not only of sex, nudity, violence and language but also intolerance to race, colour, disability and other references to groups of people. This takes the debate into the extremely thorny area of barring access to sites that are not illegal but may be offensive to one group of people or another. What price a Salman Rushdie site? Or a gay Christian site or for that matter a Christian family site that preaches that homosexuality is a perverted sin? It is a debate which suggests that new limits on the freedom of expression and new definitions of indecency and obscenity will emerge. The official position on obscenity and indecency remains in that flexible *Alice's Adventures in Wonderland* world where words mean whatever a prosecution counsel can persuade a jury or a bench of magistrates to believe them to mean. The Home Office says:

> The words 'obscene' and 'indecent' are not defined in
> UK law. It is left to the courts and their juries to act as
> the final arbiters of whether or not the material before
> them is 'obscene' or 'indecent'. The general test of
> obscenity in the Obscene Publications Act, the 'deprave
> and corrupt' test, requires the court to be satisfied that
> the material in question is harmful in its effects rather
> then merely undesirable or offensive.[4]

It stresses that this 'harmful test' avoids potential conflicts with article ten of the European Convention on Human Rights which guarantees freedom of expression and is therefore much more liberal than some of the rulings seen in British courts in the twentieth century. But as the former chief film censor, James Ferman, has demonstrated, the European Convention also allows material to be banned if it is for the 'prevention of crime and disorder' or the 'protection of health or morals'. And that is a worryingly wide loophole in the hands of politicians looking for a cheap crackdown.

One major driving force behind this push to ensure that the World Wide Web is as closely policed as any of the other traditional media has been the Internet industry itself in the shape of the Internet Watch Foundation (IWF). The days of innocence when the Net community was made up of freethinking surfers who believed they were developing some kind of anarchic new global information environment in which freedom of speech would be paramount are already long gone. Yet the origins of the Net mean that there is a significant proportion of users who have strongly held views that such interventions should be resisted.

The birth of the IWF is itself a lesson in the politics of the modern criminal justice system. The IWF was set up in September 1996 by the main Internet service providers (ISPs), including Demon Internet, BT Internet, Virgin Net, AOL, CompuServe and Dixon's FreeServe, after discussions between the Metropolitan Police, the Internet industry, the Home Office and the Department of Trade and Industry.

The official version portrays its establishment as a public-spirited move by the industry to combat the use of the Net, particularly its Usenet discussion groups and bulletin boards, by paedophiles and other child sex offenders. Its main purpose was to provide a hotline for those online to report instances of illegal child pornography on the Net when they came across them so that the ISPs could remove them.

But the actual history is rather more complex. In the summer of 1996, Chief Inspector Steve French of the Clubs and Vice Squad of Scotland Yard sent a letter to all the ISPs with a list of 133 newsgroups that contained pornographic material. He wrote:

> As you will be only too aware the content is continually changing and you will need to satisfy yourself about the nature and content before taking any action.
> Furthermore, this list is not exhaustive and we are looking to you to monitor your Newsgroups identifying and taking necessary action against those others found to contain such material. As you will be aware the publication of obscene articles is an offence.[5]

The Chief Inspector said he hoped with the cooperation of the industry to look forward to the eradication of 'this type of Newsgroup from the Internet'. Most were straightforward paedophile discussion groups or bulletin boards such as alt.sex.pedophilia.pictures and alt.binaries.pictures.boys. But there were others on the list where the argument was less clear-cut and these included alt.homosexual and alt.sex.fetish.tickling. These were sites on which illegal material had also been posted alongside more innocent items and so the police were asking for their complete closure.

The letter caused quite a stir in the Internet industry. The Conservative Science and Industry Minister at the time, Ian Taylor, underlined the explicit threat to ISPs if they did not close down the newsgroups in question. He warned that the police would act against any company that provided their users with pornographic or violent material. He went on to make it clear that there would be calls for legislation to regulate all aspects of the Internet unless and until service providers were seen wholeheartedly to embrace responsible self-regulation. 'Either the industry takes it upon itself to clean up the Net or the police intervene,' Superintendent Mike Hoskins of the Clubs and Vice Squad told the ISPs at a meeting at New Scotland Yard on 2 August 1996.[6]

The establishment of the IWF was the industry's main response. It followed an agreement – known as the R3 Safety Net Agreement covering websites and newsgroups – between the government, the police and the major UK ISPs. Set up by the energetic David Kerr, its first chief executive, its hotline is designed for users to ring, fax or e-mail about material that they believe is illegal. It opened for business in December 1996. The foundation's role is restricted to assessing whether the material is likely to be illegal – a role more usually performed by the Crown Prosecution Service. If it is thought to be illegal the IWF will try to trace its origins, tell the authors that they are acting illegally and notify the ISP that hosts the site and the police. If it involves child pornography – or the material originates from outside Britain, as most does – a report also goes to the National Criminal Intelligence Service. The third part of the agreement was that the ISPs would go one step further and help the police trace where the child pornography or other illegal material comes from. If the ISP fails to remove the material from its website, it may itself become liable for prosecution. Since the R3 Safety Net Agreement was signed in autumn 1996 no ISP has been prosecuted. The out-of-court settlement in the Demon Internet libel case in March 2000 underlined just how serious is the threat of prosecution to ISPs for the millions of items carried on their servers each day. Demon paid £15,000 and an estimated £230,000 costs to Laurence Geoffrey, a physicist who said that he had been defamed by two anonymous postings on the Net.

Indeed the main ISPs are happy to see the development of the IWF. They like it because it does for them what the British Board of Film Classification does for the film industry and cinemas. It reduces the risk of police action against them without the near impossible task of monitoring the content of their servers. It also provides a safer environment for their customers and enhances their image as responsible businesses.

The IWF's initial concern was in the highly emotional area of child pornography and paedophilia and so there was little criticism of this form of regulation. Some voices, such as the Leeds University based Cyber-Rights and Cyber-Liberties (UK), were sceptical and questioned why the police were threatening to prosecute the ISPs rather than going after those who had posted the illegal content on the sites in the first place. Nevertheless the IWF was an instant hit. It received nearly 550 reports in its first nine months of operation, relating to 2,150 items, with the police taking action over 1,200 of them. It has continued to grow. By August 1998 it had received a total of 2,146 complaints from the public. However, most were about offensive but not illegal material appearing on websites and only 453 actually related to illegal material. Nearly all were to do with child pornography (397), with the rest involving adult porn.

The volume of complaints to the IWF hotline doubled to nearly 5,000 in 1999 and rose again to pass the 8,000 mark in 2000. But while the complaints grew, the number of 'potentially illegal' items which were found to come from Britain fell sharply. The number of child pornography items which were 'taken down' in 2000 dropped from 10,189 in 1999 to only 2,498 a year later. Only 121 items which were judged to be 'potentially illegal' had originated in Britain and the IWF noted a shift towards complaints involving items contained on Eastern European websites.

For the IWF this was proof that its four years of operation was a positive sign of the impact of its work and that it was possible to deter the abuse of the Net. It is only one year's figures but the drop could also be taken as some evidence that the exploitation of the Net by paedophiles is perhaps not quite as pervasive a problem in Britain as some make out. But it also has to be said that the high number of items taken down in 1999 was partly accounted for by the fact that the police arrested two very prolific posters of child porn images to online newsgroups.

The successful international cooperation involved in closing down the Wonderland Club, an online paedophile ring, provided a major boost to all those involved in these regulatory activities. In an operation ran by Britain's national crime squad involving 180 police officers in 13 countries, the ring was broken up with the result that seven paedophiles were sent to prison in February 2001 for between 12 and 30 months after a trial at Kingston Crown Court. The two-year operation showed that it may be difficult but it is not impossible to control content on the Net which may be located on a computer server in a country with little or no ability to enforce standards. Even a huge Internet porn empire based in Antigua, the Rhino Corporation, was closed down by an international police operation.

The self-regulatory approach advocated by IWF backed up by such police action has been warmly endorsed by the Home Office and the Department of Trade and Industry:

> The government believes that self regulation by service
> providers through the IWF framework offers a positive
> way forward. It is a strategy that is being adopted by
> other European countries with a view to wider
> international co-operation, for example through the
> development of international hotline services.[7]

The self-regulation approach was confirmed by the Labour government's white paper on the communications industry published in December 2000, which also endorsed the assumption that within time media convergence would turn the Net into the mass media. The communications white paper proposed that there should be a new super media regulator, Ofcom, for telecommunications including the Internet, and radio and television. But its role as far as the Internet is concerned should be to work with the IWF in the UK and at an EU level to strengthen ways of identifying suitable and unsuitable content and to give parents control over what their children watch. It is a very promising start based on the hope that filtering packages can be developed that are sophisticated enough to avoid some of the more crass examples.

Ireland, whose censorship record is far worse and where even books such as *The Joy of Sex* were banned as recently as 1987, in particular is looking to the IWF to help it develop a similar system of self-regulation with a hotline. But despite a warm endorsement by the EU, some member states have misgivings. The French for example worry whether an association of ISPs has the right to give such wide-ranging powers, including denying access to sites, to an unaccountable hotline.

A British government review of the work of the IWF by outside consultants conducted after the election of the Labour government in 1997 has given it a glowing report. The ISPs which have signed up to the IWF and abide by its notices cover 97 per cent of the UK 'dial-up market' and the industry is trying to encourage all new entrants to join. As a result the IWF has extended its activities into the area of general education and raising awareness, particularly of the dangers to children of using the Net. In an attempt to broaden its appeal the IWF has also promised to tackle the problem of British racist sites on the Net.

But while IWF reports of illegal child porn sites in Britain have fallen sharply, the media debate about the dangers of the Net has begun to gather pace. This is in no small measure due to the efforts of Carol Vorderman, the television presenter and popular science broadcaster, who is rapidly taking on the mantle of a modern Mary Whitehouse in her efforts to clean up the Net. A celebrity who can command prime-time television slots and full-page newspaper features, including in the pages of the *Daily Express* and the *Daily Mail*, she has made tackling the paedophile presence on the Net a personal crusade. In one interview she claimed that only 12 per cent of convicted child sex abusers are given a prison sentence because many judges are paedophiles.[8] In others she attacks the government and ISPs for not doing enough to protect children from the dangers of the Net, particularly the unsupervised nature of many chat rooms.

> I am appalled by images of children as young as 18 months being abused and being forced to engage in oral sex with adults. I am appalled by the lack of police officers with any understanding of cybercrime or the resources to tackle this. I am appalled that BT charges £130 each time that the police make an inquiry. The attitude of the judiciary is wholly inadequate. Some 26,000 items taken down from UK hosts is nothing. Chat room moderation is very poor. Even in MSN.co.uk dedicated children's chat room I found references to shagging. No warning and no protection. What is being offered is a joke.[9]

Vorderman told an Internet 'summit' in the House of Lords in 2001 hosted by the IWF which brought together the Internet companies, the police and the government. The responsible Home Office minister, Lord Bassam, agreed that Vorderman had a point but argued that there was already a robust legal framework and the formation of the hi-tech crime unit would put more money and officers onto the case:

> A few very disturbing cases have recently come to light where children have been lured from home. In one case a 13 year old girl was sexually abused by a much older man who was prosecuted and sentenced to five years' imprisonment for this offence. We are aware that there have been a number of cases where it is believed the police have had difficulty in investigating these cases. There have also been a number of successful prosecutions which show that the law can work in this area, but the government does recognise that this can be a complex area for the police.

He said the government was satisfied that the existing armoury of law was sufficient to protect children from abuse. The penalty for taking and distributing indecent photographs of children had been raised from three years to ten years' imprisonment and a new offence covering attempts by adults to lure children while they are online to agree to meet them to commit indecent acts had been created. The difficulty arose, said Lord Bassam, when those such as Vorderman wanted to make it illegal to 'groom' a victim online when the initial exchanges between an abuser and a child might amount to no more than harmless chat about pop groups or football. Bassam made clear that trying to make it a criminal offence to talk to a child about football or pop music even as a prelude to a meeting involving abuse would amount to a 'thought crime' and could not be regarded as acceptable.

Nevertheless the problem of chat rooms raised by Vorderman was one that was taken seriously. ISPs were officially urged to ensure that chat rooms were monitored and to set up more supervised dedicated children's chat rooms with easy to use systems to report any unusual or alarming behaviour.

At the same time the Department for Education and Employment issued new anti-paedophile guidelines for schools telling them not to identify pupils featured in photographs on their websites and to use anonymous email addresses such as class4@ambleside.cumbria.sch.ac.uk on external school networks. The idea was to prevent sex offenders targeting individual pupils.

The national hi-tech crime unit was also launched in April 2001 and although its efforts are mainly aimed at tackling the threat of computer viruses and hackers to e-commerce it was also charged with dealing with the activities of paedophiles on the Net.

David Kerr says that the kinds of chat rooms that concern the IWF are those which are not illegal but where children may get into trouble. He cites the growing anxiety in the United States over enticement cases over the Net, but says the worries

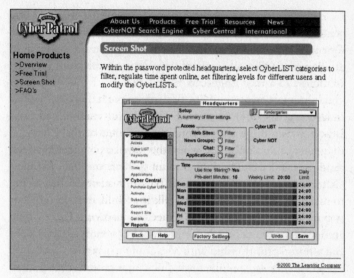

CyberPatrol, *a market leader in the future of censorship and regulation on the internet.*

also include children coming across sites about how to commit suicide or how to make bombs, as well as those containing porn. Kerr says that one of the IWF's answers is to develop rating and filtering systems which he believes are rapidly becoming more sophisticated. Civil liberties campaigners ridiculed early versions.

In one case involving CyberPatrol (one of the most popular blocking systems), the Censorware project highlighted some of the victims of its very rough and ready approach to classification. CyberPatrol is not only used to protect children in schools and libraries but also used at AOL to prevent access to inappropriate material by its 6 million plus customers, at CompuServe for its 4 million customers and for countless other businesses who want to screen their employees or their customers.

Censorware identified 64 sites it believed had been wrongly blacklisted by CyberPatrol. Among those which were listed as either 'full nude' or 'sex acts' sites was a Creature's Comfort Pet

Care Service ran by Ken and Nancy Holley, who provide a dog walking service, the Department of Computer Science at Queen Mary and Westfield College in London, the National Academy of Clinical Biochemistry and a site belonging to the US Army Corps of Engineers.[10]

Although CyberPatrol has cleaned up its act, the case does illustrate the shortcomings of the blacklisting method, particularly if poorly or untrained reviewers are used or there is a lack of quality control. Also such products have to be updated all the time to take account of the rapid growth in new websites. Others such as Net Nanny use a keyword system that allows the user to block out certain sites according to the preselected keywords. But often the more simplistic versions fail to take account of context. When Kenneth Starr's report on President Bill Clinton's relationship with Monica Lewinsky was posted on the US Congress website, several blocking programs, including the popular Net Nanny and Cybersurf, stopped their users getting access because of its sexual explicitness.

Some blocking software programs operate by banning access to sites with particular words or letters. So searches for Scunthorpe, sextuplets or shitake mushrooms may all end in blocked sites. Blocking sites with the letters s, e and x in the title stops access not only to sex sites but also to those to do with Mars exploration. Some programs could not differentiate between sites that were about breast cancer and those that merely displayed naked breasts. It was not a one-way street. The American Family Association (AFA), a conservative religious organisation, found its site blocked by CyberPatrol because of its opposition to homosexuality. In turn the AFA helped market its own brand of blocking software, X-Stop. Among those who found themselves censored by this programme were the Religious Society of Friends (also known as the Quakers). X-Stop is included in the list of filtering software packages that the Department for Education and Employment recommends for British schools.

David Kerr believes it is now possible to take a more sophisticated approach that avoids this kind of rough justice:

Any content provider can put hidden labels on their site which say what's there in a coded form. Browsers can read that label and can be programmed to act on what's on that label. What we are working at is a label which says this site contains x amount of sex, y amount of violence, z amount of bad language and quite a few other things.

Because of the way the technology works the browser can be set to read quite sophisticated information and make quite sophisticated decisions based on that information. It is a much finer filter. For example you can divide how sex is categorised between erotic sites and sex education sites. You can put an indicator in that says the perspective on sex on this site is heterosexual or homosexual so there can be much more information available to the browser. Each individual user can decide what sites they want to restrict.

You might say I don't mind my children seeing naked bodies at all but I don't want them to see any violence or the other way around. The Scandinavian naturist can accept all nudity but an Islamic fundamentalist can reject all nudity and accept all violence. That can be done at the individual level.[11]

Kerr says that the IWF tries to avoid adopting a moralistic stance:

Our position is a neutral one. What we are about is allowing responsible parents to make decisions on their own views as to what they would like to restrict access for the children they are responsible for. Ideally it will serve as a tool that can be used both by a fundamentalist Christian community as well as by a gay community.[12]

But it does not stop there. This self-regulatory body is also playing a key role in a European Commission funded project to create a generic rating and filtering system of European users of the Internet. This international initiative on content rating is known as Incore – Internet content rating for Europe. David Kerr is the general secretary to Incore. The chairman and vice-chairman are both German. The Home Office says:

> Incore is looking at how access can be controlled by users, allowing them the ultimate decision over what is seen, particularly where children are concerned. Possible categories included in a rating and filtering system – apart from the obvious ones such as sex, nudity, violence and language – are intolerance (to race, colour, disability and other references to groups of people), and potentially dangerous subjects, such as illegal drugs, bomb-making advice or suicide.[13]

One of the most difficult areas will be the enforcement of the British legislation banning incitement to racial hatred. The IWF at the suggestion of the Home Office has taken on this role in Britain but given the very sparse history of prosecutions of racist material, it is likely to prove a difficult, albeit worthwhile, task.

The German magazine, *Der Stern*, has carried a series of articles that illustrate the problem. They documented the rise of the neo-Nazis on the Net with more than 300 sites; some of them go far beyond simply inciting racial hatred. Their contents have a new quality,' Peter Frisch of the Cologne Federal Office for the Protection of the Constitution was quoted as saying:

> There has been a disturbing development from simply blackening the name of political opponents on hate lists to calling for their murder. Who can rule out that one day some fanatical idiot won't do it.[14]

Such incitement to murder on the Internet is taken seriously by the German authorities. One anonymous young surfer who faced a death threat after repeatedly insulting other online users in a right-wing chat room named Resistance was alarmed to discover that his would-be murderers had acquired his real name, home address and telephone number.

One German neo-Nazi who operates out of his American home page under the pseudonym of Meck88 is direct:

> This is a page where I publish the names, addresses, telephone numbers, etc of people who have earned a proper beating. If an activist who is prepared for violence sees this, then he doesn't need to hesitate in finishing off these people in any way he can. If he wants to have the names of any of the bastards published here, then send me an e-mail with the reason.[15]

Some offer rewards with requests that a hacked-off hand be sent to a post office box address in Belgian as proof. NPDnet, the National Democratic Party of Germany's website, advises those who wish to post really violent addresses to get an Internet address ending in .org, .com, or .net on international fast servers. The US server, Geocities, is a favourite. The reason is that the German authorities find it very difficult to block access to such sites and cannot trace the German operators.

The neo-Nazis are also playing an increasing role in the political chat rooms of the main ISPs, often using nicknames that are easily spotted such as HH (for Heil Hitler), Wotan, hooly88 and NS. In Britain extreme right-wing groups have also been quick to embrace the Net and its chat rooms with sophisticated sites operated by the British National Party and the National Front.

The key to the success of such a system must be a question of how much control over access to 'adult sites' on the Internet parents or other adult users would actually be able to exercise. There must also be a question of whether going down this road will inevitably lead to government legislation if only allegedly in the name of protecting those children whose feckless parents cannot be bothered to regulate their Internet habits.

These issues have already started to emerge. Incore held an Internet Content Summit in Munich in September 1999 organised by a non-profit social policy offshoot of the German media giant, the Bertelsmann Foundation. This meeting was a major landmark in the development of the Internet. It brought together more than 300 major 'Net heads', including senior figures in AOL, British Telecom, IBM, Microsoft, the British Home Office, the Australian Broadcasting Authority, the German police and the US Civil Liberties Union.

The work that the IWF has done was fed into a working group of experts that included Professor Jack M. Balkin of Yale University Law School, a US First Amendment 'free speech' scholar. The working group produced a proposal for the creation of an internationally recognised rating and filtering system for the Internet. It was put forward as part of an EU action plan to promote safer use of the Net. 'Parents can't be looking over their shoulders all the time to make sure that what they are finding is harmless and suitable for them,' says the Incore memorandum.[16]

It is being developed on the same basis as the work being done at Britain's IWF; the Incore memorandum says:

> We want to keep the tradition of free speech on the Internet so it is essential that the choice to use the system is made by the Internet providers themselves and that content providers can choose whether or not to describe their content. Under the proposed system any individual can set a high tolerance for any category that they are not concerned about.[17]

Professor Balkin made clear at the Munich summit that he believes that filtering is now an inevitable feature of the Internet given the glut of information available and the need to protect children from potentially harmful content. 'Like it or not we are going to have filters. The questions then becomes, what is the best design for a filter so that it preserves civil liberties?'

The Bertelsmann proposal envisages a three-layer cake. In the first layer, website operators around the world voluntarily describe their content using an internationally agreed standard set of labels. Among the suggested categories are sex, nudity, violence including sports violence, language including vulgar and 'hate' speech, intolerance, potentially dangerous subjects such as taking drugs, smoking cigarettes, making bombs or committing suicide, sites that ask for personal details or employ pressured marketing methods, those that involve credit card transactions, and interactive sites such as chat rooms or online gaming. The list is not exhaustive and some filtering systems even go so far as to block sites that advertise alcohol.

Within each category there would be several levels. So in the sex category level one would include romance/affection; level two covers passion; level three groping/touching (erogenous), clothed/unclothed; and level four masturbation, intercourse, sexual violence and deviance.

The proposed category of tolerance is a further illustration. The IWF says it has found concerns in this area to be sufficiently strong to warrant a separate category. This covers references to groups of people defined by race, ethnicity, nationality, colour, creed, (dis)ability, gender, sexual orientation or appearance. In this category level one would cover neutral references, that is non-prejudicial, to groups or attitudes to them. Level two would include references that implied or asserted a degree of inferiority or superiority by virtue of real or imagined membership. Level three includes material that maligned or deprecated one group and/or advocated discriminatory treatment of its members (not including physical harm or violence). Finally level four advocated action which would cause physical, psychological or economic harm or violence against a group. The IWF admits there will be difficulties in self-rating this category as some authors will be blind to their own prejudices, or would not see anything wrong with them. 'Accurate rating therefore depends on the definitions being non-judgemental,' it says optimistically.[18]

The second layer of the cake involves groups voluntarily creating 'templates' that combine and rank combinations of the content labels to produce a filter that reflects that group's or community's ideology. So there might be templates from the Church of England or the Roman Catholic church, or drawn up from a Jewish or Islamic perspective or from a libertarian or conservative viewpoint. Internet users would choose a template and their browsers would use the selected content site descriptions to determine which sites should be blocked. 'The scheme is set up to make a thousand flowers bloom,' says Balkin. If any government tried to require that a particular filter was used on computers in its country, it would be clear that it was an attempt at censorship because there is no standard template, runs the argument. The British IWF suggests that while sophisticated users could create their own templates, 'off-the-shelf' profiles will also be available such as those which accord with the U certificate for film or the 9 o' clock watershed for television.

The third layer of the cake would allow groups to issue 'white lists' of approved sites that would provide a more sophisticated filter than the second layer of the process. For example, a template which banned on-screen violence could permit a white list of news organisations' sites so that reports of acts of violence would be allowed. Bare flesh banned when found on erotic sites would be permitted if on a reputable art gallery site.

The underlying assumption of such a system is that parents would ban access for their children to all unrated sites. Only about 120,000 websites are currently rated under the leading rating system, the Recreational Software Advisory Council, out of the millions of sites already in existence. So such a move without a major registration drive would have the effect of drastically reducing the size of the accessible web. The IWF admits that to gain the initial momentum it will need such a concerted campaign by governments, ISPs, browser producers, search engines and other pressure groups.

The need for diversity and flexibility in any central classification system is demonstrated by Bertelsmann's own survey of public opinion in Germany, the United States and Australia. The results highlight the difficulties involved in trying to tame the web in this way. They show strong support – over 90 per cent – in all three countries for a system of rating websites to protect children. But there is huge disagreement on what those controls should be.

Germans generally want racist sites banned but do not take offence at the nudity that so upsets American parents. The US First Amendment tradition of free speech ensures that extreme political propaganda is tolerated online yet the web presence of both radical left- and right-wing sites is opposed by 58 per cent of Germans. Australians also want to ban racist sites but are unperturbed by violence with only 41 per cent supporting their removal from the web.

Dr Mark Wossner of the Bertelsmann Foundation said that society had learned to live with the risk posed by television, the cinema and video films; however, the Internet was different because it was rapidly becoming a mass medium and could be accessed from anywhere by anyone at any time. Porn accounted for only 2 per cent of the content of the Net but could now be found by children at any time and that was a new factor in the debate.

The Bertelsmann proposal not only puts forward a new global system of self-assessment of the Net but also wants to see codes of conduct which oblige ISPs to remove illegal content from their servers and for hotlines, such as the IWF's, to be established so the public can report what they find when patrolling the frontiers of cyberspace. He compared it to a system of food labelling. He said: 'I want to know what the content of my breakfast muesli is before I eat it'.[19]

But the contribution of the German Minister of the Interior, Otto Schily, was a reminder that politicians have different priorities. He told the gathered corporate Net heads that by German law each ISP was obliged to appoint a Commissioner for the Protection of Minors to shield young people from harmful material. Schily warned that it was not good enough for Internet companies to use a filter control system simply to delegate their legal responsibility to parents. He said:

> Particular problems are to be expected in socially underprivileged families where parents will hardly know how to apply such technologies responsibly. At risk are mainly those families where violence is an accepted means to push through one's interests and to solve conflicts. Because these parents lack the necessary sensitivity towards the presentation of violence it is unlikely they will filter out the relevant contents.[20]

The 'feckless parent' argument has probably been rarely made with such sophistication but the political message was clear that if the Internet industry does not go down the road of self-regulation then other measures would have to follow.

This was certainly the fear raised by civil liberties campaigners at the Munich summit. The Global Internet Liberty Campaign (GILC), which includes the American Civil Liberties Union (ACLU), and British groups such as Liberty, Index on Censorship and Cyber-Rights UK, voiced concern that, far from staving off government regulation of the Internet, this well-intentioned plan will have the opposite effect. John Perry Barlow of the Washington-based Electronic Frontier Foundation, a member of the GILC coalition, said:

> Once this system is established, it will be very easy for governments to require every web site within their jurisdiction to self-rate. It will then be a short step to government-mandated filter use. I think Jack Balkin is creating a dangerous tool, with the best of intentions. Give a government a tool and they will use it.[21]

The implication is that those sites that refuse to rate themselves will face exclusion from schools, homes and offices. There will be a tendency, as with television, for content providers to tone down their material to conform to the lowest cultural common denominator in order to secure the largest audience.

The British-based Cyber-Rights and Cyber-Liberties UK organisation believes that there will be immense difficulties with the enforcement of a common European standard as much of the material on the Net originates in the United States and South-East Asia. The significant cultural variations in Europe alone make developing a common standard almost impossible. Yaman Akdeniz, Cyber-Rights director, said:

> The wish of the lazy to allow unsupervised access to their children should not reduce all adults browsing to the level of suitability of a five year old.[22]

British critics believe that the responsibility for providing appropriate content should rest with those who run the websites and not the ISPs who should realise they have a duty under the European Convention on Human Rights to guarantee freedom of expression. They believe that these developments are as much about making the web safe for large media companies as it is about making the web safe for children.

Such critics argue that they would prefer to see government energy going into doing something about the real-life dangers that children face every day such as domestic violence, poverty and family breakdown than trying to clean up the Net. They claim that the number of occasions that a child surfing the Net has actually been enticed into a real-life meeting by a predatory adult are far fewer than might be imagined. But the supporters of such filtering and rating systems are convinced that if they do not go ahead and provide a means to parents to protect their children from what they consider to be inappropriate material, then governments will act and with a far heavier hand.

The issue is a question of regulating access to the web not only at home but also at work. Individual adults and parents want to be able to control the kind of material coming into their homes but what Bertelsmann refers to as 'corporate executives with consciences' also feel the need to keep an eye on the kinds of sites their staff are visiting during working hours. Company directors are increasingly worried that they may be liable for prosecution if staff download illegal material at work. So they are anxiously looking for effective blocking systems that will provide a sanitised version of the Net.

It is no academic matter. The roll-call of British employees who have been sacked for downloading material ranging from the tasteless to the obscene is growing daily. It goes far beyond the clear-cut question of the illegal act of a paedophile downloading child pornography pictures, as in the Gary Glitter case. While it is not a criminal offence to view computer porn, it is illegal to download obscene material on to a computer disk or to print it out, even on a home personal computer. But with the kind of hard-core porn that is legal in the rest of Europe now easily available to British Net surfers for the first time, the pressure must be building for a complete overhaul of Britain's obscene publications legislation if it is not to fall even further into disrepute.

For many companies the question also takes in material that falls far short of that which is technically obscene and has far more to do with age-old debates about whether tatty topless pin-ups should be displayed in the workplace. Nowhere is immune. In 1998 three administrative staff were dismissed from Number 10 Downing Street for downloading pornographic images on government machines. They were disciplined under Cabinet Office civil service rules and moved to other jobs. Their activity had been discovered during 'routine monitoring' of their use of the Internet. The BBC has guidelines that tell its staff that anybody using the Internet should remember they are representing the BBC and inappropriate use is not allowed. An internal BBC memo says:

> Offensive material from the Internet must not be loaded, stored or displayed on company equipment, and failure to observe this policy will treated as a serious breach of discipline.[23]

It is this definition of inappropriate use that is now being embraced by employers. Even the liberal *Guardian* newspaper has told its staff they must not visit 'offensive' sites without first giving their head of department a legitimate reason. Such guidelines are not untypical.

In the United States a furious debate over Net censorship has been raging since the mid-1990s. In 1995 a Democrat senator from Nebraska, James Exon, began his campaign to regulate the Net in a bill which became known as the Communications Decency Act (CDA). It became part of federal law in 1996 and made the distribution of 'indecent' materials via telecommunications media punishable by up to two years' imprisonment and a $250,000 fine. In this case the US Internet companies, AOL, CompuServe, Apple and even mighty Microsoft joined forces with the ACLU, the Electronic Frontier Foundation, and significantly the American Libraries Association. Together they launched a challenge to a law that was trying to impose the rigid moral code of the pervasive television networks onto the chaos of the Internet. US network television is denied the free-speech protection of the First Amendment and required to ensure that its broadcast output is not inappropriate for children.

The initial challenge came in a federal court in Philadelphia which in June 1996 struck down the CDA on the grounds that it 'went way too far in criminalising protected speech.' In his ruling Judge Dalzell said:

> As the most participatory form of mass speech yet developed, the Internet deserves the highest protection from government intrusion. Just as the strength of the Internet is chaos, so the strength of our liberty depends upon the chaos and cacophony of the unfettered speech the First Amendment protects.[24]

The judgment was upheld in a landmark Supreme Court ruling in June 1997. In *Reno* v. *ACLU* the CDA was struck down as an unconstitutional restriction on free speech by seven judges to two. Unlike network television and radio, the Net was not an 'invasive medium' and so should not be subject to the same kinds of controls, said the Supreme Court. The difference was that the user had to take 'affirmative steps', that is click the mouse quite a few times to find the objectionable material. The user rarely encountered the offensive content 'by accident' and nearly all sexually explicit sites were preceded with a warning.

The ACLU had successfully demonstrated that the Communications Decency Act would not only criminalise porn but also make illegal talking on the Net about safe sex, abortion and even cases in which prisoners had been raped. Shares in Net Nanny and other filtering packages soared. As the civil libertarian and free speech campaign groups celebrated, so the setback at federal level sparked a bushfire of anti-porn bills across the United States at state level. In Florida there was an attempt to legally require the Net purveyors of adult material to pay reparations to the victims of sex crimes. But some of the battles centred on whether public libraries could provide filtered Internet access for their adult and juvenile patrons. The civil liberties campaigners and social authoritarians fought out a series of legal actions over whether public libraries had to give both adults and children a choice of filtered or unfiltered access to the Net.

But by 1999 a renewed attempt was made at a federal level to introduce state regulation of the Net. The Child Online Protection Act, widely seen as 'spawn of CDA', required commercial websites to ensure that children do not come into contact with material deemed harmful to minors. This legislation also quickly ran into constitutional trouble when the ACLU led a coalition that included Warner Bros Online as well as sex site operators and secured a Philadelphia court ruling that the new law was also flawed on free-speech grounds.

The judge involved in the case, Judge Lowell A. Reed Jr, acknowledged that many parents would be disappointed by his ruling. But he added: 'we do the minors of this country harm if First Amendment protections, which they will with age inherit fully, are chipped away in the name of their protection.'[25] Conservative groups complained that once again children and families were left entirely on their own to protect themselves against the pornography industry. In this situation there appeared to be a political hunger in the United States for a system such as that outlined at the Munich summit. In December 2000 an Arizona senator, John McCain, persuaded Congress to pass a new bill that forces virtually all US schools and libraries to use Internet filtering software on their computers to screen out pornography and 'other moral pollutants.' President Clinton signed it into law.

To avoid a repeat of the First Amendment debate the bill's drafters ensured that the schools and libraries would voluntarily sign up to filtering by making it a condition of their federal funding. The success or failure of such back-door policing will, as with the two previous measures, be fought out in the US courts. In March 2001 the American Library Association and the American Civil Liberties' Union started a legal action in a Philadelphia court which will have to be resolved by the US Supreme Court. Among those who supported the case were the Planned Parenthood Federation and Planetout.com, whose sites were blocked by the approved filters.

Australia is also trying to go down the road of state regulation. Legislation pushed through the Canberra parliament by Senator Brian Harradine in 1999 in the name of protecting the children of 'hard-pressed mums' required ISPs to block content which is deemed offensive by the Office of Film and Literature Classification or face penalties of A$27,500 a day. It proposed sweeping restrictions on adults providing or gaining access to material deemed unsuitable to minors as determined by the Australian film and video classification standards. The Australian Broadcasting Authority was to be given the job of enforcing the legislation.

It proposed a fairly unsophisticated system using the simple old film categories of X- and R-rated guidelines to classify sites and rule on complaints. Its critics complained that the costs of the technology needed to carry out this relatively simple task could be afforded by only 20 to 30 of the 100 plus ISPs operating in Australia. They also pointed to the simple fact that there will always be a hole in the software and highlighted the case of the computers in 1,500 schools in Victoria, Australia, which were equipped with filtering software yet the pupils could still view hard-core porn.

The new law provoked a public outcry in Australia and it was claimed that it would introduce the most draconian system of Internet censorship in the world. The widely reported protests had their effect and when the Australian Broadcasting Authority approved its final code of practice, Australian ISPs were not required to block adult content sites on overseas servers. Instead it asked each ISP to use approved filters or to ask each of their customers to declare they were using them before they could access adult sites. In the first six months of its Internet operations the ABA banned 93 online items as a result of complaints from the public. At the same time a monitoring organisation, NetAlert, was set up with state funds to advise the community on managing children's access to the Net. But as in the United States the advocates of state intervention do not give up easily and have started a new campaign at the level of individual Australian states which are each responsible for book, film and video regulation. In South Australia an Internet censorship bill is being debated which would make it illegal to make available online material which is unsuitable for children, even if it is only actually accessible by adults.

David Kerr of the British IWF says the huge battles in the United States and Australia over unfettered access to the Net in public institutions like schools, universities and libraries are unlikely to be repeated in Britain.

> For schools and libraries we have this notion of in loco
> parentis and the school or library, particularly a children's
> library, makes decisions on behalf of parents. What I
> couldn't understand for a long time was that in the
> United States they argued that completely the other way

around. It comes down to the free speech amendment to the constitution. There's very much a reaction against McCarthyism and that era and a reaction against government-funded bodies imposing any restriction on access to information or free speech. Schools and libraries are regarded as government-funded agencies and it is illegal for them to bar access to anything. So they are taking the position of the state rather than the position of the parent.[26]

Kerr believes that in Britain concerns about child protection will outweigh the arguments about free speech. But he argues the IWF is essentially neutral on these questions and is about providing the tools to allow rating and filtering of sites so that the responsible individual citizen rather than the state can make such choices.

What will limit that choice in Britain is the fact that in the words of the Home Office 'what is illegal offline, is illegal online.' Which brings us back to the operation of the Obscene Publications Act. Kerr confirms that the law is a contradictory shambles:

> We have sat down at the Home Office with the BBFC, the customs and the police and talked about how will they draw the line under the Obscene Publications Act on these issues. There are quite different positions between each of these bodies.[27]

The IWF chief executive cited the difficulties that the last chief film censor, James Ferman, faced when he tried to say 'Let's just make it a harm test.'[28] As Chapter 11 shows, Customs and Excise certainly was not prepared to abandon its stricter interpretation of its separate obscenity laws.

Kerr says that when it comes to the police their attitude to the Obscene Publications Act varies around Britain. The Metropolitan Police Clubs and Vice Squad is the most relaxed in terms of what it will prosecute. They will seize films under the forfeiture procedure but will not prosecute the owner, while the Manchester police and courts take a very different view and will probably prosecute over the same material. This difference in attitude was most clearly seen in the late 1980s when the born-again Christian Chief Constable, James Anderton, decided to ban the sale of magazines such as *Penthouse* and *Men Only* in the whole of the Greater Manchester area. It was seen again in the 1990s when the West Midlands police decided to seize two photographs by the internationally known artist, Robert Mapplethorpe, in a book on the shelves of the University of Central England. It was the case of Jean Genet and Enoch Powell all over again. The photographs depicted consenting adults taking part in unorthodox sexual practices were part of a book that had been published in Britain several years before. The university authorities waged a principled struggle for academic freedom that ended with the Crown Prosecution Service declining to agree with the police that the material was likely to deprave or corrupt the students and artists who had access to it.

Andreas Whittam Smith says that when he took over as the President of the British Board of Film Classification it was this wide variation in the interpretation of the law that shocked him most.[29] David Kerr says that the 1978 Protection of Children Act provides a clear test when it comes to dealing with child porn. All the prosecution has to show is the age of the child and whether there is any sexual involvement. The law is clear with the result that juries and magistrates produce much more consistent decisions.

However, even the supposed 'clarity' of this law can in practice still generate confusion. As the police threat to the Saatchi Gallery in March 2001, to remove several photographs by the artist, Tierney Gearon, of her naked children, aged six and four, from their *I Am a Camera* exhibition, or face prosecution, demonstrated the question of whether or not they were 'indecent' proved hugely controversial. The episode itself, which echoed the police raids on art galleries in the 1960s, was a sharp reminder that the lessons of censorship have to be relearned by each succeeding generation. Inspector Brian Ward of the Metropolitan Police's obscene publications and Internet unit first visited Saatchi's north London gallery after receiving three complaints 'from members of the public' about the exhibition. It had been running for eight weeks without public controversy and indeed had been well reviewed in the broadsheets and colour supplements from the *Tatler* to the *Daily Telegraph*.

The police refused to name the complainants except to say that one came from a journalist on a 'health and leisure magazine'. Although the Sunday newspaper, the *News of the World*, denied it was behind the complaints, Jenny Blyth, the curator of the Saatchi gallery firmly believes it played a decisive role. Within a few hours of Inspector Ward and his colleague calling at the St John's Wood gallery to warn them that they faced possible prosecution under the 1978 Protection of Children Act, two journalists turned up at Gearon's unlisted west London home address. They falsely claimed to be from the *Daily Telegraph* and said they knew the police had been at the gallery earlier that afternoon.

The police told Jenny Blyth that they would be back within days to seize the two 'offending' pictures if they were not removed from the exhibition. The first showed Gearon's two children standing naked together on a sandy beach with masks over their faces and the blue sea behind. The second showed her son urinating in the snow, his trousers around his knees and his face covered by goggles. The critics said that but for the strangeness of their obscured faces they could pass as family snaps.

Soon after Inspector Ward had warned the Saatchi Gallery, he also telephoned the art publisher, Edward Booth-Clibborn, to tell him that thousands of copies of his book, *I Am a Camera*, should be removed from the shelves of Waterstones and the rest of Britain's bookshops. The 436-page volume showcases Charles Saatchi's personal collection of photographs and includes images by Tracey Emin, Andy Warhol and Cindy Sherman as well as the pictures by Gearon. The police said they were also concerned about a tiny 3 cm by 4.5 cm image by the American photographer, Nan Goldin, of a young girl standing over a naked child.

My public disclosure in the *Guardian* that the police had launched their inquiry and had warned the gallery to remove the pictures or face prosecution under the 1978 Act, which carried a possible prison sentence of up to ten years' stole the thunder of the *News of the World*. Its next issue made clear the hidden agenda of its editor, Rebekah Wade. 'Child Porn They Call Art' ran the headline over a two-page article which began:

> Upper-crust 'art lovers' are paying £5 a head to ogle degrading snaps of naked children plastered across the walls of one of Britain's most exclusive galleries.[30]

An accompanying editorial called for the closure of the exhibition and attacked the *Independent* newspapers for their criticism of the *News of the World*'s 'crusade' to name and shame paedophiles by forcing the public disclosure of the sex offenders' register. What was the *Independent*'s crime? It had sponsored the Saatchi show or as the *News of the World* put it, had backed 'a revolting exhibition of perversion under the guise of art'. A police source was quoted as saying:

> These pictures could fuel the sick fantasies of paedophiles. Soon they could end up on the Internet. We've all taken pictures of our children naked but would you want the rest of the world, including perverts, seeing them? It's time somebody decided what is art and what is porn and looked after the interests of the children who have been photographed.

The police action sparked an enormous media debate which raged while the Crown Prosecution Service considered whether or not to prosecute. Alan Yentob, the BBC's director of drama, asked if the police did not have better things to do while the moral philosopher, Baroness Warnock, also described it as 'a monstrous interference on behalf of the police'. The feminist writer, Germaine Greer, agreed with Gearon's critics that the pictures could be misused but, she argued, then so could images of the Virgin Mary. Surprisingly the libertarian *Daily Telegraph* came out in strong support of the exhibition. The culture secretary, Chris Smith, also voiced some thinly veiled criticism of the police investigation saying that while it was always difficult to strike a balance between free speech and protecting children from exploitation. 'We must be very careful in this country before we start censoring things that are happening, either in newspapers or in art galleries ... I am much more worried about paedophile material that's available on the Internet than about an art gallery somewhere in the middle of London.[31]

The President of the British Board of Film Classification, Andreas Whittam Smith, however, supported the police action. He said he would not personally take any risks where images of children were concerned:

> I think the Protection of Children Act is a very
> important piece of legislation which should be taken
> very seriously. It is very specific about what is not
> correct, that being pictures of children in sexually
> compromising positions. I don't think the fact it is a
> parent taking the pictures gives them any authority to do
> this.[32]

Others backed up his view including Labour and Tory MPs.

The most unexpected voice of support for the gallery came from the former Labour Chancellor, Lord Healey, whose own photograph of a Chinese boy eating an ice lolly with his willie hanging out of his trousers was on display in the House of Commons annual photographic exhibition. He recalled that the naked statute of a boy pissing in a fountain had been happily on public display in Brussels for many years.

While the argument raged, the Saatchi Gallery asked one of Britain's leading legal experts on freedom of expression,

Geoffrey Robertson QC, to submit a written legal opinion to the Director of Public Prosecutions on their behalf. It argued that nudity did not necessarily mean indecent or obscene. For a photograph to be indecent the court precedents showed, it said, that there had to be an element of lewdness and pictures of naked children without any sexual overtones did not amount to indecency. The 1978 Act also contains a clause allowing a defence for legitimate possession of such images which legal experts had interpreted to mean people such as forensic scientists in the course of their duties.

The decision issued by the Crown Prosecution Service on 15 March 2001 stated simply that it had advised the Met police that proceedings should not go ahead against the gallery. The evidence submitted by the police was insufficient to provide a realistic prospect of a conviction under the 1978 law. The statement added:

> In reaching this decision, the CPS considered whether the photographs in question were indecent and the likely defence of the gallery, i.e. whether they had a legitimate reason for showing them.[33]

The Saatchi affair demonstrated how much scope for misunderstanding there is in just the definition of 'indecency' and over a law that many regard as among the most clear-cut in this area. The 1959 Obscene Publications Act itself is so indefinite in its nature that the police themselves despair that they cannot convince British juries to convict on even some of the most outrageous kinds of scenes such as the insertion of a fire extinguisher into a woman's vagina.

As long ago as 1979 the official Williams committee pointed out, and it is a message that this book is designed to reinforce, that while there is the 'deprave and corrupt' test applying to what cannot be sold, other tests still apply to what may not be imported, sent by post, publicly displayed and now posted on the Internet. The 1839 Metropolitan Police Act and the 1847

Town Police Clauses Act with their simple and unqualified 'indecent or obscene' tests may still be invoked against anything that is sold. Customs legislation has yet to catch up with the Obscene Publications Act. In Northern Ireland the common law offence of obscene libel is still used instead of the more enlightened 1959 Act. Meanwhile the 1984 Video Recordings Act bases its threshold for prosecution on a 'harm' test. The British Board of Film Classification, which derives its powers from local authorities, has its own 'making morally bad' interpretation of the classic 'deprave and corrupt' test for film while applying the 'harm' test for video.

David Kerr says that at present most of the public think that when you talk about censorship or removing illegal pictures from the Net, they assume that what is under discussion is what is seen in a *Playboy* centrespread or something slightly above that: 'They do not realise we are talking about young children being raped.'

Public concern in Britain over pornography cannot just be dismissed as some kind of puritanical hangover. The politicians who articulate public unease about a completely deregulated environment, and the impact, in particular on the exploitation of children, rightly reflect popular concerns. The abuse of children is a terrible crime that needs all kinds of measures to prevent it. But these sites should be recognised for what they are, that is evidence of child abuse, and should be vigorously prosecuted as such, as the police have done in Operation Cathedral, in which they broke up the online Wonderland Club.

Such successful operations against child-abuse rings demonstrate that Britain already has strong enough laws to curb the activities of paedophiles. The Labour government has undertaken a major review of the laws relating to sex offences in Britain, but specifically excluded the obscenity laws. But the time for a major shake-up is long overdue. The longer the law remains in its present shambles, the deeper will become public scepticism about its operation and the more difficult it will be for police officers to persuade juries to convict the real traders in human misery. It is time to resurrect the Williams committee report as a piece of unfinished business hanging over from the last Labour government.

It is not just an academic point. The incorporation of the European Convention on Human Rights into British law in the Human Rights Act means that policy-makers are going to have to recognise that it prescribes 'harm' and not just 'offensiveness' as the legal test as to whether it is legitimate to restrict freedom of expression. It is highly likely that if politicians do not act then a series of high profile legal actions will eventually trigger a complete overhaul of the law in this area but one shaped by our unelected and unaccountable judges and not by democratic politicians. It is time to bring in a comprehensive obscenity law that faces up to the challenge of the Internet and recognises freedom of expression while restricting access to material that actually causes harm rather than some imagined corruption or depravity. That should be harm in the sense of producing lasting harm or injury and not just simply shock, outrage or offence to those who regard it as their mission to find immorality wherever changing technologies might create a new audience.

A note on sources

Chapter 1

A useful overview of the history of the subject can be found in *Obscenity in England*, a submission by the Society of Authors to the Home Secretary in the late 1950s, which can be found as an appendix to the Public Record Office (PRO) document CUST 49/4712.

Chapter 2

The *Ulysses* discussion draws heavily on the Public Record Office files. The main papers can be found in HO 144/20071. This Home Office bundle contains nine separate files. Files 1 and 2 contain the papers that deal with the first seizure of a copy of *Ulysses* by Customs at Croydon Airport in December 1922 and includes Sir Archibald Bodkin's legal opinion. File 3 deals with F.R. Leavis's request to obtain copies to use in his Cambridge University lectures. Files 4–6 deal with the Home Office's response to requests from individuals for permission to import individual copies. File 7 contains details of the US court ruling in 1934 lifting the US ban on *Ulysses*. File 8 deals with the 1936 decision by John Lane of the Bodley Head to publish the book. File 9 contains the papers dealing with the decision to lift the ban. A separate Metropolitan Police file, MEPO 3/930, covers police investigations into individuals who had been named as owning or selling illegal copies of *Ulysses*. The material

describing the Foreign Office's attitude to Joyce is in FCO
395/209/128688. For this chapter I have also drawn on material
in Bruce Arnold's *The Scandal of Ulysses* (St Martin's Press, New
York, 1992) and Paul Vanderham's *James Joyce and Censorship: The
Trials of Ulysses* (Macmillan, London, 1998).

Chapter 3

Most of the quoted passages used come from the Home Office
case files, HO 144/22547. The file was not due to be made
public until 2047 but was opened in 1998. The Home Office
case papers include more than 60 sub-files but a significant
number are missing, including Files 21–39, which have been destroyed. The quotations from newspapers are mainly drawn from
cuttings in the Home Office files, although the extracts from
William Joynson-Hicks's speeches came directly from back
numbers of *The Times* and the *Daily Telegraph*. See Viscount
Brentford's *Do We Need a Censor?* (Faber & Faber, London, 1929)
for Jix's own apologia. For Evelyn Waugh's more accurate view
read his *Vile Bodies* (Penguin, London, 1938). Diana Souhami's
excellent *The Trials of Radclyffe Hall* (Virago, London, 1999) has
also proved an invaluable source.

Chapter 4

This chapter is almost entirely based on state files in the Public
Record Office. The case of Kate Meyrick, the night-club
Queen of Soho, is in the MEPO files. The way the Home Office
dealt with Compton Mackenzie's *Extraordinary Women* is de-
tailed in HO 45/15727. D.H. Lawrence's poems, *Pansies*, are in
HO 144/20642. The activities of the London Public Morality
Council, including its attack on Isadora Duncan, are contained
in HO 45/15139. The story of how Norah James and Radclyffe
Hall ended up being sent to Scotland Yard's basement guillotine

is to be found in MEPO 3/383. The police papers, MEPO 2/1707, contain the British Museum's plea for banned books with literary merit to be sent to them.

Chapter 5

The HO 302 series of files in the Public Record Office contain the main postwar Home Office records on indecent publications. They include 66 files covering the period from 1953 to 1974. The first group 302/1 to 302/23 include the period of the early 1950s purge and the run-up to the 1959 Obscene Publications Act, including the Whitehall papers on Sir Alan Herbert's private member's bill. The Home Office list of banned books can be found at DPP 6/59, which includes all those against which magistrates' courts had issued destruction orders. The separate Customs and Excise banned list is at CUST 49/4357. See also CUST 49/4712 for the later list. In the police files, MEPO 2/9626 includes the proposed 'white list' of classics. DPP 6/61 has a further discussion of this issue, and DPP 6/73 gives the prosecutor's views on the Herbert bill. HO 300/6 contains the Home Office view of the arrival of rock 'n' roll. HO 302/10 gives the official response to complaints on the *Kinsey Report on Sexual Behaviour in the Human Female*. The story of Jean Genet and the Birmingham Libraries committee is contained in CUST 49/4614.

Chapter 6

D.H. Lawrence's early persecutions at the hands of the authorities are to be found at HO 45/13944, which contains details of the suppression of *The Rainbow*. The papers on the raid on Lawrence's paintings at the Warren Galleries in 1929 are to be found at MEPO 2/9428 and HO 45/24788. The *Pansies* case is at HO 144/20642. The main *Lady Chatterley* papers are contained in

DPP 2/3077, which comes in four parts, including a transcript of the trial. Complaints to the Home Office about *Lady Chatterley* are at HO 302/11. C.H. Rolph (ed.) *The Trial of Lady Chatterley*: *Regina v. Penguin Books Limited* (Penguin, London, 1961) provides a transcript of the case. C.H. Rolph's *Books in the Dock* (André Deutsch, London, 1969) provides authoritative background to the entire subject, as does Alec Craig's *The Banned Books of England* (George Allen & Unwin, London, 1937 and 1962).

Chapter 7

The main case papers on Henry Miller's *Tropic of Cancer* are to be found in DPP 2/3610. The police report on *Tropic of Cancer* is at MEPO 2/10400. The seizure of Miller's book, *Sexus*, is at HO 302/36. The postwar history of the censorship of *Fanny Hill* is at CUST 49/4357. The note from Alec Douglas-Home to Henry Brooke warning of the flood of US pulp fiction is to be found at PREM 11/4848, where the Prime Minister voices concerns about 'purple hearts and obscene publications'. Examples of the treatment of pulp fiction novels are at DPP 2/3558. The trial papers on the *Last Exit to Brooklyn* case are at CRIM 1/4694. The papers on Mary McCarthy's *The Group* are at DPP 2/3981.

The question of guaranteeing trial by jury for works of literature is discussed at HO 302/37. The ramifications of the police raids on the Tate Gallery and the Victoria and Albert Museum are contained in HO 302/40 and of the police raid on the *International Times* magazine at HO 302/41. The difficulties facing the Aubrey Beardsley exhibition are at HO 302/42. The library at Chelsea Art College also contains material that I have drawn on for Beardsley and Jim Dine. More material on Jim Dine and *Last Exit* appears in HO 302/40.

Chapter 8

For the Lord Chamberlain's verdict on individual plays, the collection of his papers in the British Library was consulted. The main papers on the end of theatre censorship are to be found in the Public Record Office HO 300 series, which also contains papers on cinema as well as the licensing of other forms of 'entertainments', including hypnotism and boxing. HO 300/12, HO 300/56 and HO 300/60 contain the main papers on the final days of the Lord Chamberlain. HO 300/56 includes the official verdict on Edward Bond's *Saved* and John Osborne's *A Patriot for Me*. PREM 13/1395 documents how the script of *Private Eye*'s *Mrs Wilson's Diary* was censored. The file concerning the Jackdaw on the Kennedy assassination is at FCO 7/858 and the papers on Gerald Scarfe's New York exhibition are at FCO 7/805. The details of the row over Ronald Millar's *Number 10* are to be found at PREM 1394.

Chapter 9

The correspondence between the Prime Minister and Mary Whitehouse over 'profanity on television' can be found at HO 256/719. The papers on the aftermath of the *Oz* trial and the prosecution of the *Little Red Schoolbook* are based on HO 302/49, which had been due to be kept secret until 2003 but was opened early on my application by the Home Office. As well as correspondence between the Home Secretary and the Metropolitan Police Commissioner about the *Oz* trial, it contains papers on the detailed allegations of corruption made against the Scotland Yard Obscene Publications Squad. I also read the incomplete collection of *Oz* magazines in the British Library and drew on Professor Tim Newburn's invaluable *Permission and Regulation: Law and Morals in Post-War Britain* (Routledge, London, 1992) and Barry Cox, John Shirley and Martin Short's *The Fall of Scotland Yard* (Penguin, London, 1977). Also useful are James Callaghan, *Time and Chance* (Collins, London, 1987) and Duncan Campbell's *The Underworld* (Penguin, London, 1994). Richard Neville's *Hippie Hippie Shake* (Bloomsbury, London, 1995) gives a defendant's view of the *Oz* trial. Geoffrey Robertson's *The Justice Game* (Chatto and Windus, London, 1998) and his *Obscenity* (Weidenfeld and Nicolson, London, 1979) provide the perspective of a brilliant human rights lawyer. *Playpower* was a book by Richard Neville (Jonathan Cape, London, 1970).

Chapter 10

This section draws heavily on contemporary press coverage, particularly from the *Guardian*, and on John Sutherland's *Offensive Literature* (Junction Books, London, 1982). Also useful are Mary Whitehouse's *Whatever Happened to Sex* (Hodder and Stoughton, London, 1972), the Williams committee's *Report on Obscenity and Film Censorship* (HMSO, London, 1979) and Lord Longford's *Pornography: The Longford Report* (Coronet, London, 1972).

Chapter 11

Tom Dewe Mathews, *Censored* (Chatto and Windus, London, 1994) is now the standard text on cinema censorship in Britain. I have also drawn on James Ferman's own lectures and an interview that I did for the *Guardian* with Andreas Whittam Smith. The BBFC's website (www.BBFC.co.uk) is a useful source as well as its annual reports. A good account of the research into the existence of a link between juvenile crime and video violence is to be found in Ann Hagell and Tim Newburn's *Young Offenders and the Media* (Policy Studies Institute, London, 1994).

Chapter 12

A good basic guide to civil liberties and the Internet is Yaman
Akdeniz's *Sex on the Net* (South Street Press, Reading, 1999).
Akdeniz is the founder of Cyber-Rights and Cyber-Liberties
(UK). See Laurence O'Toole, *Pornocopia* (Serpent's Tail, London,
1998) for good background on the development of the sex industry in cyberspace. In the Home Office's *Testing Obscenity*
(HMSO Research Study 157, London, 1996), Sharon Grace pro-
vides useful international comparisons of the state of the law. *In-
ternet Detective: An Investigator's Guide* by Detective Inspector
David J. Davis of the West Midlands Police (Home Office, Police
Research Group, 1998) demonstrates that there are few parts of
the Web that are beyond the modernised reach of the law. My
thanks to David Kerr of the Internet Watch Foundation, Lynda
Jackson of the Home Office and Andreas Whittam Smith of the
British Board of Film Classification for briefings and interviews.
There is already a wide range of websites that cover these issues.
See particularly www.eff.org of the Electronic Frontier Foun-
dation. That will also take you into the Global Internet Liberty
Campaign. In Britain www.cyber-rights.org will take you
to Yaman Akdeniz's site. For more on the European debate see
www.incore.org.

The *Melon Farmers* home page provides an excellent censorship link page on:
http://www.dtaylor.demon.co.uk/links.htm.

Books are still in trouble, particularly in the United States.
See the Banned Books online project to get an idea of just
how much: http://digital.library.upenn.edu/books/
banned-books.html.

Notes

Chapter 1

1 John Milton, *Areopagitica*, London, 1643.
2 *R v. Hicklin*, LR 3 QB 360 1868.
3 Quoted in Alec Craig, *The Banned Books of England and Other Countries*, George Allen & Unwin, London, 1962, p. 63.
4 *Superhighway Safety: Children's Safe Use of the internet*, Becta/DfEE, London, 1999.

Chapter 2

1 *The Times*, 12 December 1928.
2 Quoted in Bruce Arnold, *The Scandal of Ulysses*, St Martin's Press, New York, 1992.
3 Public Record Office, FCO 395/209/128688.
4 Ibid.
5 Ibid.
6 PRO, HO 144/20071.
7 Shane Leslie, *Quarterly Review*, London, 1922.
8 James Joyce, *Ulysses*, Shakespeare and Co., Paris, 1922, pp. 704–5. Three extracts from Episode 18, 'Penelope', reproduced with permission of the Estate of James Joyce. © Copyright estate of James Joyce.

9 Ibid.

10 Ibid.

11 George Orwell, *An Age Like This, 1920–1940*, Secker and Warburg, London, 1968.

12 F.R. Leavis, letter to the *Times Literary Supplement*, May 1963.

13 Ibid.

14 Ibid.

15 Theodore Francis Powys's *Wolf Select* was targeted by Joynson-Hicks in 1929: 'Well written but the foulest concoction of vileness I have ever read. Humorous jokes about one boy being seduced by another,' said one protester to the Home Office.

16 Leavis, op. cit.

17 PRO, MEPO 3/390.

Chapter 3

1 James Douglas, 'A Book That Must Be Suppressed', *Sunday Express*, 19 August 1928.

2 Diana Souhami, *The Trials of Radclyffe Hall*, Virago, London, 1999.

3 Leonard Woolf, *Manchester Guardian*, quoted in Home Office file, HO 144/22547.

4 Radclyffe Hall, letter to *Daily Herald*, 21 December 1928.

5 Radclyffe Hall, *The Well of Loneliness*, Jonathan Cape, London, 1949, p. 144.

6 L.P. Hartley, *Saturday Review*, 28 July 1928.

7 Arnold Dawson, *Daily Herald*, 20 August 1928. Copies of this and the other reviews quoted are to be found in HO 144/22547.

8 Beaverbrook certainly did not share Douglas's indignation. He later wrote to a friend: 'You must read the *Well of Loneliness*. It is a very good book. But of course you must read it in the unexpurgated edition.'

9 Sir Guy Stephenson, the deputy DPP to Under-Secretary of State, Home Office, 21 August 1928.

10 This simple fact seems to have been overlooked by Jix, despite the fact he was a prominent supporter of a well-backed but futile attempt in 1921 by the Conservative MP, Frederick McQuiston, to 'raise the status of lesbianism under the criminal law' on the grounds that it was 'a deformity of the brain'.

11 *The Journal of Arnold Bennett*, entry for 24 August 1928, London, 1933.

12 As can be seen from the case of the Stepney miller and *Ulysses*, the Post Office has long had powers to detain and open mail coming from overseas if it has reason to believe that it is indecent or obscene. The power dates back to the 1884 Post Office (Protection) Act, but the authorities soon abandoned the pretence that the power was there to protect the morals of Post Office staff. The Post Office powers are even more draconian than those used by Customs. In the case of Customs it has to notify the apparent owner that the books have been seized and give him/her an opportunity to challenge the decision in the courts. The Post Office Act simply allows any postal packet opened to be 'destroyed or otherwise disposed of'. Although the official files give no hint, it is presumed that the GPO was already on the lookout for parcels sent by the Pegasus Press in Paris and did not need a Home Secretary's warrant to open a small parcel of books. The arrangements for the modern-day interception of telephone calls and e-mails by the police and the security services are safeguarded by codes of conduct with judicial and ministerial oversight built into the process. Major political battles are going over the right to 'open' encrypted e-mails amidst police fears of organised crime.

13 Reported in *The Times*, 16 October 1928.

14 *Evening Standard*, 9 November 1928.

15 Virginia Woolf to Quentin Bell, 1 November 1928, in *A*

Change of Perspective: The Letters of Virginia Woolf 1882–1941,
Hogarth Press, London, 1977.

16 Quoted in Diana Souhami's *The Trials of Radclyffe Hall*,
   based on Radclyffe Hall's handwritten notes for a lecture
   on the trial.
17 *Evening Standard*, 9 November 1928.
18 Ibid.
19 *Evening Standard*, 16 November 1928.
20 *Manchester Guardian*, 16 December 1928.
21 *Daily Telegraph*, 17 November 1928.
22 C.H. Rolph, *Books in the Dock*, André Deutsch, London,
   1969.
23 *Daily Telegraph*, 12 December 1928.
24 *Evening Standard*, 16 November 1928.
25 Ibid.
26 *Manchester Guardian*, 17 December 1928.
27 Leonard Woolf, *Manchester Guardian*, 20 December 1928.
28 *Daily Herald*, 21 December 1928.

Chapter 4

1 P.R. Stephenson, *Policeman of the Lord: A Political Satire*,
  Sophistocles Press, London, 1929.
2 Evelyn Waugh, *Vile Bodies,* Penguin, London (copyright
  1930), pp. 19–20.
3 Isadora Duncan, *My Life,* London, 1928.
4 Rebecca West, *Time and Tide*, 22 March 1929.
5 Victor Gollancz, 'Banning', *Time and Tide*, 22 March 1929.
6 Viscount Brentford, *Do We Need a Censor?*, Criterion
  Miscellany, Faber & Faber, London, 1929.
7 Ibid.

Chapter 5

1 PRO DPP 2/3682.
2 C.H. Rolph, *Books in the Dock*, André Deutsch, London, 1969, p. 102.
3 Ibid., p. 103.
4 PRO DPP 6/73.
5 *Birmingham Evening Mail*, 8 January 1957.
6 *The Times*, 24 December 1956.
7 *Birmingham Post*, 24 December 1956.
8 *Birmingham Mail*, 1 January 1957.
9 *Birmingham Evening Despatch*, 2 February 1957.
10 *Hansard*, col. 166, House of Commons, 18 February 1957.
11 *Hansard*, cols. 168/169, House of Commons, 18 February 1957.
12 *Hansard*, col. 174, House of Commons, 18 February 1957.
13 Herbert Committee on Obscene Publications, PRO HO 302/12.
14 *Sunday Express*, 29 January 1956.

Chapter 6

1 D.H. Lawrence, *Pornography and Obscenity*, Faber & Faber, London, 1929.
2 D.H. Lawrence, Foreword to *Pansies*, Faber & Faber, London, 1939.
3 *Daily Express*, 15 August 1929.
4 PRO MEPO 2/9428; HO 45/4788.
5 D.H. Lawrence, *Pornography and Obscenity*, p. 31.
6 *Nettles: The Collected Poems of D.H. Lawrence*, Heinemann, London, 1972, p. 582.
7 Germaine Greer, 'Sex, Lies and Old Pork Pies', *Independent on Sunday*, 3 June 1990, p. 9.
8 D.H. Lawrence, *Lady Chatterley's Lover,* Penguin, London, 1993 edition, pp. 218–19.

9 C.H. Rolph, *The Trial of Lady Chatterley*, Penguin, London, 1961.

Chapter 7

1 Philip Larkin, *Collected Poems*, Faber & Faber, London, 1988, p. 167.
2 Henry Miller, *Obscenity and the Law of Reflection*, quoted in *Selected Prose* I, MacGibbon & Kee, London, 1965, p. 358.
3 Henry Miller, *Tropic of Cancer*, John Calder, London (copyright 1934), 1963, pp. 5–6, 16.
4 Henry Miller, *Sexus*, Grove Press, New York, 1965, p. 180.
5 PRO DPP 2/3981.
6 John Cleland, *Fanny Hill:Memoirs of a Lady of Pleasure*, Penguin, London, 1985, p. 86.
7 Anthony Burgess, quoted in PRO CRIM 1/4694.
8 Hubert Selby, *Last Exit to Brooklyn*, Calder and Boyars, London, 1966, p. 83.
9 Robert Maxwell, quoted in PRO CRIM 1/4694.
10 Gordon Honeycombe and Adam Acworth, *Adam's Tale*, Hutchinson, London, 1974, pp. 199–202.

Chapter 8

1 Peter Brook, *US:The Book of Royal Shakespeare Theatre Production*, Calder and Boyars, London, 1968.

Chapter 9

1 *Guardian*, 28 April 1970.
2 *The Times*, 26 August 1970.
3 Geoffrey Robertson, *Obscenity*, Weidenfeld and Nicolson, London, 1979, p. 216.

4 John Sutherland, *Offensive Literature*, Junction Books, London, 1982, p. 105.

5 *Guardian*, 9 August 1999.

6 *Time Out's Book of London*, Time Out, London, 1972, p. 192.

7 *The Little Red Schoolbook*, Stage One, translated by Berit Thornberry, London, 1971, p. 95.

8 Ibid., p. 95.

9 Ibid., p. 127.

10 Ibid., p. 29.

11 Lord Longford, *Pornography: The Longford Report*, Coronet, London, 1972, p. 26.

12 Richard Neville, *Hippie Hippie Shake*, Bloomsbury, London, 1995, p. 203.

13 Ibid., p. 204.

14 *Daily Telegraph* 6 April 1971.

15 *Oz* 28, Schoolkids Issue, London, 1970.

16 Tony Palmer, *The Trials of Oz*, Bland and Briggs, London, 1971, p. 169.

17 Ibid., pp. 103–4.

18 Ibid., p. 146.

19 Ibid., p. 71.

20 Ibid., p. 72.

21 *Hippie Hippie Shake*, p. 292.

22 Palmer, op. cit., pp. 238–52.

23 Geoffrey Robertson, *The Justice Game*, Chatto and Windus, London, 1998.

24 Mary Whitehouse, *Whatever Happened to Sex*, Hodder and Stoughton, London, 1972, p. 239.

25 *Hippie Hippie Shake*.

Chapter 10

1 James Kirkup, 'The Love That Dares to Speak its Name', *Gay News* 96, 13–30 June 1976.

2 John Sutherland, *Offensive Literature*, Junction Books, London, 1982, p. 154.

3 *Report of the Committee on Obscenity and Film Censorship*, HMSO, London, 1979.

4 Ibid., p. 124.

5 Ibid., p. 132.

6 Ibid., p. 102.

7 Ibid., p. 63.

8 Ibid., p. 57.

9 Quoted in Mary Whitehouse, *A Most Dangerous Woman?*, Lion, Tring, 1982, p. 233.

10 Howard Brenton, *The Romans in Britain*, Eyre Methuen, London, 1980, Part one, scene three, pp. 41–2.

11 Andrea Dworkin, *Pornography: Men Possessing Women*, Women's Press, London, 1981; Susan Griffin, *Pornography and Silence: Culture's Revenge Against Nature*, Harper and Row, New York, 1981.

Chapter 11

1 James Ferman, *Annual Report*, British Board of Film Classification, London, 1998, p. 7.

2 Ibid., p. 7.

3 Ibid., p. 6.

4 Ibid., p. 7.

5 An Evening with James Ferman, BAFTA, London, 26 February 1999.

6 Ibid.

7 Interview with BBC TV Panorama, 'Porn Wars', 2 November 1998.

8 Ibid.

9 BBFC 1998 *Annual Report*.

Chapter 12

1 Tony Blair interview with Bun.Com, 25 October 1999.
2 Home Office briefing for author, July 1999.
3 Ibid.
4 Ibid.
5 See cyber-rights.org.uk/documents/themet.htm
6 Ibid.
7 Home Office briefing for author.
8 *Sunday Times*, 25 March 2001.
9 Carol Vorderman, IWF meeting at House of Lords, 23 January 2001.
10 See www.censorware.org.
11 Interview with author, 3 September 1999.
12 Ibid.
13 Home Office briefing to author.
14 *Der Stern*, July 1999.
15 Ibid.
16 See www.incore.org., 9 September 1999 (European Internet content regulation).
17 Ibid.
18 See www.iwf.org.uk (Internet Watch Foundation)
19 see papers archived at www.stiftung/bertelsmann.de/Internetcontent
20 Ibid.
21 www.gilc.org (Global Internet Liberty Campaign).
22 www.cyber-rights.org.uk
23 *Observer* 27 September 1998.
24 Ruling archived at aclu.org/issues/cyber the website of the American Civil Liberties Union.
25 Ibid.
26 Interview with author.
27 Ibid.
28 Ibid.
29 Interview with Andreas Whittam Smith, October 1999.
30 *News of the World*, 11 March 2001

31 Chris Smith interviewed on Sky Television's *Sunday with Adam Boulton* programme.
32 *Independent on Sunday*, 11 March 2001.
33 Crown Prosecution Service, press notice 106/00, 15 March 2001.

Index